Ordnance Survey/Jarrold
**Landranger Guidebook
to**

Snowdonia,
Anglesey and The Lleyn Peninsula

Compiled by Peter Titchmarsh, M.A., F.R.G.S.

Companion to Landranger Maps 114, 115, 123, 124 and parts of 116, 125 and 135

Jarrold Colour Publications

How to use this Guide

Space has not allowed us to include every place on the relevant Landranger Maps in the 'Places of Special Interest' section (pages 28-109). The items have been selected however, to provide you with a varied and interesting companion during your travels around Snowdonia, Anglesey and the Lleyn Peninsula. Places of exceptional interest have been highlighted by being printed in blue.

Each entry is identified first with the number of the Landranger map or maps on which it appears (eg. 114, 115, etc). This is followed by two letters (eg. SH) and by a 4-figure reference number (eg. 07-37). The first two figures of this number are those which appear in blue along the north and south edges of Landranger maps; the other two appear in blue along the east and west edges.

Therefore, to locate any place or feature referred to in this guide book on the relevant Landranger map, first read the two figures along the north or south edges of the map, then the two figures along the east or west edges. Trace the lines adjacent to each of the two sets of figures across the map face and the point where they intersect will be the south-west corner of the grid square in which the place or feature lies. Thus the Pass of Aberglaslyn falls in the grid square 59-48 on Landranger map 115.

The Key Maps on pages 4-9 identify the suggested starting points of our ten tours and twelve walks, and in the 'Tours' and 'Walks' sections, all places which also have a separate entry in the 'Places of Special Interest' section are in bold type. Each tour and walk is accompanied by a map, and there are cross-references between Tours and Walks on both the maps and in the text.

Acknowledgements

We would like to thank Mr Reg Jones for his most interesting article on *Natural History*. We are most grateful to Mr Frank Skelcey, Mr Alan Shorrock and Mr Ramsey Clarke, all of whom are members of the Ramblers' Association, for their work on the sixteen *Walks*. This work included walking over the routes concerned and provision of the detailed directions for walkers which will be found in the guide. We would also like to thank the staff of the Snowdonia National Park, the Gwynedd County Planning Office, and a great number of Tourist Information Centres, for all their help and advice.

First published 1986 by Ordnance Survey and Jarrold Colour Publications

Ordnance Survey	Jarrold Colour
Romsey Road	Publications
Maybush	Barrack Street
Southampton SO9 4DH	Norwich NR3 1TR

© Crown copyright 1986

Printed in Great Britain by Jarrold and Sons Ltd., Norwich. 186

Contents

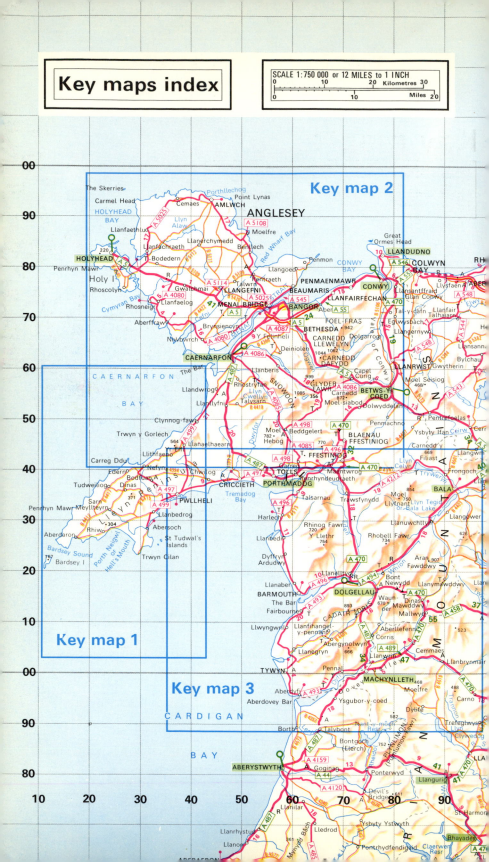

Key map 3

SCALE 1:250 000 or 4 MILES to 1 INCH

0 1 km = 0·6214 mile · 5 · 10 · Kilometres 15

0 1 mile = 1·61 kms · 5 · Miles · 10

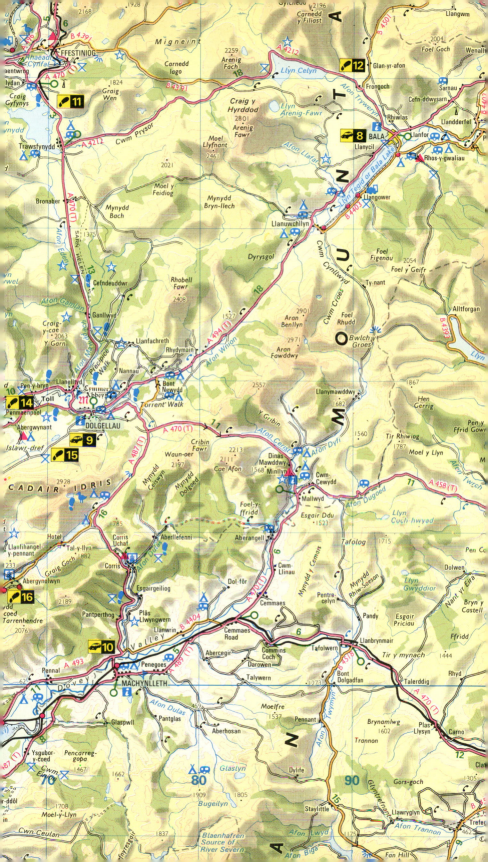

Introduction

This guide covers almost the entire county of Gwynedd, and although not essential to its enjoyment, Landranger Maps 114, 115, 123, 124, and parts of Landranger Maps 116, 125 and 135 could go hand-in-hand with the book, to provide a companion without equal. The area covered ranges from the northern coast of Anglesey, southwards to the broad Dyfi Estuary, from the Lleyn's south-western tip to the lovely Conwy Valley, and to the lakes and mountains extending as far eastwards as Bala.

Anglesey, the largest of Britain's offshore islands, has a long and splendid coastline, with bird-haunted cliffs and islands, and a succession of beautiful sandy bays, many of which are deeply indented between rocky headlands. Its inland countryside lacks the drama of most of our area, but its gently rolling country has wide open skies and an ever-present backdrop provided by the distant skyline of Snowdonia. This gentle landscape also has many secrets, including two pleasant reservoirs, many small medieval churches, and a series of fascinating prehistoric monuments. The towns of Holyhead and Llangefni are both worth visiting, and neither Beaumaris, with its splendid castle, nor the National Trust's Plas Newydd, should be missed.

Snowdonia itself hardly needs special praise here. It contains some of the most splendid scenery in the British Isles, and offers a bewildering range of activities to the visitor — from the exploration of its mountains, an activity only for those with experience or with proper guidance — to visits to slate caverns and hydro-electric stations, rides on little railways, walks in forests and beside lakes, rivers and waterfalls, or ambles around small towns, villages and ancient monuments. Snowdon itself may be climbed with care, or visited on its own mountain railway starting from Llanberis, an interesting village which should certainly be visited.

Snowdonia's northern coast has several fine castles; Conwy Castle, sheltering an equally fine old town at the seaward end of the delightful Conwy Valley; Penrhyn Castle, not medieval, but a fascinating neo-Norman structure; and of course the magnificent castle of Caernarfon. Between Conwy and Penrhyn, the coast is dominated by the northern end of the great Carneddau Range, and further west it is bounded by the narrow and very beautiful Menai Strait, with Anglesey just beyond.

Beyond Caernarfon, the lovely Lleyn Peninsula is not far away. Here will be found a coastline very similar to that of Anglesey — long sandy bays, high cliffs and quiet coves. Its quiet interior is well served with small roads, and there are medieval churches to be visited and several prominent and quite dramatic hill and mountain-tops, some of which reveal signs of occupation in Celtic times.

Eastwards, beyond broad Tremadog Bay, is the great castle of Harlech, overlooking a wide sweep of dune country, and backed by the hills of the Ardudwy and the Rhinog mountains beyond — a most attractive piece of country. South from here is the outstandingly beautiful Mawddach Estuary, and beyond it, the mountain mass of Cadair Idris, and the charming old towns of Dolgellau and Machynlleth, with Aberdyfi yet further south at the head of the lovely Dyfi Estuary.

The eastern, inland fringes of our area are taken up with the great forests of Dyfi and Coed-y-Brenin, and the lonely mountain ranges of Aran and Arenig, with the three great lakes of Trawsfynydd, Celyn and Tegid (Bala) adding further sparkle and interest to a largely desert scene.

To guide you to the very best features which the area as a whole has to offer, we have devised a series of ten tours. They are, like the guide as a whole, self-contained, but if you purchase the relevant Landranger map or maps you will be able to vary these tours to suit your own requirements. They have been designed primarily for motorists, but most are also suitable for cyclists.

Walkers would of course find these tours too long and too 'road-orientated', but to whet your appetite, we have also provided a series of sixteen walks in widely varied countryside, and each of these link on to at least one of the tours.

History Revealed ...
A Short Survey of the Area's Past

Moving up the western coastlands of Europe from the Iberian peninsula and the Mediterranean, Neolithic (or Stone Age) farming communities had begun to settle in North Wales, as in other parts of upland Britain, by the mid-fourth millenium BC. Evidence of this occupation is to be found in the many 'megalithic' chambered tombs (used for multiple burials) in North Wales, two of the finest specimens of which are both on Anglesey — **Bryncelli Ddu** and **Barclodiad y Gawres**. Although devoted largely to stock rearing, they also had at least one thriving industry in North Wales, the so-called 'axe factory' on a hillside above **Penmaemawr**, the products of which have been found in many other parts of Britain.

About 2000 BC the so-called 'Beaker Folk' moved westward from the Continent, heralding the Bronze Age. This culture was characterised by the worship of its peoples at stone circles or henges, the most famous of which are far to the south at Stonehenge and Avebury. The finest specimen in the area (although a pale shadow of Stonehenge) is the 'Druid's Circle', not far to the south of the Penmaenmawr 'axe factory' (see above), but there was also probably a stone circle associated with **Bryncelli Ddu**, and there are the remains of several other circles in the mountains behind the northern coast, in the Ardudwy hills behind Harlech (124) (SH 61-32) and behind Dyfrynn Ardudwy (124) (SH 60-23) (SH 61-20). The Bronze Age dead were buried singly in 'round barrows' and many of these will be found in the area, in the form of tumuli or cairns. Many of the area's numerous standing stones also date from the Bronze Age, although some may be rubbing or marker stones of a much later date.

A third wave of settlers, the Celtic Iron Age peoples, moved westward from the Continent between about 550 BC and AD 50, bringing with them a form of speech which was to provide the origins not only of the Welsh language, but also that of the related tongues of Gaelic, Manx and Cornish. They organised themselves into larger and more cohesive groups, and were able to construct and maintain many large, well-sited settlements, such as the oustandingly impressive Tre'r Ceiri above **Llanaelhearn**, and **Din Lligwy** to the north-west of Benllech. Many other groups of huts built by these Celtic peoples have survived, and are still known in North Wales as Cytiau'r Gwyddelod, or Muriau'r Gwyddelod (Irishmen's Houses, or Irishmen's Walls).

By the time the Romans landed in Britain in AD 43, Celtic Britain was split into a number of tribal areas and northwest Wales was occupied by the Ordovices, with the Druids exerting a particularly strong influence in Anglesey. By AD 58 the Roman legions had finally defeated the Silures, the tribe occupying South Wales, and it was only a matter of time before the Roman Governor, Suetonius Paulinus, was able to push right across North Wales from the legionary fortress at Chester. His legions first defeated the neighbouring Deceangli, and then in AD 61 crossed the Menai Strait in flat bottom boats and

Bryncelli Ddu Burial Chamber.

crushed the Ordovices and the Druid priests, who, with their customs of human sacrifice, had so disgusted the far-from-squeamish Roman troops . For a graphic account of Suetonius Paulinus's crossing of the Menai Strait see *The Annals of Tacitus*.

To retain control of the area, something which had to be postponed a few years until Queen Boadicea's rebellion in the south-east had been crushed, the

Romans built a network of roads linking their permanent fortresses at **Caerhun** (Canovium), **Caernarfon** (Segontium), **Holyhead** (Caer Gybi), **Tomen- y-mur** and at **Caer Gai**, near Bala. Life in many of the Celtic, 'Iron Age' settlements must have continued much as before, with a Celtic tradition still very much alive. However, some facets of the Romano-British way of life certainly existed even in this remote corner of the Empire (see the pillar in **Llangian** churchyard, and the inscribed stone in **Llansadwrn** church).

It is not surprising that the next period of history has been called the 'Dark Ages', as our knowledge of what really took place in the centuries following the departure of the legions is still extremely scanty. But there is no doubt that in Wales, Christianity brought here by the Romans continued to flourish after their departure, and even to grow, and that this was the heroic age of the Celtic Church. Homespun missionary saints, among them St Beuno, St Cadfan, and even possibly St Patrick, established cells here and some set out to 'convert the heathen' in lands across the sea,

including Ireland, Scotland and the West Country. It was many years before the practices of Rome were able to supersede those of the Celtic Christian Church with any degree of success, and its strength was borne out by the continuing popularity as a place of pilgrimage for many centuries to come, of **Bardsey Island**, the so-called 'Island of 20,000 Saints'.

The Anglo-Saxons probably never penetrated far into the mountain fastness of North Wales, but both they, and much later the Norsemen, frequently raided the Welsh from the sea, plundering the monasteries of **Penmon** and **Bardsey** in the process. These external threats helped to unite the north-west Welsh into the kingdom of Gwynedd, and Rhodri Mawr was their first great leader against the marauding Danes, while his grandson Hywel Dda established the first laws of the Welsh.

The period that followed, between the 9th and 13th centuries, was the great age of the Welsh Princes. Due largely to their geographical situation these Princes were tolerated by the Norman kings of England, who even left

Caernarfon Castle — one of Edward I's great coastal fortresses.

the policing of the less remote border country (the Welsh Marches) to their 'Marcher Lords'. The Wales of this time was visited in 1188 by a Norman-Welsh monk, Gerald of Barry, or Giraldus Cambrensis, and his *Itinerary of Wales* describes the land through which he travelled and the people he encountered on the way.

From their court at **Aberffraw** on Anglesey, the Welsh Princes succeeded in extending their power and influence, this reaching its peak during the reign of Llywelyn the Great, grandly titled 'Prince of Aberffraw and Lord of Snowdon'. It was probably at this time that the four very different 'native castles' of **Castell y Bere**, **Criccieth**, **Dolbadarn** and **Dolwyddelan** were built. Llywelyn the Great's grandson, subsequently known as 'Llywelyn the Last', at one time appeared to be faring as well as his ancestor, but he then misjudged the new English king, Edward I, and refused to pay homage to him on his accession. For this miscalculation, he eventually paid with his life, and in the years that followed Edward I finally put paid to further Welsh ambitions, not only by defeating them in the campaigns of 1276 and 1277, but also by building his six great coastal castles, four of which still stand in our area — **Beaumaris, Conwy, Caernarfon and Harlech**, the other two being Aberystwyth and Flint.

Apart from a brief moment of glory, during the 'rebellion' of Owain Glyndwr between 1400 and 1412, and his short-lived Welsh parliaments, Welsh aspirations had to make do with the ascent to the English throne by one of their own — an Anglesey man, Henry Tudor of **Penmynydd**, who became Henry VII. The loyalty of the Welsh to their Tudor masters seems to have been transferred without much effort to the Stuarts, and during the Civil War the gentry of north and west Wales supplied a contingent of Welsh troops large enough to form an effective core for the army of the King.

Due at least in part to the earlier struggles that took place in this area, medieval architecture, apart from the great castles and massive town walls, is not as well represented here as in the more settled parts of the country. However, despite widespread and often

Cymmer Abbey, near Dolgellau.

over-enthusiastic restoration in Victorian times, a number of medieval churches are still well worth visiting. There are fine examples at **Clynnog-fawr**, **Conwy**, **Llanengan**, **Llaniestyn** and **Llanegryn**; but especially in Anglesey and the Lleyn, where there are many other simple, unspoilt churches to be found. The remains of the monastic institutions on **Bardsey** and **St Tudwal's Islands** are not accessible, but **Penmon Priory** and the ruins of **Cymmer Abbey** are both of considerable interest.

Secular building work in the form of manor houses and mansions have survived from the 15th, 16th and 17th centuries, and may be seen at **Penarth Fawr**, **Cochwillan Old Hall** and **Plas-yn-Rhiw** respectively, while the late 18th and early 19th centuries are well represented by **Plas Newydd** and **Penrhyn Castle**. Aberconwy, a fine example of a medieval merchant's house may be visited at **Conwy**, and in contrast, elegant late 18th and early 19th century town houses are to be seen in Beaumaris, at that time a fashionable resort for the gentry of Anglesey and the nearby mainland.

The Agricultural Revolution had a considerable impact on some areas, with the enclosure of the lowland parts of Anglesey and the coastal country of the mainland, and the reclamation of the Glaslyn Estuary, near **Porthmadog** and the marshes near **Maltraeth**. On the other hand, the Industrial Revolution saw the opening-up of the great copper mines on **Parys Mountain** and its port at nearby **Amlwch**. Less dramatic

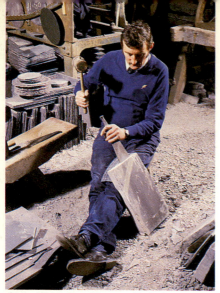

At the Welsh Slate Museum, Llanberis.

developments included the establishment of water-powered woollen mills, examples of which may still be found today at **Felin Isaf**, **Trefriw**, **Penmachno** and **Brynkir**. However, the greatest industrial impact upon the area in the 19th century was the creation of a demand for cheap house-roofing material. This demand was met by the development of the massive slate quarries around Llanberis, Corris, Blaenau Ffestiniog, and Abergynolwyn; an activity which was literally to change the face of the areas in which it took place. The slate industry, which in its time spawned railways, ports, mines, vast quarries, waste tips, mining villages, non-conformist chapels and even great country houses, has now all but gone. Despite this collapse there are many fascinating remains still to be seen at **Llanberis** and **Blaenau Ffestiniog**, and railways which were originally built for slate-carrying still run, including **the Ffestiniog**, **the Llanberis** and **the Talyllyn**. A smaller, but more romantic industry was also established further south, the extraction of gold from the Mawddach Valley, part of the area now covered by the **Coed-y-Brenin**, **Cwmmynach**, and also in the hills to the north of **Bontddu**, the latter still being partly productive.

The need for improved transport through the area was answered by the development of the London-to-Holyhead road by the engineering genius, Thomas Telford. His outstanding works in the area, the great bridges across the Conwy Estuary and the Menai Strait, were later paralleled by the two fine railway bridges of Robert Stephenson.

The landscape is now already recovering from the ravages of slate-quarrying, but other activities have made their mark in recent years — forestry, water supply, and both hydro-powered and nuclear-powered electricity generation. Although some of these developments have made positive contributions to the landscape, critical comments have been levelled at all three. It is likely however that the growing pressures of tourism may yet prove to be more harmful than any of them.

Visitors have been coming to Snowdonia for a very long time. In the 18th century the mountains of North Wales, along with those in the Lake District and Scotland, became the subject of much interest to the newly flourishing Romantic movement, and a number of visitors came here well in advance of the great mass of holidaymakers brought here by the railways in the later years of the 19th century and the early years of the 20th. The creation of the Snowdonia National Park has drawn even greater attention to the attractions of much of the area covered by this guide, but constant efforts are being made to reconcile the interests of the inhabitants of the area with those of the visitor. The Park authorities have worked hard to protect its most fragile elements — worn footpaths, eroded grass slopes, etc. — and have campaigned ceaselessly to protect the area against over-development. But there is one point that cannot be stressed strongly enough — the vast majority of the land in the National Park is privately owned, and no special rights for visitors are implied by the words 'National' or 'Park'. This then is Snowdonia, Anglesey and the Lleyn in the 20th century, the result of nature's creation and the impact upon it of man's fascinating and varied activities over many thousands of years. There is a wealth of interest and beauty to be absorbed, and if all who come this way act with consideration and thoughtfulness, there should be many more years in which this may be savoured with undiluted pleasure.

Natural History

By Reg Jones

Snowdonia, Anglesey and the Lleyn Peninsula embrace a wide variety of habitats ranging from the highest mountains in Wales to lush lowland marshes and fens. In addition there is a coastline which includes broad estuaries with open sandy flats, while in complete contrast there are impressive sea cliffs and rocky offshore islands.

Snowdonia — The Uplands. The name Snowdonia conjures up a vision of mountains and this is indeed an upland area punctuated by rugged peaks and crags with steep-sided slopes, often scree-covered, plunging down towards dark narrow lakes. While the area has been formed by natural forces, most recently by glaciers, man too has left his imprint, not least by his use of grazing animals, especially sheep. Sheep feed by nibbling and any plant which cannot regenerate itself from ground level is destroyed. Thus, those parts of the uplands used for grazing sheep are, for the most part, rather monotonous stretches of grasses with few brightly coloured flowering plants apart from low-growing species such as yellow-flowered tormentil and wispy heath bedstraw.

Fortunately sheep cannot reach everything and where there are north-facing cliffs with damp and inaccessible ledges more interesting plants like purple saxifrage and rose-root may be established. These are examples of 'arctic-alpines' because of their usual association with

Wheatyear — a summer resident on scree-covered slopes.

Alpine and Arctic situations but there are other species such as the Welsh Poppy which are also to be found at lower levels. One plant, the Snowdon Lily, grows nowhere else in Britain other than on ledges in the Glyder and Snowdon ranges. Rocky screes, usually limeless, may appear almost barren but where there are shady recesses these may also be occupied by parsley fern or tufts of heather and bilberry. Wet and boggy places can be relatively colourful with, amongst others, butterwort, sundew, bog asphodel and marsh orchids.

Well-cropped grassy terrain does not attract a great variety of nesting birds apart from skylarks and meadow pipits with a few curlews in rougher and quieter parts. However, where there are rocky features, other species are soon noted. Ravens flight from lofty crags emitting gutteral calls, 'pruk-pruk', as they go, sometimes soaring on outstretched wings or occasionally engaging in aerobatic manoeuvres. The smaller carrion crow is present at lower altitudes and parties of red-legged and red-billed choughs, which may have nested in disused copper mines, occasionally alight to probe in the turf for grubs. Of the birds of prey, a buzzard, circling aloft, mewing plaintively, is often in view while kestrels, probably nesting on cliff ledges, hover in the air. Regrettably, the peregrine, another crag-nesting bird, must be considered somewhat rare. Of the smaller species, ring ouzels and wheatears occur locally in stony gullies or on rocky hillsides, usually being accompanied by the ubiquitous wren. Where there are

Welsh Poppy — widely distributed in damp, rocky places.

lakes with pebble-fringed shores, common sandpipers are often in residence, while other species as varied as cormorants and grey wagtails may be regular visitors.

The general features of upland Snowdonia can be appreciated by following a nature trail, such as the one at Cwm Idwal (see page 56). It is approached from the A5 at Ogwen Cottage (115) (SH 65-60). The trail proceeds around the shallow glacial lake, Llyn Idwal, which lies partly encircled by impressive cliffs and peaks.

Snowdonia — The Woodlands. In earlier times, broad-leaved woodlands covered much of Britain and in Snowdonia many of the hillsides were clothed with trees, mainly sessile oaks. Regrettably, largely as a result of man's activities, most have disappeared and apart from isolated specimens sprouting from inaccessible crags, true native woodland is restricted to a relatively few places, usually in the valleys.

A typical lowland oakwood has a rich ground flora including many common flowers such as primrose and dog's mercury. In Snowdonia, where, very often, the soil is thin and there is grazing by sheep, the ground cover consists mainly of grasses with possibly some heather and bilberry in the drier parts. The presence of bracken indicates a deeper soil and where there are steep gullies with bubbling streams the plant life will be decidedly richer and will include a number of ferns.

Oak trees play host to a variety of organisms. In damp and unpolluted atmospheres, lichens quickly adorn the bark and ferns may grow from damp crotches. Few trees support a greater population of insects, including countless moth caterpillars which feed in the leafy canopy. These attract insect-eating birds: common species such as tits, willow warblers and chaffinches, together with rarer pied flycatchers, redstarts and wood warblers. Several of these are hole-nesting, utilising cavities which have developed over the years in mature trees after branches have become detached. In addition, there are the acorns, and these are greedily consumed by jays and squirrels, mice and voles, the last two being, in turn, the prey of tawny owls. Other predators,

Pied Flycatcher — a hole-nesting bird in broad-leaved woodlands.

nesting aloft, are buzzards and the dashing sparrow hawk. All this is just a part of a thriving community.

While deciduous woods are small and few in number extensive planting of conifers has taken place during the present century. Being largely evergreen and closely arranged, little light reaches the ground to encourage the development of other plants. Consequently, coniferous woods of this type never appear to support as much life as broad-leaved woodland. Nevertheless, some species do well. Coal tits and goldcrests are very much in evidence and it is here, in summer, that siskins are to be seen. New plantations can be extremely interesting. Less shady conditions prevail and, sheep being excluded by fencing, a vigorous ground cover develops. In addition the young trees make excellent song posts for numerous small birds including yellowhammers, redpolls, whinchats, tree-pipits and willow warblers.

Good examples of broad-leaved woods can be seen around the Mawddach estuary. Further north the Coed Llyn Mair Trail (124) (SH 65-41) (see Tan-y-bwlch, page 106), near Maentwrog, proceeds through an oak wood, while the Coedydd Aber Trail (115) (SH 66-71) (see page 29) embraces both deciduous and coniferous woodland. There are several instructive walks in the Gwydyr Forest (115) (SH 79-55 etc.) (see page 64) around Betws-y-Coed.

Anglesey. While much of Anglesey consists of gently undulating country devoted to agriculture there is a great deal to interest the naturalist. Inland there are a number of fertile lakes or meres, such as Llyn Coron (114) (SH 37-70) (see page 77), with a rich flora and fauna including as typical breeding birds, great crested grebe, coot and tufted duck. In addition there are marshes and fens renowned for the quality of their plant life. However, probably the greatest attractions lie around the coast. The north-eastern peninsula based on Penmon is limestone country and this is apparent in the flowers as seen at the Iron Age settlement, Bwrdd Arthur (114) (SH 58-81) (see page 76), where there are rock-roses, bloody cranesbills, green-winged orchids and many other lime-loving plants. In this area, there are several seabird colonies, some situated in quarries, with herring, lesser black-backed and great black-backed gulls and, sometimes common gulls. Offshore is Puffin Island which can be viewed from boats sailing from Beaumaris. Nowadays it is renowned for the huge herring gull colony but there are auks, kittiwakes and fulmars on the cliffs with cormorants and shags at lower levels.

West of Moelfre (114) (SH 51-86), the limestone is replaced by limeless rocks and the coast is more rugged with the headlands clothed with gorse, heather and bracken rather than the richer chalk flora further east. At the same time, rocky slopes inclining towards the sea are often bright with spring squills, thrift and sea campion. Seabirds nest here and there, but the largest numbers are to be seen on Anglesey's highest cliffs at South Stack on Holy Island (114) (SH 20-82) (see page 104). Here are hundreds of guillemots and razorbills together with puffins, fulmars, shags and cormorants. This is an R.S.P.B. reserve and there are good viewing facilities. Offshore, terns may be seen fishing but they need level shores where

they can nest undisturbed. Anglesey provides one or two such sites as at Cemlyn Lagoon (114) (SH 33-93) (see page 49), and at Inys Feirig, off Rhosneigr (114) (SH 30-73) (see page 102).

In contrast to the South Stack cliffs, there is distinctly flatter ground in the south-east of the island, the area known as Newborough Warren (114) (SH 42-63 etc). (See also page 91, for map and

Herring Gulls — commonest of the larger gulls found around the coast.

further details.) Lying between the estuaries of the Cefni and Braint rivers it embraces a variety of habitats including an extensive dune system and a salt marsh. A significant portion has been planted with conifers, mainly Corsican Pine, creating Newborough Forest, but the remainder is a National Nature Reserve.

In the east, where the Braint flows into the Menai Strait, there are open sandy flats from which sand, blowing inland, has created dunes, those closest to the shore being bound together by marram grass. The dunes further inland, being older, are carpeted with an appreciable variety of plants, the flora on the landward side being heath-like with some shrubs such as hawthorn. As in typical dune systems, there are hollows or slacks between adjacent dunes and, offering moister conditions, there are a number of distinctive species such as creeping willow, round-leaved wintergreen, grass of Parnassus, butterwort and orchids including the rare dune helleborine. Of the animal life in the dunes, the large number of nesting gulls is most apparent but there are other breeding birds: oystercatcher, lapwing,

Bloody Cranesbill — a characteristic plant found on calcareous soils.

Kittiwake — an oceanic bird nesting on precipitous cliffs.

curlew, skylark and meadow pipit.

The salt marsh (114) (SH 40-66) lies on the southern bank of the Cefni estuary. At the north-eastern end is a shallow, brackish pool, Malltraeth Pool (114) (SH 40-68), which is a good place to watch wading birds, especially in spring and autumn when they are on passage. Finally, and quite different from the rest of the reserve, there is Llanddwyn (114) (SH 38-62) (see page 70), a rocky peninsula projecting outwards from the south-western shore, with a flora typical of rocky terrain and a colony of shags and cormorants on an offshore islet. Newborough Warren can be reached on the A4080, south-westwards from Menai Bridge. Six well signed access routes allow for its exploration. (See also page 88.)

The Lleyn Peninsula. Much of the Lleyn Peninsula is lowland pasture interrupted here and there by domed hills of hard lime-free rocks — the monadnock hills. The term monadnock means 'an isolated peak'. Some of the drier slopes are heather clad although much has disappeared over the years as a result of burning and grazing. One such group of peaks is Yr Eifl, lying close to the western coastline. Nearby, and close to Penrhyn Glas (123) (SH 33-43), the massive cliff, Carreg y Llam, rises from the sea, its ledges being occupied by the largest colony of guillemots and razor-

bills in North Wales. With them are the other common cliff-nesting species: kittiwakes, fulmars, shags, cormorants and some gulls. The cliff is approached by leaving the A449 coast road at Llanaelhaearn and after following the B4417 for three miles, a minor road heads off towards the coast. It is also possible to reach this by referring to Tour Six, page 120, well beyond Nefyn.

For other seabirds it is necessary to visit offshore islands. Bardsey (123) (SH 12-21) (see page 36), lying two miles out to sea off the southern tip of the peninsula is a haven for 2-3000 pairs of manx shearwaters which nest in burrows below ground. By day, they are silent and unseen but during the hours of darkness the air is filled with their weird cackling and birds flying in from the sea tumble out of the sky before moving clumsily to join their mates. The chough is another familiar resident and the island is also home for a number of grey seals. Bardsey is approached by boat from Aberdaron within whose bay are two smaller rocky islets, Ynys Gwylan-fawr and Ynys Gwylan-bâch (123) (SH 18-24), the former having a variety of seabirds, but being particularly noted for its puffins. Further east are St Tudwal's Islands (123) (SH 34-25), but they are less well populated.

The greatest variety of plants occurs along the southern border fringing Cardigan Bay and this is a result of variation in the nature of the underlying rock. In the extreme west, on the lime-free slopes of Mynydd Mawr (123) (SH 13-25) there are unrelieved stretches of heather and gorse, but on moving a couple of miles eastwards towards Aberdaron, where less acid conditions prevail, a more diverse flora is in evidence. To emphasise this change, a few miles further east, on the slopes of Mynydd Rhiw (123) (SH 24-29), the ash, a lover of wet calcareous soils, flourishes and the ground supports lime-seeking plants. The trend is reversed at Trwyn Cilan (123) (SH 29-23), acid rocks being dominant, and in the shallow pools on the peaty headland are aquatic plants such as pillwort and velvety-leaved marsh St John's wort which characterise non-calcareous waters. This is a coastline well worth exploration.

Leisure Activities . . . A Brief Summary

The area covered by this guide provides a bewildering variety of sport and leisure activities and we have listed some of those which we feel will be of particular interest to visitors.

Motoring. You will probably have arrived in your own car, but if you wish to hire a self-drive car or chauffeur-driven car, there is a wide choice available. Self-drive cars are available from the following garages:

Aberconwy Car Hire, Llandudno, *Tel: (0492) 74669*

British Car Rentals, Llanfairpwll, *Tel (0248) 714355*

Caernarfon Motors, Caernarfon, *Tel: (0286) 2475*

Castle Rentals, Criccieth, *Tel: (076671) 2085/2807*

Garth Service Station, Bangor, *Tel: (0248) 353640*

Gordon Ford, Colwyn Bay, *Tel: (0492) 2201*

Swan National, Holyhead, *Tel: (0407) 4614*

If alternative services are required, or if you require a chauffeur-driven car, use the local Yellow Pages, or Thompson Directory, as there are many other services available. A list of self-drive hire operators is also available at T.I.C.s.

Path to Llyn Idwal (see Cwm Idwal, page 56).

Bus. Local bus services can be fun if you are prepared to fit in with their schedules, which in many parts of the country are governed by local transport needs. In Snowdonia, however, great efforts have been made to provide a number of special services for visitors. Timetables giving details of times and routes (including a splendid bus map of the area) may be obtained from most T.I.C.s, or from the Public Transport Unit, County Planning Department, County Offices, Caernarfon LL55 1SH. Special 'unlimited travel' tickets are on offer, either *Gwynedd Bus Rovers*, or *Crosville Wanderers*. A very special service has also been developed to provide access in and around the Snowdon massif itself, and this is called *The Snowdon Sherpa*. This service is a great help to walkers and climbers, and overcomes the problem of overcrowding on the small car parks in the mountains (leaflet available at most T.I.C.s).

Train. Details of British Rail's train services in the area may be obtained from most T.I.C.s, or from any British Rail Station. As in the case of the bus services, great efforts have been made to provide a range of special services for the visitor. Those staying in Llandudno are especially well served, with a series of interesting day trips during the season, and a special 'Sunday Shuttle' down the Conwy Valley, to link with the Ffestiniog Railway, and on to the Cambrian Coast Line. This British Rail coastal line is a most useful feature in its own right, and runs along the

coast between Aberystwyth and Pwllheli, with links not only with main-line trains from London, Birmingham and Shrewsbury, but also with some of the famous 'Great Little Trains of Wales'. These are the Ffestiniog, the Welsh Highland, the Fairbourne, and the Talyllyn, all of which have very different personalities of their own. Also in our area are the Llanberis Lake Railway and the Bala Lake Railway. For further details including those relating to 8-day 'Wanderer Tickets', ask at any T.I.C. for the leaflet, *Great Little Trains of Wales*.

Caravanning and Camping. There are so many suitable sites in the area covered by this guide, that it would be impossible, in a publication of this nature, to provide a list that could be judged to be adequately representative. There is a useful series of guide leaflets which include details of sites in the various areas covered, and all the T.I.C.s can provide further help. If you wish to plan in advance, there are a number of excellent countrywide booklets on sale nationally from early January each year. But if you wish to have the very best camping and/or caravan site information, you would be advised to join one of the national clubs covering these activities. These include: *The Camping and Caravanning Club, 11 Lower Grosvenor Place, London SW1W 0EY*, and *The Caravan Club, East Grinstead House, East Grinstead, West Sussex RH19 1UA*.

Cycling. This is a splendid way of looking around the area, and once off the main routes (which is the object of most of our listed tours) the little 'unclassified' roads (yellow on the Landranger map) are relatively peaceful. Many of the roads in the mountains are unavoidably demanding, but if you are reasonably fit you should not be deterred. If you do not have your own machine, these can be hired from: Maglona Garage, *Maengwyn St., Machynlleth. Tel: (0654) 2019*, and Lakeside Services, *10, Lakeside Estate, Rhosneigr. Tel: (0407) 810338*.
If you still have difficulty in making arrangements, the very helpful *Cyclists Touring Club. 69 Meadrow, Godalming, Surrey GU7 3HS. Tel: (048 68) 7217*, may have other addresses. Why not become a member?

Walking and Climbing. Walking is the ideal way of exploring the area, and may be combined with any of the above means of transport. You will find sixteen walks described on pages 130-161, and we hope that these will provide a pleasant introduction to the pleasures of walking with map and guide in this often dramatic mountain country. However, do not attempt, either as walker or climber, any forays into the mountains without proper equipment, experience and advice. If in doubt, first refer to the advice

given on the inside of the rear cover, and remember that every year without exception, there are a number of tragedies in this area. So, please make sure that Landranger Guide readers are never found to be at risk themselves, nor a menace to others.

Those without experience wishing to go into the hills would be advised to first go on some guided walks. As their helpful annual leaflet explains, the Snowdonia National Park provides a series of 'informal walks led by capable leaders, whose knowledge of the area will help you to learn more about the National Park, its history, scenery and people'. Most details will also be found in the tourist 'newspaper', *Dragon Times*.

Advice on clothes and equipment will be found on the inside of the rear cover. To help you overcome to some extent the vagaries of the weather, the National Park provide an automatic telephone **Weather Forecast Service**. This is available from 7.30am each day on Llanberis 870120. Do please make use of it, if you are heading into the hills, however capable you feel you may be. There is a wealth of detailed advice available on walking and climbing, but we would suggest that you first read W.A. Poucher's *The Welsh Peaks*, and/or Terry Marsh's *The Mountains of Wales*. They are both excellent, but to gain further experience, why not go on a course at the National Centre for Mountain Activities at Plas-y-Brenin? (see Capel Curig, page 47).

Although there is a network of clearly signed walks in the Snowdonia National Park, and a series of forest and nature trails, do not always expect to find well defined paths in other areas. If walking on non-waymarked paths, rights of way are clearly shown on both the Landranger map and on the Pathfinder extracts, but these may not show up too clearly on the ground. If in doubt, do try to ask locally regarding rights of way, and at all times do make sure that your dog is on a lead if livestock are anywhere near, and that all gates are left as you found them, which will normally be closed. One thing which should be made clear to every visitor — almost all land in the National Park is privately owned, and the status of 'National Park' does not water down the rights of farmers and other landowners — so please respect the privacy of the resident population.

Horse Riding. Details of the very wide range of available riding facilities may be obtained from any of the T.I.C.s, and the Wales Tourist Board publish a useful booklet entitled *Wales - Pony Trekking and Riding*. All levels of skill are catered for, from the complete expert to the novice; but for full details see the booklet, which may be obtained at the nearest T.I.C.

Pony Trekking along the shore of Llyn Geironydd.

The Best of the Beaches. There are a bewildering number of beaches in this area, but some of our favourites are in Anglesey and the Lleyn. See 'Places of Interest' section for details, but why not visit some of these — On Anglesey: Llanddwyn Bay, Porth Trafadog, Ynys y Fydlyn, Traeth yr Ora, and Traeth Bychan — On the Lleyn: Abersoch, Porth Neigwl, Porth Iago, Porth Towyn, and Porth Nefyn. There are many other pleasant stretches of sandy beach in other areas, notably at Penmaemawr, Llandudno, Colwyn Bay on the north coast, and Black Rock Sands, Barmouth, Tywyn and Aberdyfi further to the south.

Water Sports. This area has much to offer those who, in some way or other, love to 'mess about in boats'. There are many points along the coast where small boats may be launched, but if you are inexperienced in matters concerning the sea, do ask for local advice. Well-known sailing centres include Abersoch, Aberdyfi (home of the GP14 class of sailing dinghies), Red Wharf Bay, Beaumaris, Borth-y-Gest and Portdinorwic. Sailing courses are run at the new Sports Centre at Plas Menai, and at Plas Rhiwaedog, near Bala. Windsurfing has now also become very popular in the area, both on the lakes and on the sea. Bala is now a nationally recognised centre for 'White Water' canoeing, and an information pack on the available facilities may be obtained by sending an S.A.E. to the *Council Offices, High St., Bala, Gwynedd.*

Golf. There are no fewer than 23 courses in the area covered by this guide. They are: The Aberdovey, *Tel: (065472) 210.* The Abersoch,

Tel: *(075881) 2622.* The Anglesey, at Rhosneigr, *Tel: (0407) 810219.* The Bala, *Tel: (0678) 520539.* The Baron Hill, near Beaumaris, *Tel: (0248) 810231.* The Betws-y-Coed, *Tel: (06902) 556.* The Bull Bay, near Amlwch, *Tel: (0407) 831188.* The Caernarfon, near Caernarfon, *Tel: (0286) 3783.* The Caernarfonshire, near Conwy, *Tel: (0492) 633400.* The Criccieth, *Tel: (076671) 2154.* The Dolgellau, *Tel: (0341) 422603.* The Ffestiniog,

Canoeing on Llyn Gwynant.

Tel: (076676) 2587. The Holyhead, at Treard-dur, *Tel (0407) 3279.* The Nefyn & District, *Tel: (0758) 720218.* The North Wales, Llandudno, *Tel: (0492) 75325.* The Machynlleth, *Tel: (0654) 2246.* The Old Colwyn, *Tel: (0492) 515581.* The Penmaenmawr, near Conwy, *Tel: (0492) 623330.* The Porthmadog, *Tel: (0766) 2037.* The Pwllheli, *Tel: (0758) 612520.* The Rhôs on Sea, *Tel: (0942) 49641.* The Royal St David's, Harlech, *Tel: (0766) 780361.* The St Deiniol, near Bangor, *Tel: (0248) 353098.*

Fishing. There are a wealth of fishing opportunities in the area covered by our guide. Much valuable information relating to coastal, river and reservoir fishing may be obtained from the various Tourist Information Centres, and the Wales Tourist Board publishes a really excellent *Wales Angling Guide*, (edited by Clive Gammon). This contains detailed information and guidance relating to angling from beaches, estuaries, headlands and jetties, and of course, from boats. Wales' rich game-fishing rivers are also described in detail, and there is also a section on coarse fishing in the reservoirs.

Places to Visit .... A summary list showing page number followed by map number/s and map reference.

Castles and Castle Earthworks.
Beaumaris (38) (114,115) (SH 60-76)
Caernarfon (46) (114,115) (SH 47-62)
Castell Aberlleiniog (78) (114,115) (SH 61-79)
Castell y Bere (48) (124) (SH 66-08)
Conwy (52) (115) (SH 77-77)
Criccieth (54) (123,124) (SH 50-38)
Dolbadarn (59) (115) (SH 58-59)
Dolwyddelan (60) (115) (SH 73-52)
Domen Ddreiniog (73) (135) (SH 59-03)
Harlech (65) (124) (SH 58-31)
Tomen y Bala (34) (125) (SH 92-36)

Craft Centres and Craft Activities.
Blythe Farm, Llandwrog (73) (115, 123) (SH 44-57)
Bodvel Hall (42) (123) (SH 34-36)
Bryn Melyn Studio, Dolgellau (60) (124) (SH 72-17)
Cae Ddafydd (90) (115) (SH 61-45)
Corris Craft Centre (53) (124) (SH 75-07)
Cwm Pottery, Trefor (108) (123) (SH 37-46)
Llanberis Craft Workshops (69) (114,115) (SH 58-60)
Maes Artro Tourist Village (68) (123) (SH 43-36)
Penmachno (village) (92) (115) (SH 79-50)
Porthmadog Pottery (97) (124) (SH 56-38)
Portmeirion (99) (124) (SH 59-37)

Factories, Mills, Power Stations, Quarries, etc.
Bethesda Slate Quarries (40) (115) (SH 62-65)
Bodeilio Weaving Centre (41) (114,115) (SH 49-77)
Braichgoch Slate Slab Quarries (53) (124) (SH 74-08)
Brynkir Woollen Mill (43) (124) (SH 52-42)
Centre For Alternative Technology (49) (135) (SH 04-75)

Clogau St David's Gold Mine *(Not open at time of writing)* (42) (124) (SH 66-19)
Dinorwic Power Station (58) (115) (SH 59-59)
Felin Isaf (62) (116) (SH 80-74)
Ffestiniog Hydro-Electric Scheme (63) (124) (SH 67-44)
Gloddfa Ganol Slate Mine (64) (115) (SH 69-47)
Llechwedd Slate Caverns (81) (115) (SH 70-47)
Meirion Woollen Mill (58) (124,125) (SH 85-13)
Old Llanfair Quarry Slate Caverns (74) (124) (SH 57-28)
Parys Mountain (32) (114) (SH 44-90)
Pemmachno Woollen Mill (92) (116) (SH 80-52)
Tudor Slate Works, Groeslon (64) (123,115) (SH 47-55)
Trawsfynydd Nuclear Power Station (107) (124) (SH 69-38)
Trefriw Woollen Mill (108) (115) (SH 78-63)
Welsh Slate Museum (69) (114,115) (SH 58-60)
Wylfa Nuclear Power Station (109) (114) (SH 35-93)

Forests and Forest Walks.
Afon Eden Trail (50) (124) (SH 71-27)
Beddgelert Forest Walks (40) (115) (SH 56-49 etc.)
Bishop Morgan Trail (108) (115) (SH 77-52)
Cabin Wood Walk, Llanystumdwy (81) (123) (SH 46-38)
Cae'n-y-Coed (44) (115) (SH 76-57)
Coed-y-Brenin (50) (124) (SH 73-26 etc.)
Cwm Cadian Forest Walks (55) (124) (SH 75-05)
Dyfi (Dovey) Forest (61) (124,135) (SH 80-10 etc.)
Foel Friog (63) (124) (SH 77-09)
Garth Falls Walk (64) (115) (SH 77-56)
Gwydyr Forest Walks (64) (115,116) (SH 78-58 etc.)
Hendai Forest Trail (70) (114) (SH 40-63)
Nant Gwernol (31) (124) (SH 68-06)
Newborough Forest (91) (114) (SH 40-64 etc.)
Penllyn Forest (92) (125) (SH 96-30 etc.)

Gardens and Forest Gardens.
Bodnant (NT) (41) (116) (SH 80-72)
Cae'n-y-Coed (44) (115) (SH 76-57)

Visitor Centre at the Ffestiniog Hydro-Electric Scheme.

Glasdir Forest Garden (50) (124) (SH 74-22)
Glynllifon (64) (115,123) (SH 45-55)
Hafoty House (40) (115) (SH 53-57)
Happy Valley Gardens, Llandudno (71) (115) (SH 78-83)

Historic Houses, etc.
Aberconwy House (NT) (52) (115) (SH 78-77)

Beaumaris Assize Court (38) (114,115) (SH 60-76)
Beaumaris Gaol (38) (115) (SH 60-76)
Bryn Bras Castle (38) (114,115) (SH 54-62)
Cochwillan Old Hall (50) (115) (SH 60-69)
Cymmer Abbey (57) (124) (SH 72-19)
Foel Fawr Windmill (NT) (68) (123) (SH 30-32)
Gelert's Grave (39) (115) (SH 59-47)
Gwydir Castle (64) (115) (SH 79-61)
Gwydir Uchaf Chapel (65) (115) (SH 79-60)
Hen Capel Lligwy (58) (114) (SH 49-86)
Marquess of Anglesey's Column (87) (114,115) (SH 53-71)
Penarth Fawr (92) (123) (SH 41-37)
Penmon Priory, Dovecote, etc (93) (114,115) (SH 63-80 etc.)
Penrhyn Castle (NT) (94) (115) (SH 60-71)
Plas Newydd (NT) (95) (114,115) (SH 52-69)
Plas-yn-Rhiw (NT) (96) (123) (SH 23-28)
Pont Minllyn (58) (124,125) (SH 85-13)
Portmeirion (99) (124) (SH 59-37)
St Cybi's Well (121) (123) (SH 42-41)
Telford Bridge (NT) (52) (115) (SH 78-77)
Tu-hwnt-i'r-bont (NT) (79) (115) (SH 79-61)
Ty-hyll (Ugly House) (108) (115) (SH 75-57)
Ty Mawr (NT) (108) (115) (SH 77-52)

Mountain Ranges.
Arans (33) (124,125) (SH 86-22 etc.)
Ardudwy (33) (124) (SH 60-22 etc.)
Arenigs (33) (124,125) (SH 81-41 etc.)
Cadair Idris (44) (124) (SH 71-13 etc.)
Carneddau (47) (115) (SH 68-64 etc.)
Glyders (64) (115) (SH 65-58 etc.)
Hebog (66) (115) (SH 56-47 etc.)
Rhinogs (101) (124) (SH 65-30 etc.)
Siabod & the Moelwyns (103) (115,124) (SH 70-54 etc.)
Snowdon Massif (103) (115) (SH 61-54 etc.)
Yr Eifl (109) (123) (SH 36-44 etc.)

Museums, Art Galleries, etc.
Aberdyfi Maritime Museum (30) (135) (SN 61-95)
Bangor Art Gallery (36) (114,115) (SH 57-71)
Bangor Museum of Antiquities (36) (114,115) (SH 57-71)
Bod Deiniol Visitor Centre (81) (114) (SH 37-85)
Caernarfon Maritime Museum (46) (114,115) (SH 47-63)
Conwy Valley Railway Museum, Betws-y-Coed (41) (115) (SH 79-56)
Conwy Visitor Centre (53) (115) (SH 78-77)
Corris Railway Museum (53) (124) (SH 75-07)
Felin Faesog Museum (62) (115,123) (SH 44-50)
Holyhead Maritime Museum (66) (114) (SH 24-82)
Llandudno Doll Museum & Model Railway (71) (115) (SH 78-82)
Llanfairpwll Tourist Centre (75) (114,115) (SH 53-71)
Lleyn Historical & Maritime Museum (90) (123) (SH 30-40)
Lloyd George Memorial Museum, Llanystumdwy (80) (123) (SH 47-38)
Maesgwm, Forest Visitor Centre (86) (124) (SH 71-27)
Mostyn Art Gallery, Llandudno (71) (115) (SH 78-82)
Museum of Childhood, Beaumaris (39) (114,115) (SH 60-76)
Oriel Eryri (Welsh Environmental Centre (69) (114,115) (SH 58- 60)
Owain Glyndwr Centre, Machynlleth (85) (135) (SH 74-00)

At the Conwy Valley Railway Museum, Betws-y-Coed.

Plas Mawr, Conwy (52) (115) (SH 78-77)
Quarry Hospital Visitor Centre (69) (114,115) (SH 58-60)
Royal Welsh Fusiliers Museum, Caernarfon Castle (46) (114,115) (SH 47-62)
Tal-y-bont Country Life Museum (105) (124) (SH 58-21)
Tegfryn Art Gallery, Menai Bridge (88) (114,115) (SH 55-72)
Tudor Maritime Exhibition, Barmouth (36) (124) (SH 61-15)
Tywyn Narrow Gauge Museum (109) (135) (SH 58-00)
Welsh Slate Museum (69) (114,115) (SH 58-60)
Y Stablau (The Stables) Centre, Betws-y-Coed (41) (115) (SH 79- 56)

Nature Reserves Etc.
Bardsey Island (36) (123) (SH 12-21)
Cemlyn Bay (NT) (48) (114) (SH 33-93)
Coedydd Aber (29) (115) (SH 66-71)
Cwm Idwal (56) (115) (SH 64-59)
Cwm Llan (57) (115) (SH 62-53)
Garth-gell Bird Reserve (RSPB) (56) (124) (SH 68-20)
Morfa Dyffryn (89) (124) (SH 56-24)
Morfa Harlech (66) (124) (SH 57-32)
Newborough Warren (91) (114) (SH 42-63)
Penmaenpool Nature Information Centre (92) (124) (SH 69-18)
Penrhos (94) (114) (SH 27-81)
Rhinog Fach (101) (124) (SH 66-28 etc.)
Snowdon (104) (115) (SH 61-54 etc.)
South Stack Bird Reserve (RSPB) (104) (114) (SH 20-82)
Tan-y-bwlch (106) (124) (SH 65-40 etc.)

Nature Trails *(See also Forests & Forest Walks).*
Cemaes Bay (48) (114) (SH 35-93)
Coed Llyn Mair (106) (124) (SH 65-41)
Coedydd Aber (29) (115) (SH 66-71)
Bryneuryn Scenic Trail (51) (116) (SH 83-79)
Cwm Idwal (56) (115) (SH 64-59)
Cwm Nantcol (56) (124) (SH 60-27)
Great Orme Nature Trail (71) (115) (SH 78 83)
South Stack (104) (114) (SH 20-82)
Penmaenpool-Morfa Mawddach Walk (93) (124) (SH 69-18 etc.)

Prehistoric Sites.

Sites marked with an asterisk are in the care of the Welsh Office (Cadw), and are normally open at any reasonable time. Most of the other sites are on private ground and permission must therefore be sought before any visit is considered.

Abererch *(Burial Chamber & Standing Stones)* (30) (123) (SH 39-38)

Arthur's Quoit *(Burial Chamber)* (108) (123) (SH 22-34)

Bach Wen *(Burial Chamber)* (49) (115,123) (SH 40-49)

Barclodiad y Gawres* *(Burial Chamber)* (36) (114) (SH 32-70)

Barclodiad y Gawres *(Burial Mound)* (43) (115) (SH 71-71)

Bodowyr* *(Burial Chamber)* (42) (114,115) (SH 46-68)

Bryn Cader Faner *(Cairn Circle)* (88) (124) (SH 64-35)

Bryncelli Ddu* *(Burial Chamber)* (43) (114,115) (SH 50-70)

Bwrdd Arthur *(Iron Age Settlement)* (76) (114,115) (SH 58- 81)

Caer Engan *(Iron Age Settlement)* (79) (115,123) (SH 47-52)

Caer y Twr *(Iron Age Settlement)* (66) (114) (SH 22-82)

Capel Garmon* *(Chambered Long Cairn)* (47) (116) (SH 81-54)

Carn Bentyrch *(Hill Settlement)* (78) (123) (SH 42-41)

Carneddau Hengwm *(Burial Cairns)* (105) (124) (SH 61-20)

Carn Fadryn *(Iron Age Fort)* (47) (123) (SH 27-35)

Carreg Leidr *(Standing Stone)* (73) (114) (SH 44-84)

Castell Bryn-gwyn* *(Stone Age/Iron Age Settlement)* (43) (114,115) (SH 46-67)

Castell Odo *(Iron Age Settlement)* (29) (123) (SH 18-28)

Castell y Gaer *(Iron Age Settlement)* (81) (124) (SH 59-09)

Cist Cerrig *(Burial Chamber)* (42) (124) (SH 54-38)

Coetan Arthur *(Burial Chamber)* (61) (124) (SH 60-22)

Dinas Dinlle *(Iron Age Settlement)* (57) (115,123) (SH 43- 56)

Dinas Dinorwig *(Iron Age Settlement)* (79) (114,115) (SH 54- 65)

Dinas Emrys *(Iron Age Settlement, etc.)* (90) (115) (SH 60- 49)

Dinas Gynfor *(Iron Age Settlement)* (58) (114) (SH 38-95)

Din Dryfol* *(Burial Chamber)* (58) (114) (SH 39-72)

Din Lligwy* *(Iron Age/Roman Village)* (58) (114) (SH 49-86)

Din Sylwy *(See Bwrdd Arthur — above)*

Druid's Circle *(Henge Monument)* (75) (115) (SH 72-74)

Dyffryn Ardudwy* *(Burial Chamber)* (61) (124) (SH 58-23)

Garn Boduan *(Iron Age Settlement)* (42) (123) (SH 31-39)

Giant's Stick *(Standing Stone)* (102) (115) (SH 73-71)

Llandegfan *(Standing Stone)* (70) (114,115) (SH 55-73)

Llanfechell *(Standing Stones & Burial Chamber)* (76) (114) (SH 36- 91)

Lligwy* *(Burial Chamber)* (58) (114) (SH 50-86)

Maen-y-bardd *(Burial Chamber)* (102) (115) (SH 74-71)

Moel Goedog *(Standing Stones, etc.)* (88) (124) (SH 61-32)

Pant-y-Saer *(Hut Group & Burial Chambers)* (68) (114,115) (SH 50-82)

Penmaenmawr *('Axe Factory')* (92) (115) (SH 70-75)

Penrhosfeilw* *(Standing Stones)* (94) (114) (SH 22-80)

Pen-y-Dinas *(Iron Age Settlement)* (105) (124) (SH 60-20)

Pen-y-Gaer *(Iron Age Settlement)* (69) (115) (SH 75-69)

Plas Newydd *(Burial Chamber)* (95) (114,115) (SH 52-69)

Porth Dinllaen *(Iron Age Settlement)* (96) (123) (SH 27-41)

Presaddfed* *(Burial Chamber)* (99) (114) (SH 34-80)

Rhoslan *(Burial Chamber)* (81) (123) (SH 48-40)

Tan-y-Muriau *(Burial Chamber)* (101) (123) (SH 23-28)

Trefignath* *(Burial Chamber)* (67) (114) (SH 25-80)

Tregwehelydd *(Standing Stone)* (76) (114) (SH 34-83)

Tre'r Ceiri *(Iron Age Hill Fort)* (67) (123) (SH 37-44)

Trwyn Du *(Cairn)* (30) (114) (SH 35-67)

Twt Hill, Caernarfon *Iron Age Settlement)* (46) (114,115) (SH 48-63)

Ty Mawr* *(Hut Circles)* (66) (114) (SH 21-82)

Ty Mawr* *(Standing Stone)* (67) (114) (SH 25-80)

Ty-Newydd* *(Burial Chamber)* (74) (114) (SH 34-73)

Railways.

Bala Lake Railway (36) (125) (SH 92-34 etc.)

Cambrian Coast Railway (Part of BR) (46)

Corris Railway (53) (124) (SH 75-07)

Fairbourne Railway (62) (124) (SH 61-13)

Ffestiniog Railway (62) (124) (SH 57-38 etc.)

Llanberis Lake Railway (58) (114,115) (SH 57-61)

Llandudno Tram & Cabin Lift (71) (115) (SH 77-83)

Snowdon Mountain Railway (104) (115) (SH 59-57 etc.)

Talyllyn Railway (106) (124,135) (SH 58-00 etc.)

Welsh Highland Railway (109) (124) (SH 57-39)

Roman Sites.

Sites marked with an asterisk are in the care of the Welsh Office (Cadw), and are normally open at any reasonable time. Most of the other sites are on private ground and permission must therefore be sought before any visit is considered.

Brithdir *(Fort)* (42) (124) (SH 77-18)

Caer Gai *(Fort)* (44) (124,125) (SH 87-31)

Caer Gybi*, Holyhead *(Fort)* (12) (114) (SH 24-82)

Caerhun *(Fort)* (44) (115) (SH 77-70)

Caer Leb *(? Villa)* (43) (114,115) (SH 47-67)

Caer Llugwy *(Fort)* (45) (115) (SH 74-57)

Cefn Gaer *(Fort)* (93) (135) (SH 70-00)

Sarn Helen *(Roads)* (103) (124, etc.) (SH 72-41)

Segontium*, Caernarfon *(Fort)* (46) (114,115) (SH 48-62)

Tomen-y-mur *(Fort, etc. near medieval mound)* (106) (124) (SH 70-38)

Sports Centres and other Leisure Facilities.

Arfon Leisure Centre, Caernarfon (46) (114,115) (SH 48-63)

Amlch Leisure Centre (32) (114) (SH 44-93)

Bangor *(Heated Swimming Pool)* (36) (114,115) (SH 57-71)

Bodvel Hall *(Horse Riding)* (42) (123) (SH 34-36)

Butlin's Holiday Camp (101) (123) (SH 43-36)

Canolfan Aberconwy, Llandudno (71) (115) (SH 78-82)

Sunset over Bardsey Island from Pen y Cil (SH 15-24).

Eiras Park Leisure Centre, Colwyn Bay (50) (116) (SH 86-78)
Holyhead Leisure Centre (66) (114) (SH 24-81)
Plas Arthur Leisure Centre, Llangefni (77) (114,115) (SH 46-75)
Plas Menai *(Watersports)* (95) (114,115) (SH 50-65)
Plâs Tan-y-Bwlch *(National Park Study Centre)* (95) (124) (SH 65-40)
Plas-y-Brenin *(National Mountain Centre for Mountain Activities)* (47) (115) (SH 71-57)

Special Walks *(See also Nature Trails, Forest Walks).*
The Dingle, Llangefni (77) (114,115) (SH 45-76)
Glan Faenol (NT) (64) (114,115) (SH 53-69)
Llwybr Coed Walk, Llanystumdwy (81) (123) (SH 47-38)
Panorama Walk (38) (124) (SH 62-16)
Torrent Walk (107) (124) (SH 75-18)
Vivian Trails (69) (114,115) (SH 58-60)

Waterfalls.
Aber Falls (28) (115) (SH 66-70)
Blaen-pennant (41) (115) (SH 89-21)
Ceunant Mawr (49) (115) (SH 57-59)
Conway Falls (53) (116) (SH 80-53)
Dolgoch Falls (60) (135) (SH 65-04)

Machno Falls (53) (116) (SH 80-53)
Pistyll Cain (95) (124) (SH 73-27)
Pistyll Gwyn (80) (125) (SH 88-19)
Rhaeadr Cynfal (62) (124) (SH 70-41)
Rhaeadr Du (101) (124) (SH 66-38)
Rhaeadr Mawddach (95) (124) (SH 73-27)
Rhaeadr y Cwm (101) (124) (SH 73-41)
Rhaiadr Du (NT) (101) (124) (SH 72-24)
Swallow Falls (105) (115) (SH 76-57)

Wildlife Parks, Farm Parks, Farm Trails, etc.
Anglesey Sea Zoo, Brynsiencyn (43) (114,115) (SH 47-65)
Cae Ddafydd *(Rare Breeds)* (90) (115) (SH 61-45)
Cefn-Isa Farm Trail (56) (124) (SH 60-27)
Cyffdy Farm Park (57) (124,125) (SH 88-34)
Penrhos Nature Reserve (94) (114) (SH 27-81)
Pili Palas *(Butterflies)* (95) (114,115) (SH 54-72)
Tal y Waen Farm Trail (106) (124) (SH 69-17)
Trefrifawr Farm Trail (30) (135) (SH 63-97)
Tyn Llan Farm Museum (93) (124) (SH 54-39)
Welsh Mountain Zoo (50) (116) (SH 83-78)

Special Events.
For a list of events, dates of which change annually, see the relevant leaflets which are available from the various Tourist Information Centres listed overleaf.

Further Information

Tourist Information Centres.

Aberdyfi (Aberdovey). *The Wharf. Tel: (0654) 72321*
Bala. *High St. Tel: (0678) 520367*
Bangor. *Town Hall. Tel: (0248) 352786*
Barmouth (Abermaw). *Marine Parade. Tel: (0341) 280787*
Beddgelert. *Llywelyn Cottage (NT). Tel: (0766) 86293*
Betws-y-Coed. *Y Stablau. Tel: (06902) 665 or 426*

Rhaeadr-fawr, the best of the Aber Falls.

Blaenau Ffestiniog. *Isalt. Tel: (0766) 830360*
Caernarfon. *Y Maes. Tel: (0286) 2232*
Colwyn Bay. *Prince of Wales Theatre. Tel: (0492) 30478*
Conwy. *Castle St. Tel: (049263) 2248*
Criccieth. *The Green (Summer only). Tel: (076671) 2489*
Dinas Mawddwy. *Meirion Mill. Tel: (06504) 311*
Dolgellau. *The Bridge. Tel: (0341) 422888*
Harlech. *In centre. Tel: (0766) 780658*
Holyhead. *Marine Square, Salt Island. Tel: (0407) 2622*
Llanberis. *Oriel Eryri. Tel: (0286) 870765*
Llandudno. *Chapel St. Tel: (0492) 76413*
Machynlleth. *Owain Glyndwr Centre. Tel: (0654) 2401*
Menai Bridge. *Coed Cyrnol, on A4080 beyond bridge. Tel: (0248) 712626/713923*
Porthmadog. *High St. Tel: (0766) 2981*
Pwllheli. *Y Maes. Tel: (075861) 3000*
Tywyn. *High St. Tel: (0654) 710070*

Other Useful Addresses and/or Telephone Numbers.

Forestry Commission, *Gwydyr Uchaf, Llanrwst, LL26 0PN. Tel (0492) 640578)*
National Trust, *Trinity Square, Llandudno, LL30 2DE. Tel: (0492) 74421*
National Park Daily Weather Forecast, *Tel: Llanberis 870120*
Nature Conservancy Council, *Penrhos Rd., Bangor, LL57 2LQ. Tel: (0248) 355141*
North Wales Tourism Council, *77, Conway Rd., Colwyn Bay, Clwyd, LL29 7LN. Tel: (0492) 31731*
Snowdonia National Park, *Penrhyndeudraeth, LL48 6LS. Tel: (0766) 770274/770701*
Snowdonia National Park Society, *Capel Curig, Betws-y-Coed, Gwynedd.*
A.A. 24 Hour Breakdown Service, Caernarfon. *Tel: (0286) 3935*
A.A. 24 Hour Breakdown Service, Llandudno. *Tel: (0492) 79066*
R.A.C. 24 Hour Breakdown Service, Liverpool. *Tel: (051 709) 0707*
Police, Bangor. *Tel: (0448) 352222*
Police, Caernarfon. *Tel: (0286) 3333*
Police, Colwyn Bay. *Tel: (0492) 517171*
Police, Dolgellau. *Tel: (0341) 422222*
Police, Holyhead. *Tel: (0407) 2323 or 2325*
Police, Llandudno. *Tel: (0492) 78241*
Police, Porthmadog. *Tel: (0766) 2226 or 2426*
Police, Pwllheli. *Tel: (0758) 612721 or 612277/8*

Ordnance Survey Agents.

Bookland & Co Ltd, 288, High St., Bangor *Tel (0248) 353039*
Sheldons, 8, Penrhyn Rd., Colwyn Bay *Tel: (0492) 2395*

Black Rock Sands, near Porthmadog.

A Few Welsh Place-Names

Aber — *estuary, or confluence*
Afon — *river*
Allt — *hill, slope*
Bach — *little*
Bedd — *grave*
Betws — *chapel of ease*
Bod — *dwelling place*
Bont — *bridge*
Bryn — *mound*
Bwlch — *pass or gap*
Bychan — *small, the lesser*
Caer — *camp or fort*
Capel — *chapel*
Carn — *cairn, rock, mountain*
Carnedd — *cairn, tumulus, mountain*
Carreg — *stone or rock*
Castell — *castle*
Cefn — *ridge*
Celli — *grove or copse*
Ceunant — *ravine or gorge*
Coch — *red*
Coed — *forest, wood, tree*
Cors — *bog*
Craig — *crag*
Croes — *cross, cross-roads*
Cwm — *valley*
Cymmer — *junction or confluence*
Din — *town or hill fort*
Drws — *gap or narrow pass*

Du (or Ddu) — *black*
Dyffryn — *valley*
Fach — *little*
Fawr — *great, large*
Felin — *mill*
Fford — *way or road*
Ffynnon — *spring*
Foel — *bare hill*
Fynydd — *mountain*
Gaer — *camp or fort*
Garn — *a prominence*
Garth — *hill or headland*
Glas — *green or blue*
Glyn — *glen*
Goch — *red*
Graig — *crag*
Groes — *cross, cross-roads*
Gwaun — *common or moor*
Gwyn — *white*
Hafod — *summer dwelling*
Hendre — *winter dwelling*
Hen — *old*
Isaf — *lower, lowest*
Llan — *enclosure, sacred enclosure, hence a church*
Llech — *flat stone*
Llyn — *lake*
Maen — *stone*
Maes — *open field, or open place*
Mawr — *great, large*
Mign — *bog*

Moel — *bare hill*
Mynach — *monk*
Mynydd — *mountain*
Nant — *brook or dingle*
Newydd — *new*
Ogof — *cave*
Pant — *hollow, or valley*
Pen — *head, or top*
Pistyll — *spouting waterfall*
Plas — *hall or mansion*
Pont — *bridge*
Porth — *gateway or harbour*
Pwll — *pool or hollow*
Rhaeadr — *waterfall*
Rhiw — *slope*
Rhyd — *ford*
Sarn — *causeway*
Tal — *brow of hill, or headland*
Tomen — *mound*
Traeth — *strand, beach or shore*
Tre — *dwelling or village*
Twyn — *small hill, or knoll*
Ty — *house*
Uchaf — *higher, highest*
Waun — *common or moor*
Wyn — *white*
Y, Yr — *the, of the*
Yn, Ym — *in*
Ynys — *island*
Ysbyty — *hospital or hospice*

Places of Special Interest

Places of outstanding interest are printed in blue.

Aber (115) (SH 65-72) *7m E Bangor.* The name of this minute village lying just to the south of the busy A55 is short for Abergwyngregyn (The Mouth of the River of White Shells). In the wide waters between here and Beaumaris lie Traeth Lafan (the Lavan Sands), the legendary site of the drowned palace of Llys Helig. Regrettably the extended lines of stones exposed at low tide, which gave rise to this legend, have long ago been proved to be of natural origin. There is an attractive 17th century house, Pen-y-bryn visible from the A55, just to the east of the village.

The village itself is situated on the Afon Aber, a little river flowing between steep mountain slopes, which are especially well wooded to the east. The mound in the village is almost certainly of Norman origin, and is the site of a palace built here in the 13th century by the Princes of Gwynedd. The best known of these was Llywelyn the Great, whose wife Joan was the natural daughter of King John. She is believed to have had an affair with a Norman Marcher lord, William de Braose, while he was held captive here by her husband. Following the payment of a large ransom, de Braose was released and invited to attend a banquet to celebrate his departure, only to be immediately hanged before Llywelyn's wife, whose infidelities had unfortunately not gone unnoticed. However let us pass on to happier things and explore further up the valley to the Aber Falls (see below).

Aber Falls (115) (SH 66-70) *7m E Bangor.* Drive south through Aber and park at Bont Newydd (SH 66-71). Then walk south for just under two miles, up the beautifully wooded valley of the Afon Goch, a National Nature Reserve, to visit the spectacular Rhaeadr-fawr (The Big Fall), a 170-foot waterfall, also known as the Mare's Tail. A waymarked return walk, the route of which is not shown as a right of way on our accompanying map, may be made over higher ground to the east of the valley, through coniferous woodlands owned by the Forestry Commission, although this involves a fairly steep climb in its early stages. Each walk takes between 1 and 2 hours, and as the paths involved are often wet and slippery, it would be wise to wear stout shoes or

Aber and the Aber Falls

SCALE 1:25 000 or 2½ INCHES to 1 MILE

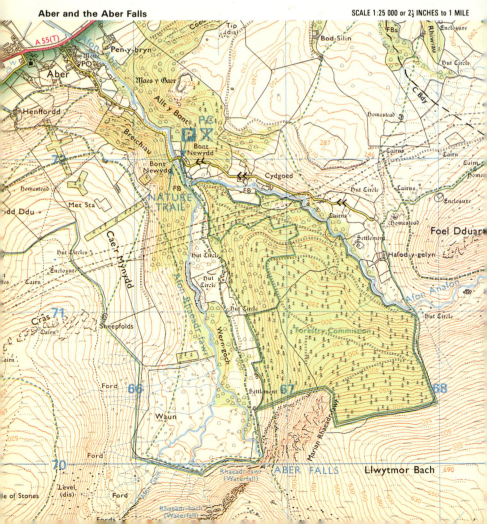

boots. As always, be sure to wear or carry warm clothes. Both walks make up the Coedydd Aber Trail, which is well described in a booklet produced jointly by the Nature Conservancy Council and the Forestry Commission, and which is available for a modest sum from an 'honesty box' at the car park.

Aberangell (124,125) (SH 84-10) *14m SE Dolgellau.* Small village in the delightfully wooded valley of the River Dovey (Afon Dyfi), and on the eastern fringes of the great Dyfi Forest. There is an interesting and beautiful forest road leading west from here to the little village of Aberllefenni, but at present there is some doubt if vehicles driven by members of the public are permitted to use it. We suggest therefore that you enquire at the village for the latest news on this situation . . . it could be well worth the trouble.

Aber-Cywarch (124,125) (SH 86-15) *10m E Dolgellau.* Pleasant hamlet close to the point where the Afon Cywarch flows into the Dyfi not far from its source (SH 86-22) below Aran Fawddwy, with two pretty cottage terraces overlooking the road down from Bwlch y Groes. During his tour of 1854 recorded in *Wild Wales*, George Borrow found this to be a place of 'trees and groves and running waters' and 'a wild and wondrous place'. See also Cwm Cywarch, page 55.

Aberdaron (123) (SH 17-26) *17m SW Pwllheli.* This attractive little fishing and holiday village is situated in a sheltered bay at the western end of the Lleyn Peninsula, in cliff-girt country with much gorse and heather. It has bright painted plaster and pebble-dashed cottages, steep hills, a sparkling stream, a medieval hump-back bridge and a mile-long sandy beach. It was the last mainland stage for pilgrims on their long journey to the Abbey of St Mary on Bardsey Island, and their 14th century rest-house, Y-Gegin Fawr (The Old Kitchen), is now a cafe and souvenir shop. The nearby Post Office was designed by Clough Williams-Ellis, of Portmeirion

fame. The large church on the cliff-edge above the beach dates from the 12th and 15th centuries, and has a late Norman doorway, weathered by centuries of storms. This building once gave sanctuary to the fugitive Gruffydd ap Rhys ap Tewdwr, during his successful flight from the allies of Henry I. Just under two miles to the north-east, the hill Mynydd Ystum (SH 18-28) is crowned by the earthworks of an Iron Age settlement, Castell Odo.

Walk south-west from Aberdaron along cliff paths, above the minute inlets of Porth Meudwy, Porth y Pistyll and Hen Borth, for fine views eastwards towards the mountains of Snowdonia. It is also possible to drive south-westwards to Mynydd Mawr and the National Trust-owned headland of Braich-y-Pwll, the 'Land's End' of North Wales (see Mynydd Mawr, page 89).

Aberdesach (115,123) (SH 42-51) *9m SW Caernarfon.* Hamlet beside the very straight A499 road between Caernarfon and Pwllheli. There is an exposed shingly beach with some sand at low tide, and it is possible to launch small boats here. The inshore fishing is usually reasonable.

Aberdyfi (Aberdovey) (135) (SN 61-95) *10m W Machynlleth.* Cheerful holiday village situated on a narrow strip of land between the mountains and the beautiful sweeping sands of the Dovey (Dyfi) Estuary. Like many other holiday resorts, its architecture is largely Victorian, but here it is much cosier in feeling than most, and it is further flavoured by a **wharf and jetty (1)** with many colourful boats at their moorings close by. The GP14 sailing dinghy was first adopted here as a club boat, and the black bell on its sails was inspired by 'The Bells of Aberdovey', a song made famous in *Liberty Hall*, the opera written in 1785 by Englishman, Charles Dibdin, part of which runs thus . . .

Pretty maidens come again
Join us in a merry strain,
To all who live on land or main
Say the Bells of Aberdovey

1 Wharf and Jetty
2 Maritime Museum
3 The Best Walk
4 Tourist Information Centre

Aberfyfi (Aberdovey)

SCALE 1:10 000 or 6 INCHES to 1 MILE

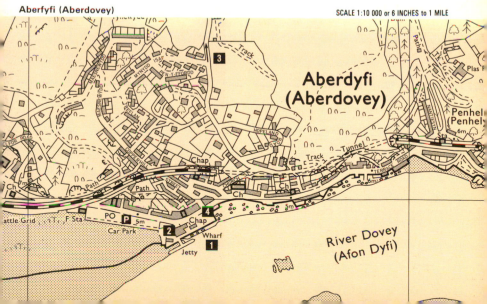

Aberdovey — between the mountains and the sea.

The bells to which Dibdin referred were supposed to have rung across the sea from the submerged and legendary land of Cantref y Gwaelod, off the coast near Llanfair (see page 75) many miles to the north.

The Dovey is noted for its salmon and sea trout, but visitors will find both bass and flat fish in the estuary channel opposite the village and off the shore beyond the dunes to the west and north. There is a small **Maritime Museum (2)** on the seafront run by the local Outward Bound Centre (an organisation which started here during the Second World War), and this illustrates the early history of Aberdyfi, which was a busy fishing village and trading port until the coming of the railways in the latter part of the 19th century. Sea fishing trips are available, and it should also be possible to hire motor boats or sailing dinghies. Courses in sailing, canoeing, windsurfing, and water-skiing are also on offer, and boats are available to ferry visitors across the estuary to the Ynyslas shore. Do not attempt to swim in the estuary mouth, where there are fast and dangerous currents, but keep to the north of the landing stage, taking the advice of the warning notices, and making use of the five miles of sands stretching west and north from the village. There are tennis courts and a bowling green, and to the west of the village there is an 18-hole golf course bordering the sea. Less than two miles to the north-east of Aberdyfi, there is a Farm Trail at Trefrifawr (SN 63-97).

The best walk from the village (3) is north up a steep road, with a pause awhile for the fine views back over the estuary, and after about a mile, moving on to a track straight ahead, where the road bears to the right. From here it is possible to walk over the mountain top and down into the Happy Valley (see page 65). It is probably best to return to Aberdovey by the same route. Details of other walks will be found in the publication, *Walks in and around Aberdyfi*, which is available from the **Tourist Information Centre (4)** on the Wharf (tel: 0654 72321).

Abererch (123) (SH 39-36) *2m NE Pwllheli*. Situated on the banks of the Afon Erch, just inland from the sea, this is a quietly attractive little village, with some unobtrusive modern development. A restored medieval church, which has some 16th century stalls within, faces the red and white

Ebenezer Chapel across a street at the top of the village. A road beyond the A497 leads to a large caravan site in the dunes behind the Morfa Abererch, a four-mile-long sand and pebble beach. In contrast, just over a mile to the north of the village, to the east of the A499, there is a prehistoric burial chamber (SH 399-385), with two standing stones not far to its north.

Aberffraw (114) (SH 35-68) *15m W Menai Bridge*. The Court of the Welsh Princes sat at Aberffraw in early Christian times, but no trace remains of the wooden buildings that they must have used. Today it is a sleepy undeveloped village, with a quiet square and a good inn. The much-restored church of St Beuno has a rough-hewn Norman arch and twin aisles divided by 16th century arcading. A single-span stone packhorse bridge in the village now only carries a footpath over the Afon Ffraw, and the village is happily bypassed by the A4080, which approaches from the east over the head of the Tywyn Aberffraw, a great expanse of grass and sand bisected by enormous dunes which hide the sands of Aberffraw Bay. There is an attractive cliff walk south-westwards from here to Porth Cwyfan (see page 96), passing a small prehistoric cairn, Trwyn Du, standing on a headland overlooking the mouth of the Afon Ffraw.

Aberglaslyn, Pass of (115) (SH 59-46) *6m NNE Porthmadog*. It is here that the Afon Glaslyn breaks through the mountains, on its way to the sea.

The Afon Glaslyn at Aber Glaslyn.

30

Aberglaslyn means 'Mouth of the River of the Blue Lake', a reference to the time when the sea reached to the foot of the pass, and ships could sail up as far as Pont Aber Glaslyn, at the foot of the pass. This was before William Madocks M.P. reclaimed the Glaslyn Estuary early in the 19th century (see Porthmadog, page 97). There are car parks at either end of the pass, with fine views on every side and seven-hundred-foot-high pine-clad cliffs enclosing river, road, and the remnants of the old Welsh Highland Railway (see page 109). See also Nantmor, page 90.

Abergynolwyn (124) (SH 67-06) *7m NE Tywyn.* This small village in the Dysynni Valley was once an important slate quarrying centre, and vast quarries lie at the head of the attractive valley to its south-east. Here is Nant Gwernol Station, the north-eastern terminus of the highly popular Talyllyn Railway (see page 106). The original purpose of this railway was for the transport of slate to the main railway line at Tywyn, just over seven miles away, but passengers were also carried, even in its early days. There are an attractive series of forest walks starting from the Nant Gwernol Station, and these are described in an interesting leaflet published by the Forestry Commission. Our own Walk 16, page 160, starts from the very useful car park and picnic site adjacent to Abergynolwyn Station, half a mile to the south-west of the village.

Aberllefenni (124) (SH 77-09) *2m NE Corris.* Slate was still being mined at this minute village on the western side of the great Dyfi Forest, when we last called here. There were old workshops where the slate was cut and trimmed, and we very much hope that this work is still being carried on when our readers call this way. There is an attractive forest road about five miles in length, leading east from here to the small village of Aberangell, but at present there is some doubt as to whether vehicles driven by members of the public are permitted to use it. May we suggest that you enquire at the village for the latest news on this situation — it could be well worth the trouble. There is a pleasant two-mile-long forest trail starting across a footbridge from the Forestry Commission's picnic site at Foel Friog (SH 77-09), on the small road into Aberllefenni from Corris. There are views of the Dulas valley, and a pleasant mixture of larch and oak woodlands, with some evidence of slate working. A study of Landranger Map 124 or Outdoor Leisure Map 23 will reveal several opportunities for longer walks in this unspoilt forest country.

Abermenai Point (114) (SH 44-61) *3m SE Newborough.* Standing at the southern entrance to the Menai Strait, this is the southernmost tip of Anglesey. Until the early 19th century one of the main routes into Anglesey used a ferry across the Strait here, and it is possible that Roman troops under Suetonius Paulinus came this way in AD 60, and that their example was followed by Agricola's men some 18 years later. The remains of an old breakwater may still be seen, and there is a safe anchorage for day picnickers from sailing dinghies, with good views across the Strait to Fort Belan (see page 63). It is also possible to walk here from Newborough, across Newborough Warren, but ask

locally for advice before setting out (See also Newborough, page 90).

Abersoch (123) (SH 31-28) *7m SW Pwllheli.* Delightful seaside resort and sailing centre with two long sandy beaches backed by dunes, and safe moorings for hundreds of yachts and boatyards to service these colourful craft. There is a lively little harbour, narrow streets lined with character shops, restaurants and inns, and a number of comfortable modern hotels. There is a good 18-hole golf course

Abersoch harbour.

behind the dunes to the south of the village, while to the north, the long 'Warren' beach is backed by an extensive complex of caravans and bungalows, with its own shops and services. This long beach may also be reached by footpaths across National Trust land nearer the village. The bay as a whole is known as St Tudwal's Road, and there are fine views south-eastwards to St Tudwal's Islands (see page 103).

Afon Gain and Afon Lliw Valleys (124) (SH 78-33) *7m SE & E Trawsfynydd.* This map reference takes us to remote mountain country which is the

Mountain country near the source of the Afon Gain.

The Abersoch Area

SCALE 1:50 000 or 1¼ INCHES to 1 MILE

watershed of these two small rivers, one of which flows into the Mawddach, emptying westwards into Tremadog Bay, and one of which joins the Dee, to flow north-eastwards to Liverpool Bay. There is an attractive mountain road heading south-eastwards from Trawsfynydd, and then eastwards over high, partly afforested country, before dropping down to Llanuwchllyn. The road reaches a height of 1743 feet above sea level, which is only 47 feet lower than Bwlch y Groes (see page 43), but here we are almost on the top of wide open country, and not within the confines of a pass. It is in areas like this that the Landranger map really comes into its own, giving the driver confidence, and providing real companionship and interest on the journey.

Amlwch (114) (SH 44-93) *18m NW Menai Bridge.* This little port owes its origins to the rich veins of copper found in the nearby Parys Mountain in 1768 (see page 92). Before this time it had been a fishing hamlet with only six houses, but by the turn of the century it had a population of six thousand people and no fewer than 1025 ale houses, a proportion that could only have been possible in a really wild mining community such as this. Its natural harbour had been enlarged in 1793 to allow the berthing of

ore-carrying ships, and for a short time it was the world's largest copper port. In more recent times Shell have built a Marine Terminal here, and oil is taken from tankers moored offshore, and pumped to a 'tank farm' at Rhosgoch (SH 41-90). From here it passes through a long pipeline to Stanilow Refinery, near Liverpool. Despite these developments, and the building of a large chemical works on a headland to the west of the town, the coastal scenery in the vicinity is outstanding, and there are often views of ships on their way between Liverpool and North America which have just rounded, or which are about to round, Point Lynas, a narrow headland about two miles to the east.

The handsome parish church was built by the Parys Mines Company in 1800, to the design of James Wyatt, the fashionable London architect best known for his ruthless neo-Gothic 'restoration' of various great buildings including the cathedrals of Durham, Hereford and Salisbury, and it is ironic that his own work here was itself Gothicized some seventy years later. Amlwch has a fine Leisure Centre *(tel: 0407 830060 or 830232)* whose facilities include a swimming pool, tennis and squash courts, and there is a good 18-hole golf course near Bull Bay, to the west of the town. Walks from Amlwch include a fine cliff path eastwards to Point Lynas.

The Arans (124, 125) (SH 86-22 etc.) *10m E Dolgellau*. This fine range of mountains runs from the head of Llyn Tegid (Bala Lake), south-westwards to Dinas Mawddwy. Its chief peaks are Aran Fawddwy (SH 86-22), and Aran Benllyn (SH 86-24), and the former is not only the highest mountain in southern Snowdonia, but also over-looks the mountain lake of Creiglyn Dyfi, the source of the Afon Dyfi (River Dovey). Best views of these peaks are to be obtained from Bwlch y Groes (see page 43), and best access for rock-climbers is up Cwm Cywarch from Aber Cywarch (see page 29). Access onto the Arans is now only by Courtesy Footpaths as a result of an agreement between the landowners and the National Park Authority. Details and map are available from the National Park Office at Penrhyndeudraeth. Do not attempt to penetrate this country without adequate experience, clothing and equipment. For further general advice, please see the inside rear cover of this guide.

The Ardudwy (124) (SH 60-22 etc.) This is a delightful area of hill country between the coast and the Rhinog Range, running southwards from Talsarnau and Harlech, almost to Barmouth. The most satisfying approach to it would be on foot, west-wards through the Bwlch Drws Ardudwy (see page 43). But a study of Landranger Sheet 124 will reveal many minor roads and pathways threading through this beautiful and unspoilt landscape. See also **Tour 7**, page 122, and **Walk 13**, page 154.

The Arenigs (124, 125) (SH 81-41 etc.) *8m NW Bala*. These two peaks are situated in wild open country at the head of Llyn Celyn, with Arenig Fach (SH 82-41) to the north of the A4212, and Arenig Fawr (SH 82-36) well to its south. Arenig Fawr is the more dramatic of the two, and is topped by a small cairn, with a plaque in memory of the crew of eight United States aircrew, who died when their Flying Fortress bomber crashed into the mountain in 1943. Both peaks have tarns close by, overlooked by dramatic rocky crags, but neither should be attempted without expert advice (see 'The Arans', above).

Arthog (124) (SH 64-14) *6m SW Dolgellau*. Small village beneath steep wooded hillsides, with a plain little 19th century church. Climb up from here past the Arthog waterfalls, to obtain fine views out over the Mawddach estuary and to visit the lakes of Cregennen. Take the old coach road from here, south-westward as far as Cyfannedd, from whence it is possible to walk on over the hills to Llwyngwril. Hardy walkers can also take the Ffordd Ddu, (the Black Road), to cross the hills to Llanegryn in the Dysynni valley, a distance of seven miles.

Artro Valley (124) (SH 61-28 etc.) *3m SE Harlech*. Beautifully wooded valley in the hills behind Harlech, situated between Cwm Bychan (see page 54) and Cwm Nantcol (see page 56). There are at least

1 Capel Tegid	3 Parish Church
2 Tomen-y-Bala	4 Visitor Centre
	5 Lake Warden's Office

Bala   SCALE 1:10 000 or 6 INCHES to 1 MILE

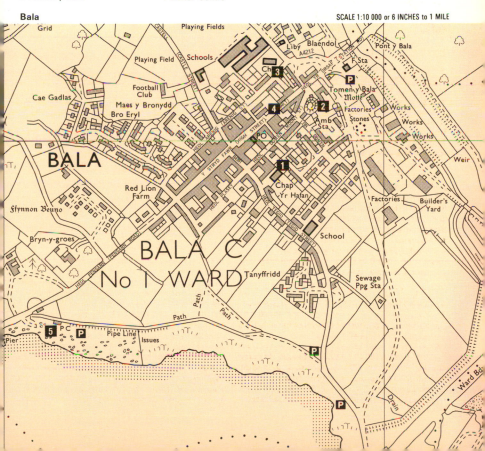

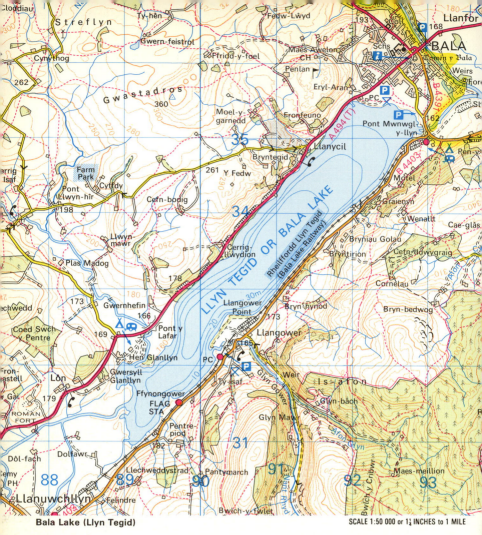

Bala Lake (Llyn Tegid)

SCALE 1:50 000 or 1¼ INCHES to 1 MILE

two car parks, one of which has a picnic site adjoining.

Bala (125) (SH 92-36) Busy little market town and tourist centre situated at the north-eastern end of Llyn Tegid (Bala Lake). It is well placed for those wishing to explore the eastern parts of Snowdonia, the Berwyn Mountains and Lake Vyrnwy. Most of its activity is concentrated on the long High Street (Stryd Fawr), which stretches from the bridge over the Afon Tryweryn almost to the shores of the lake, and which follows the exact course of the Roman road that ran from Chester to the nearby fort at Caer Gai (see page 44) and on to the coast near Dolgellau. There is a proud statue of Thomas Ellis, M.P., 'Chief Liberal Whip in 1894', a Georgian Town Hall almost opposite, and a whole series of bright and cheerful shops, restaurants and hotels.

In quieter Tegid Street will be found *Capel Tegid (1)*, outside which stands the statue of Thomas Charles, the founder of the Welsh Sunday School Movement, and the British and Foreign Bible Society. It was to here that Mary Jones made her famous twenty-eight mile walk from Llanfihangel-y-Pennant (see page 76), to collect her bible from Charles. The *Tomen y Bala (2)* lies on the north

side of the town, behind the Old Grammar School, and is almost certainly the remains of a Norman castle earthwork. The Victorian Parish Church, *Eglwys Crist (Christ Church) (3)* is not of great architectural interest to visitors.

Throughout the summer there is a most helpful *Visitor Centre (4)* run by the Snowdonia National Park in the High Street *(Tel: 0678 520367).* Bala Tennis Club has two hard courts, and there is a 9-hole golf course about a mile to the south-west, off the A494 road towards Dolgellau. See below for Bala Lake, *Warden's Office* at *(5)* and the Bala Lake Railway.

Bala Lake (Llyn Tegid) (125) (SH 90-33 etc.) *To immediate SW of Bala.* This is the largest area of natural water in Wales, being about 4½ miles long and about ⅔ mile wide. There are fine views down the lake from the north-eastern end near Bala towards the dramatic outline of Aran Benllyn. The lake is a relatively quiet place, much favoured by anglers, and sailing and windsurfing enthusiasts, with no power boating allowed. There is also a ban on shooting and consequently the lake has become a haven for wildlife, with herons, grebes, cormorants, ducks, swans and several other species being

34

Bangor (see following page)

SCALE 1:10 000 or 6 INCHES to 1 MILE

1 Pier (closed)
2 Cathedral
3 University
4 Theatr Gwynedd
5 Museum of Welsh Antiquities &
  Art Gallery
6 Tourist Information Centre
  (Town Hall)
7 Swimming Pool

regularly observed here. The lake is also unique in being the only place in Britain where the Gwyniad is to be found. This is an alpine species of fish, a member of the salmon family, which is thought to have become land-locked during the Ice Age. This is rarely caught, but the fishing on the lake is excellent generally. Boats may be hired for rowing and fishing from the jetty at the north-eastern end of the lake (SH 92-35), and swimming is also allowed. *The Lake Warden's Office (5)* is shown on our plan of Bala and there are no fewer than thirteen car parks around the shores of the lake. For further details of these and other facilities, read the leaflet, *Llyn Tegid* which is available at the Snowdonia National Park Visitor Centre in Bala High Street.

Bala Lake Railway (125) (SH 92-34 etc.) This runs along the south-eastern shore of Bala Lake for 4½ miles, from Bala Station to Llanuwchllyn, following the course of an old main railway line. From Easter to mid-October steam and diesel locomotives which once worked in the slate quarries of North Wales now haul passenger coaches, some open, some closed, so that visitors can enjoy the views of mountains and lake in all weathers. Bala Station is within walking distance of the High Street, and at Llanuwchllyn there is a free car park and light refreshments. *Tel (06784) 666 for further details.*

Bangor (114,115) (SH 57-72) Small city standing at the eastern entrance to the Menai Strait, with a well respected university, and many streets full of character and largely Victorian in flavour. Its views across the Strait to the wooded shores of Anglesey are perhaps its best feature. The long, late-Victorian *Pier (1)* , which is unfortunately closed, stretches northwards over half way to the Anglesey shore, and not far from its entrance there is a white house with bay windows which is thought to have been used by Telford when he was building the road to Holyhead and his two great bridges (see Conwy, page 53, and Menai Bridge, page 87).

There was probably a settlement here in pre-Roman times, but the present town grew up around its monastery (see below). Its strategic position, commanding the approach to Anglesey, made it the focal point of much bitter fighting during the latter part of the Civil War. The university and the cathedral have their origins in the 6th century AD, as part of a monastery founded by St Deiniol, a missionary who came from Strathclyde, and who became the first Bishop of Gwynedd. Bangor is in fact the oldest diocese in the United Kingdom, having been founded 81 years earlier than Canterbury. The original *Cathedral (2)* was destroyed by Owain Glyndwr in 1402, but was rebuilt in the 15th and 16th centuries. Writing in 1722 in his *Tour Through England and Wales*, Daniel Defoe described this building as 'old, mean looking, and almost despicable', but it was much restored by the ever-active Sir Gilbert Scott and his son between 1868 and 1880. Do not miss the 'Mostyn Christ', a large, late medieval carved wooden figure near the north door. Bangor is justifiably proud of its *University (3)*. Its buildings are some of the best to be found in North Wales, and it has a fine academic record.

Bangor is also proud of its new *Theatr Gwynedd (4)*, and it also has a *Museum of Welsh Antiquities (5)* and an *Art Gallery (5)* in Fford Gwynedd. There is a *Tourist Information Centre*

in the *Town Hall (6) Tel: 0248 52768*, a *heated swimming pool (6)* in Garth Road, and an 18-hole golf course to the south-east of the city.

Barclodiad y Gawres Burial Chamber (114) (SH 32-70) *2m S Rhosneigr*. This prehistoric passage grave, the Welsh name of which translates delightfully into 'The Giantess's Apronful', is easily accessible from the path round the headland between Porth Trecastell and Porth Nobla. It contains several incised stones similar to some found in Ireland. The covering mound has been elaborately restored and the chamber which is approached down a 20-foot-long passageway, is open during the summer. For another burial chamber with the same name, see Bwlch-y-Ddeufaen, page 43.

Bardsey Island (Ynys Enlli) (123) (SH 12-21 etc.) *5m SW Aberdaron*. This lies off the south-western tip of the Lleyn Peninsula, and is separated from it by a notorious tide-race. The English name, 'The Isle of Tides or Eddies', may have been derived from 'Birdsey', and appropriately the island is now a bird sanctuary, being visited mainly by students of natural history. At one time it supported a small farming and fishing community, but now only a ruined tower and a few stones remain of the ancient Abbey of St Mary (St Mair), which was founded by St Cadfan in the 6th century. The monks of Bangor-is-Coed, near Chester, came here for refuge when they were expelled from their original site by the Saxons. The Abbey was a place of pilgrimage for many hundreds of years and is the reputed burial place of a vast number of holy men, still being known in Wales as the 'Isle of 20,000 Saints'. It is best viewed from the National Trust-owned headland of Braich y Pwll (see Mynydd Mawr, page 89).

Barmouth, *Abermaw* (124) (SH 61-15) This charming little harbour town sits beneath steep hillsides at the mouth of the lovely Mawddach estuary. Its popularity as a holiday resort bloomed rapidly with the coming of the railway in the 19th century, and it is still well served by the delightful Cambrian Coast line (see page 46). The impressive red sandstone *St John's Church (1)*, built largely at the expense of Mrs Dyson Perrins of the Worcestershire Sauce family, is perched above most of the town, although the town's mother church was once Llanaber (see page 67).

It has a long sandy beach, bright holiday shops and hotels, and an attractive little *harbour (2)* overlooked by a small round building, put up in the 1820s to accommodate drunken sailors and gold miners from the Bontddu area, who must have turned the town into a miniature version of the notorious Dawson City when the local 'goldrush' was at its height. Near the harbour is Barmouth's oldest building, the 15th century Ty Gwyn, and here will be found the Tudor Maritime Exhibition. There is also a Lifeboat Museum on the quay, and Barmouth is justifiably proud of its lifeboat, *The Princess of Wales*. Boats leave here for inshore and deep sea fishing trips, and there is a *ferry (3)* across the estuary mouth which connects with the Fairbourne Railway. There are a variety of facilities for visitors in the Memorial Park and throughout the summer there is a *Tourist Information Centre (4)* near the Bus Station on the Marine Parade *(Tel: 0341 280787)*.

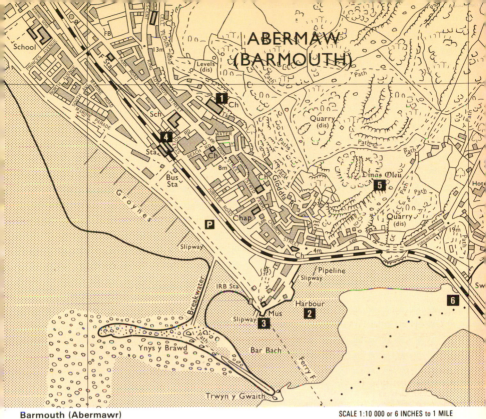

Barmouth (Abermawr)

SCALE 1:10 000 or 6 INCHES to 1 MILE

1 Parish Church   3 Ferry   5 Dinas Oleu

2 Harbour   4 Tourist Information Centre   6 Barmouth Bridge

Barmouth Toll Bridge — at the mouth of the Mawddach Estuary.

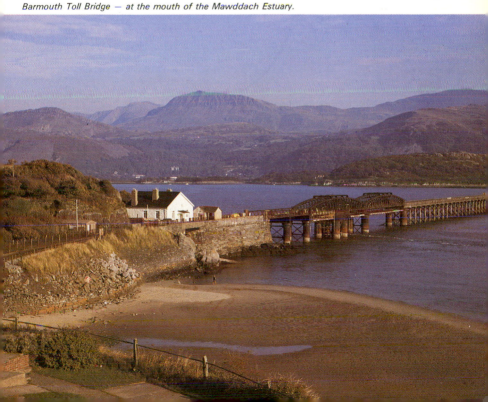

The Mawddach Estuary from the Panorama Walk, near Barmouth.

Dinas Oleu (5), an area of cliffland just above the town bright with yellow gorse all the summer, was the first property acquired by the National Trust, being given by Mrs F. Talbot in 1895, the year that the Trust was founded.

Walks from Barmouth include the Panorama Walk, well to the east of the town, which provides splendid views out over the waters of the Mawddach to Cadair Idris, and beyond the head of its estuary to the peaks of the distant Aran range. It is also possible to cross the estuary by walking across the **Toll Bridge (6)** alongside the ½-mile-long railway bridge to Morfa Mawddach Station, and then along the southern shore either to Fairbourne or Arthog.

Beaumaris (114,115) (SH 60-76) This pleasant old town is a busy holiday resort and yachting centre, with ample car parking, cheerful shops, and a number of good hotels, inns and restaurants. Situated at the north-eastern end of the Menai Strait, it was Anglesey's capital for centuries, and until the building of the Menai Bridge, its principal port of entry from the mainland. For this reason it was much used by travellers between England and Ireland, and there were several posting inns here. It was also the centre of the island's social life, and in Georgian times many of its more prosperous gentry had a town house here.

The building of **Beaumaris Castle (1)** was

commenced by Edward I in 1295, the eighth and last of his great ring of fortresses encircling the Welsh, a proud nation which he was determined to contain and subdue. Thanks to a workforce of about 2500 men, it was completed within only 3 years. It has a perfectly concentric plan, and ironically, although it is one of the outstanding examples of medieval military architecture, it never saw military action. When it was built, fully laden ships could sail up on the high tide to the dock by the 'Gate next the Sea'. Walk around the outer walls for a fine view of the castle's inner defences, with its series of round towers and two gatehouses, and do not miss the lovely vaulted chapel in the Chapel Tower, with its priest's chamber above, sadly never completed.

Opposite the castle, stands the **County Hall and Assizes (2)**, also known as the Assize Court, which was built in 1614, and which was Anglesey's principal Assize Court until as recently as 1971. The notorious Judge Jeffreys, better known for the harsh sentences imposed on the unfortunate Duke of Monmouth's followers after Sedgemoor, is believed to have also sat in justice here. The tiny courtroom's furnishings have remained unchanged since the 18th century, with the stone-flagged public area being separated from the rest by an iron grille, and with no seats provided for the common people.

The Parish Church of St Mary and St Nicholas (3), near the town centre, is of about the same age as the castle. It contains many relics from Llanfaes Friary, including choir stalls with misericords (carved seat undersides), the finely carved alabaster Bulkeley altar tomb, and the 13th century stone coffin of Princess Joan, natural daughter of King John, wife of Llywelyn the Great, and a lady of doubtful virtue (see Aber, page 28). The Bulkeleys were the island's largest landowners for many generations, and they lived at Baron Hill, a mansion just above the town. The Bulkeley Memorial, a tall 19th century obelisk, stands beyond Baron Hill, to the right of the small road to Llanddona (SH 59-77).

Behind the church will be found **Beaumaris Gaol (4)**, a grim building erected in 1829 under Robert Peel's Prison Reform Act. It was used as the County Gaol for less than fifty years, and in 1878 the few remaining prisoners were transferred to Caer-

1 Beaumaris Castle	4 Beaumaris Gaol	7 The Tudor Rose
2 County Hall and Assizes	5 The Museum of Childhood	8 Paddling Pool (on Pier)
3 Parish Church	6 The Green	

Beaumaris   SCALE 1:10 000 or 6 INCHES to 1 MILE

Beaumaris Castle — an outstanding example of medieval military architecture.

narfon. For some time after that it was used as the local police station and lock-up, but for many years since then it has been open to the public, who may see typical cells, and a treadwheel which was used to pump water into tanks on the roof. Visitors may also see, high up in one of the outside walls, the door through which condemned men stepped out to their execution.

At the north-eastern end of Castle Street, not far from the castle itself, will be found the **Museum of Childhood (5)** *(tel: 0248 810448)*. This contains a series of fascinating displays, devoted to children's toys, trains, dolls, pottery, and many other items which will rekindle affectionate memories of the past. Facing **The Green (6)** and the Menai Strait, with fine views across the water to Bangor and the mountains of Snowdonia, are several fine Georgian terraces, evidence of Beaumaris's prosperity in the 18th and early 19th centuries. Other features of interest in Beaumaris include the 17th century Bull's Head Hotel, an important posting house with 15th century origins. It has a fine old honeysuckle in its yard, and much good china, brass and other antiques within. Close by is the George and Dragon Inn, which dates from 1595, and **The Tudor Rose (7)** in Castle Street, which was built in about 1400, and which retains much of its original timber. This is one of the oldest domestic buildings in Anglesey, and now houses an antique shop and art gallery.

Beaumaris also has a **Paddling Pool (8)** (on the Pier), and a 9-hole golf course a mile to the south-west. But perhaps it is best known for its yachting activity, and a visit here is always enlivened by the number of boats to be seen offshore. There are pleasure cruises to Penmon, Puffin Island (not to land), and up the Strait to Menai Bridge. Sea fishing trips are also offered *(tel: 0248 810746)*.

Beddgelert(115) (SH 59-48) *7m N Porthmadog.* Small village deep set below splendid mountain country, at the meeting point of two rivers, the Afon Glaslyn and the Nant Colwyn. Although more

likely to have been derived from St Celert, who was associated with an early Celtic monastery on the site of the present church, the name of this village has been made famous by the apocryphal legend of Llywelyn's faithful hound Gelert, slain by its master, when it had in fact saved his child from a wolf. This story was probably the commercial inspiration of a certain David Pritchard, the first landlord of the

Beddgelert.

Goat Hotel, and it was he who erected a cairn in the meadow near the river, which is said to mark the unfortunate animal's grave. There is no doubt that Mr Pritchard's promotional talents have borne rich fruit over the years, but regardless of this Beddgelert is an ideal centre for visitors who wish to explore the splendid mountain area in which it lies. There are several hotels and guest houses, a number of craft and gift shops, a useful general store and a camping shop and clothing shop. The National Trust have an Information Centre at Llywelyn Cottage in the centre of the village *(tel: 076 686 293)*. Our **Walk 9**, page 146 starts from the main car

car park in Beddgelert. For Beddgelert Forest, see below.

Beddgelert Forest (115) (SH 56-49 etc.) *To immediate N Beddgelert.* First designated as a 'Forest Park' in 1937, this extensive area is now well-covered with firs and larches. There is a Snowdonia Forest Park Camp Site a mile to the north of Beddgelert, to the west side of the A4085 (SH 57-49), Caernarfon road, with the Glan y Gors car park and picnic site close by. There are 6 waymarked routes from 2 to 3 miles in length, and 2 longer walks starting either from the camp site or the car park, and these provide a good opportunity to explore this large forest. For further details purchase a copy of the Forestry Commission's excellent Forest Guide and Map entitled *Coedwig Beddgelert.*

Benllech (114,115) (SH 51-82) *7m N Menai Bridge.* A large and very popular holiday village above a wide sandy bay. Here will be found fine firm sand and safe bathing at every state of the tide, two ingredients that are so desirable for the family holidaymaker. There are hotels and guest houses in plenty, and a large holiday camp. The high cliffs above the beach are rich in carboniferous fossils, and it is possible to walk above them, northwards to Traeth Bychan, and beyond to Moelfre. The old parish church of Llanfair Mathafarn Eithaf (SH 50-82), attractively situated down a little lane off to the north of the B5108, has a relatively new pulpit commemorating the bicentenary of the poet Goronwy Owen. He was born in the parish in 1723, and was a student of Jesus College, Oxford. After many years as a curate in various English parishes, he emigrated to Virginia with the help of his friend Lewis Morris (see Brynrefail, page 43), and died there, probably in 1769. Owen's reputation was such that George Borrow, coming here during the tour recorded in his book *Wild Wales,* made a point of not only staying here and visiting the church, but also devoted a separate chapter to Owen's life.

Bethesda (115) (SH 62-66) *5m SE Bangor.* This busy quarrying town at one time housed more than 2000 workers from the Penrhyn slate quarries, but these now operate on a very much reduced scale. The quarries existed in the time of Elizabeth I, but were not systematically worked until the period when Richard Pennant of Liverpool married the Penrhyn heiress and himself became Baron Penrhyn in 1783. To cater for the workers' souls, several grandiose chapels were built, notably 'Jerusalem' and 'Siloam', and 'Bethesda' in the High Street, after which the town was named. The town is hemmed in on the west by enormous spoil heaps and the quarries themselves are reckoned to be the deepest in the world, with a series of 60-foot-high terraces and a total depth of over 1000 feet. These quarries, which produce a variety of coloured slate in blue, green and red, are open to groups of visitors from April to September by arrangement and under a guide. There is a caravan and camping site at Ogwen Bank, off the A5 just to the south of the town, and this busy road soon leads to the dramatic Nant Ffrancon valley, and into the mountains past Llyn Ogwen and Capel Curig.

Betws Garmon (115) (SH 53-57) *5m SE Caernar-fon.* Small village astride the A4085 Caernarfon to Beddgelert road, at the entry to the National Park area. St Garmon's Church is a simple well-proportioned neo-Norman building dating from 1841, and there are delightful gardens at Hafoty House, with azaleas, hydrangeas and flowering shrubs, and rock and water gardens, all close to the Nant Mill waterfalls. At the southern end of the village there is a graceful three-arched 18th century bridge carrying the main road over the Afon Gwyrfai, and built by local man, Harry Parry, claimed by friends to be 'the modern Inigo'.

Betws-y-Coed (115) (SH 79-56) *17m S Conwy.* Situated in the heart of the great Gwydyr Forest at the meeting point of three valleys, the Conwy, Llugwy and Lledr, this greystone village is today a natural centre for visitors, and has been so for well over 150 years. It was popular with Victorian honeymooners and was made famous by the Birmingham watercolourist, David Cox, who favoured North Wales above anywhere else. The sign he painted for the Royal Oak Hotel has for many years been carefully preserved inside this pleasant old building.

Being at the junction of three rivers, Betws-y-Coed has several bridges: the Pont-y-Pair, (Bridge of the Cauldron), a rugged five-arch bridge over the Llugwy; a suspension foot bridge hidden behind the

The Fairy Glen, near Betws-y-Coed (see page 53).

Old Church; and the genius Telford's cast-iron Waterloo Bridge, taking his Holyhead Road, now the A5, over the Conwy (see Conwy, page 51). The 14th century 'Old Church' of St Michael and All Angels is quietly located behind the railway station, and in its nave lies the effigy of Gruffydd ap Dafydd, the great nephew of Llywelyn the Last, who fought in the wars of Edward III and the Black Prince. The handsome Early English style New Church of St Mary the Virgin was built in 1873, and is one of the better examples of mid-Victorian architecture.

Being situated at a junction on the A5, Betws-y-Coed is perhaps too easily accessible, and at times it can become rather congested. However it is without doubt one of the best touring, walking and fishing centres in North Wales. It is the starting point of several easy hill walks, particularly to Llyn Elsi (SH 78-55) by the Jubilee Path, and to Llyn y

Betwys-y-Coed   SCALE 1:25 000 or 2½ INCHES to 1 MILE

Parc, making use of our **Walk 5**, page 138. But for further details see Y Stablau, below.

Y Stablau (The Stables), in the centre of the village, is the Snowdonia National Park Information Centre *(tel: 06902 665 or 06902 426)*, and this provides a general introduction to the National Park with an audio-visual theatre where slide-shows can be seen during the main summer months. Information on the Gwydyr Forest is also available here, with details of 6 walks in the immediate vicinity, and of others further afield. While in Betws- y-Coed do not miss a visit to the interesting Conwy Valley Railway Museum *(tel: 0492 640568)*, which is in the old goods yard by the BR station. There are displays covering railways in general, with special reference to North Wales, and also an interesting miniature railway.

Black Rock Sands (124) (SH 52-37) *3m SW Porthmadog.* This well known beach at the northern end of Tremadog Bay has over a mile of firm clean sand, and can be reached on two roads from Morfa Bychan.

Blaenau Ffestiniog (115) (SH 70-45) *12m NE Porthmadog.* Small town situated at the head of the Vale of Ffestiniog, between the great mountains of Manod Mawr (115) (SH 72-45) and Moelwyn Mawr (124) (SH 65-44). Its prosperity was due almost entirely to the great slate caverns and quarries nearby, and today two of these caverns provide a variety of interesting experiences for visitors. (See Gloddfa Ganol, page 64; and Llechwedd, page 81.) (See also Ffestiniog Power Station, page 63, and Tanygrisiau, page 106.)

The town is on British Rail's Conwy Valley Line, and is also served by the Ffestiniog Narrow Gauge Railway coming up from Porthmadog. There is a Snowdonia National Park and Ffestiniog Railway Travel and Information Centre at Isallt in the centre of the town *(tel: 0766 831360)*, and from here a leaflet can be purchased describing the interesting Blaenau Ffestiniog Town Trail. This is about 1 ½ miles long and should take about one hour.

Blaen-pennant Waterfalls (124,125) (SH 89-21) *(6m NE Dinas-Mawddwy).* A long series of water-falls on the Afon Dyfi, not far below its source beneath the crags of Aran Fawddwy. They are situated below the rocks of Ogof Ddu (The Black Cave), some distance from the road, but are approached by an easy footpath. The valley of the Dyfi between here and Dinas is principally devoted to farming, but there are rhododendrons in many of the hedges and on some of the mountain slopes too. To the north lies the fabulous Bwlch y Groes, see page 43. See also **Tour 9**, page 126, for a fine run through this largely unspoilt mountain scenery.

Bodedern (114) (SH 33-80) *7m E Holyhead.* When it stood on the old main road to Holyhead (before the building of Telford's new road), Bodedern was a town noted for woollen manufacture, and it still retains a towny flavour. The church has been over-restored, but there is a pleasant inn, near which stands an imposing pump under a classical pediment. This was presented by Lord Stanley of Alderley in 1897. For Pressaddfed Burial Chamber, north-east of village, see page 99.

Bodeilio Weaving Centre (114,115) (SH 49-77) *2m NE Llangefni.* The interesting exhibition here tells the story of handloom weaving, and demonstration workshops show how contemporary weavers are applying their ancient skills. There are also two shops, a separate gallery mounting month-long craft exhibitions, and a licensed vegetarian restaurant. *(Tel: 0248 722465.)*

Bodewyrd (114) (SH 39-90) *4m SW Amlwch.* Just a neat little church with three 18th century brasses, a few houses, and a gabled 18th century dovecote, which was sadly very decayed the last time we called here.

Bodnant Garden (N.T.) (116) (SH 80-72) *8m S Llandudno, 5m S Conwy.* This is one of Britain's

View from the Upper Terrace, Bodnant Garden.

outstanding gardens, and was given to the National Trust by the father of the present Lord Aberconwy, who continues to administer it on the Trust's behalf. Within its 80 acres, first laid out in 1875, there is a series of terraces leading down the hill from the house, and looking across the Conwy valley to the mountains of the Carneddau. There are fine collections of camelias, azaleas, rhododendrons, and magnolias, and buildings within the garden include the delightful Pin Mill, which is sited at the end of a formal 'canal'. This dates from about 1730, and was moved here as recently as 1938, from Woodchester near Stroud. Tea and light refreshments are available from a kiosk in the car park during the summer months. *(Tel: 049267 460.)*

Bodowyr Burial Chamber (114) (SH 46-68) *7m SW Menai Bridge.* Here is a massive capstone on three large uprights, a good specimen of the cromlechs used by the Neolithic inhabitants of Anglesey for their communal burials over 4000 years ago. Like all of them it would of course have been originally covered by a mound of earth.

Boduan (123) (SH 32-37) *4m NW Pwllheli.* Small village to the south-east of a well-wooded hill, Garn Boduan, which has the remains of an Iron Age settlement on its summit. The ambitious 19th century neo-Norman church in red sandstone contains some pleasant monuments to members of the Wynn family, who used to live at Plas Boduan (Boduan Hall), a largely 18th century building in beautiful woodlands, to the north of the village. There is a pleasant walk west and south-west from here, leading to the slopes of Carn Fadryn. A study of Landranger Sheet 123 will reveal many footpaths and quiet roads allowing for the exploration of the quiet inland countryside around here.

Bodvel Hall (123) (SH 34-36) *2m N Pwllheli, on A497.* A range of farm buildings here have been turned into a centre for Welsh crafts, with areas for displaying skilled work in wood, slate, pottery and wool. There is also a horse-riding centre and a caravan site.

The Mawddach Estuary, near Bontddu.

Bontddu (124) (SH 66-18) *4m W Dolgellau, on A496.* Small village beneath tree-clad hills on the northern shore of the Mawddach estuary. There is a picnic site at Fiddler's Elbow, on the A496 to the east of the village, and our **Walk 14**, page 156 starts from here. There is also a picnic site on the A496 to the west of the village, and a car park beside a small road into the hills, just to the north of Llechfraith (SH 66-19). Near this little road up Cwm-Hirgwm is one gold mine, the Clogau St David's, which was still working when we called here last, and which has been the traditional source of Royal wedding rings since the turn of the century. At the time of writing this was not open to the public, and does not at present appear as exciting as it sounds, but it provides a good reason for a walk in this attractive little valley. It is situated about 200 yards downstream of a bridge over the Hirgwm stream, on the west side of the road up from Bontddu. It is also possible to walk from Llechfraith, eastwards over the hills to Cwm-mynach (see page 56), or west and south-west to Barmouth, first using the public road.

Borth-y-Gest (124) (SH 56-37) *1m S Porthmadog.* A largely unspoilt little seaside resort, clustered around a small bay, and looking out over the Afon Glaslyn estuary, with its multitude of sailing dinghies and other boats. There are small sandy coves tucked away nearby and the wide range of accommodation makes Borth-y-Gest an ideal place for a quiet family holiday. There is a pleasant walk north-westwards passing between Cist Cerrig (SH 543-384), three upright stones which are the remains of a Stone Age burial chamber, and Moel-y-Gest, a rocky hill with fine views from its summit.

Botwnnog (123) (SH 26-31) *9m WSW Pwllheli.* Small village with a school founded in 1616 as a Free Grammar School by Henry Rowlands, Bishop of Bangor, a memorial to whom may be found inside the gate of the nearby church of St Beuno. Beyond the church there is a pleasant lane running north-eastwards to Garnfadryn, from whence there are attractive walks around the dramatic hill of Carn Fadryn (SH 27-35). Use Landranger Sheet 123 to explore this pleasant countryside.

Brithdir (124) (SH 76-18) *3m E Dolgellau.* Small hamlet in the hills above the Afon Wnion Valley with, on its east side, the earthworks of a Roman fortlet, which was situated on the Roman road running south-eastwards from Chester to the coast near Dolgellau. To the west of Brithdir is its unusual late Victorian church. This was designed by Henry Wilson, a junior partner of the well-known architect, J. D. Sedding, who had designed the Vicarage a few years earlier. Wilson, most noted for his metalwork, has left his mark in the form of an altar and pulpit, both of beaten copper, and doors inlaid with mother-of-pearl. Further to the south-west, along the B4416, is the Torrent Walk, but for this attractive feature see page 107.

Bryn Bras Castle (114,115) (SH 54-62) *5m E Caernarfon.* This mansion was built as a castle in about 1830 in extravagant neo-Norman style, around an earlier structure. It is romantically sited against a background of high mountains, and lies in a splendid 30 acre garden, with rhododendrons, roses and hydrangeas, a walled knot garden, woodland walks, pools and waterfalls. There is also a 'mountain walk' with fine views of Snowdonia and Anglesey. Part of the very much 'lived-in' interior is open to view, and this includes hall, galleried staircase, drawing room, morning room and library. Refreshments are available in the Garden Tearoom and on the lawns, and there is also a picnic area. *(Tel: 0286 870210.)*

Bryncelli Ddu Burial Chamber (114,115) (SH 50-70) *2m SW Llanfair P.G.* Situated about a mile to the east of Llanddaniel Fab Church, this is without doubt the best preserved Neolithic monument in North Wales. During its construction sometime between 3500 and 4000 years ago, earlier circles of upright stones were partially destroyed by its creators. What now remains is a great mound of earth covering a burial chamber in which there is a single 8-foot upright stone with faintly carved patterns just visible upon it, and which is reached by a long, narrow passage. Key is available at nearby farmhouse.

Brynkir Woollen Mills (124) (SH 52-42) *At Golan, 3m NW Porthmadog, to N of A487.* A working woollen mill where visitors may see machines in action, and then browse in the mill shop, where mill products on display include blankets, bedspreads, travelling rugs, tweeds and flannels. There is also a water wheel to be seen. *(Tel: 076 675 236.)* This is on our **Tour 5**, page 118.

Bryncroes (123) (SH 22-31) *6m W Abersoch.* Quiet hamlet below the northern end of Mynydd Rhiw, with Ffynnon Fair, a well which was one of the watering places for medieval pilgrims heading for Bardsey Island. Walk south from here, up over the steep slopes of Mynydd Rhiw.

Brynrefail (114) (SH 48-86) *4m NW Benllech.* This hamlet on the A5025 is in the parish of Penrhoslugwy, and is at the start of our **Walk 1**, page 130. It has a chapel on the main road, but the pleasant little parish church of St Michael is situated at Ty-mawr, ½ mile to the south (SH 481-859). Also on our **Walk 1**, this medieval building, although restored in 1865, contains a Jacobean communion table, and a 6th century inscribed stone. On a hillside above the Pilot Boat Inn, a short distance along the A5025 to the north-east of Brynrefail, will be found the Morris Memorial. This monument commemorates three 18th century brothers who were born at Pentre Eirianell, just to its north. They were all intellectuals with a wide variety of interests, and founders of the Cymmrodorion Society. Lewis Morris, the eldest of the three, was a highly practical and scientific person and is still remembered for his hydographic survey of the Welsh coast.

Brynsiencyn (114,115) (SH 48-67) *4m SW Llanfair P.G.* This compact village sits astride the A4080, but there is a small road south-west from here leading to the Menai Strait's shore at Barras, from whence there are fine views across to Caernarfon Castle and the ancient town walls. Not far away (SH 478-654) is the Anglesey Sea Zoo, based at an oyster hatchery. Here are many examples of local

sealife in a series of large tanks, from sharks to shrimps, and everything is under cover. There is a craft shop, a tea-room and seafood snacks are available. *(Tel: 024 873411.)*

To the west of the village will be found Caer Leb (SH 473-675), rectangular earthworks, probably occupied during the 3rd century AD, and thought to be the local equivalent of a Roman villa. A little further to the west (SH 465-671) are the defensive earthworks of Castell Bryn-Gwyn. This site was probably first developed as a henge monument in Neolithic times, and then adapted as a fortified site in the 1st century AD.

Bwlch Drws Ardudwy (124) (SH 66-28) *8m E Harlech.* Apart from the Roman Steps (see page 102) this pass is the best crossing of the Rhinog Range (see page 101), but it is a wild and rugged place and only recommended to those with experience of hillwalking. Thomas Pennant, in his famous book *Tour in Wales*, published in 1778, wrote that he — ' was tempted to visit this noted pass, and found the horror of it far exceeding the most gloomy idea that could be conceived of it.' Bwlch Drws Ardudwy may be approached from our **Walk 13**, Point D (see page 154).

Bwlch Oerddrws (124) (SH 79-17) *5m E Dolgellau.* Bwlch is the Welsh name for a pass, and this one is appropriately named 'The Pass of the Cold Door'. The A470 from Dinas Mawddwy to Dolgellau runs through here, and once this road starts to descend, fine views open up westwards to Cadair Idris. Near the top of the pass there is a small car park below the crags of Craig y Bwlch.

Bwlch y Ddeufaen (115) (SH 71-71) *8m SW Conwy.* This ancient pass in wild mountain country to the west of the Conwy Valley was used by the Romans for their road between Chester and Caernarfon, and more locally between the fort of Canovium at Caerhun (SH 77-70) and the coast near Gorddinog (SH 66-73). In the pass, at SH 716-716, there is a prehistoric cairn, Barclodiad y Gawres (The Giantess's Apronful), probably the remains of a burial mound. This is not to be confused with the better-known Barclodiad y Gawres, in Anglesey (see page 36). Bwlch y Ddeufaen means 'The Pass of the Two Stones', and must refer either to the two standing stones to its east (see Roewen, page 102), or to the two Roman milestones that once stood on this section of road, and which are now in the British Museum.

There is a minor road up from the Conwy Valley, reaching almost to the pass, and from here it is possible to walk north-west to Llanfairfechan, or west to Aber. The pass itself has unfortunately been marred by power lines.

Bwlch y Groes (125) (SH 91-23) *8m NE Dinas Mawddwy.* This pass in the mountains between Llanuwchllyn and Dinas Mawddwy stands at 1790 feet above sea level, and is the highest pass crossed by a road in Wales. From the car park just to its north there are splendid views northwards down Cwm Cynllwyd towards the Arenigs, and westwards to Aran Fawddwy and Aran Benllyn. At the very top of the pass, just to the south of the car park, the road between Llanuwchllyn and Dinas is joined by an equally delightful road coming up from

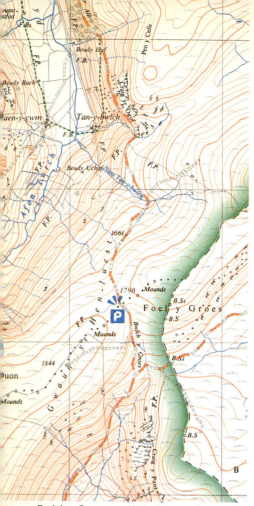

Bwlch y Groes   SCALE 1:25 000 or 2½ INCHES to 1 MILE

the wooded valley in which Llyn Efyrnwy (Lake Vyrnwy) lies. Although outside the scope of this guide, it is possible to loop back to Bala, by turning northwards from the lake over further mountain country, and down Cwm Hirnant (all on Sheet 125). South of Bwlch y Groes the road drops southwards, steeply down into the valley of the Afon Rhiwlech and it is dominated by the sweeping black rocks and scree of Craig y Pant. This is on our **Tour 9**, page 126.

View northwards down Cwm Cynllwyd, from Bwlch y Groes.

Cadair Idris (124) (SH 71-13) *3m S Dolgellau*. This rugged mountain range is made up of volcanic rocks eroded by glacial action over millions of years, and takes its name from one of the great hollows created thus, the legendary 'Chair of Idris', which shelters the waters of Llyn y Gadair. Idris remains a shadowy figure, possibly a local poet, philosopher and astronomer much given to brooding thoughts while sitting in his chair on the mountain top, or possibly a local hero who fought against the Saxon invaders in the 7th century, and paid for this with his life. As early as the 18th century, visitors were being taken up the mountain by a guide from Dolgellau, and at the height of the Victorian era, there was even a refreshment hut on Penygadair, its highest summit.

Our **Walk 15**, page 158 follows the Pony Path for part of its ascent to, and descent from Penygadair. The Fox's Path is dangerous and is not recom-

Cadair Idris — a view from Lynnau Cregennen.

mended, but there are leaflets available from the National Park Information Centres describing the Minffordd Path, up from the A487 (SH 73-11) in the south, the Pony Path from Ty Nant (SH 69-15), and the Pony Path from Llanfihangel-y-pennant (SH 67-08) in the south-west.

Cae'n-y-coed (115) (SH 76-57) *2m W Betws-y-Coed, just off A5*. This is a Forestry Commission picnic site, with toilets, on a grassy slope with birch trees. From here a waymarked walk, steep in places, leads through a Forest Garden where over a 100 different species may be seen.

Caer Gai (124,125) (SH 87-31) *5m SW Bala*. Here, not far from the point where the Afon Lliw flows into the Afon Dyfrdwy (River Dee), are the earth-works of a Roman fort that once stood at the junction of the Roman road running from Chester to the coast near Dolgellau, with another one running north-westwards to the fort, Tomen-y-mur (see page 106), and possibly on from there to Caernar-fon. These earthworks are on private land, and are not open to public view.

Caer Gybi (See Holyhead, page 66)

Caerhun (115) (SH 77-70) *5m S Conwy*. The earthworks of the 1st century Roman fort of Canovium are beautifully sited on a small hill overlooking the Afon Conwy. This fort was built, probably during Agricola's campaign of AD 78, to guard the crossing of the Conwy, by the road from

Chester to Caernarfon. Situated in the north-east corner of the earthworks is a long narrow medieval church, much restored in 1850. It is best to visit both earthworks and church by walking south-westwards from a point near the Tal-y-cafn bridge over the Conwy (SH 78-71), and we suggest that you obtain the Gwynedd County Council's leaflet, *Caerhun in the Conwy Valley*, which provides details of a pleasant circular walk of about 4 miles, extending as far west as Pontwgan. If you do not have time to obtain this, use Landranger Sheet 115.

Caer Llugwy (115) (SH 74-57) *4m W Betws-y-Coed*. Small Roman fort on the banks of the Afon Llugwy. This stood on the Roman road running south from Caerhun to Tomen-y-mur, but little of interest remains above ground.

Caernarfon (114,115) (SH 48-62) Busy holiday town and market centre for the Lleyn Peninsula, southern Anglesey and much of Snowdonia, Caernarfon is also the administrative capital of the

1 Twt Hill Fort
2 Segontium
3 St Peblig's Church (off map, to south-east)
4 Caernarfon Castle

5 Aber Brige (Pont-yr-Aber)
6 Coed Helen Recreation Ground, etc.
7 Slate Quay
8 Y Maes

9 Maritime Museum
10 Arfon Leisure Centre (off map, to north-east)

Caernarfon

SCALE 1:10 000 or 6 INCHES to 1 MILE

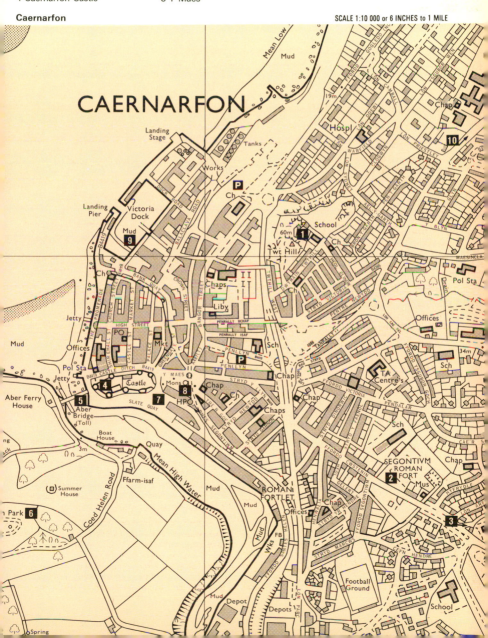

county of Gwynedd. Its strategic importance is emphasised by the location within its bounds of an Iron Age hill fort at Twt Hill, a Roman fort, Segontium, and the greatest of Edward I's Welsh castles.

The remains of **Twt Hill Fort (1)** are not of great interest to visitors, but the picnic possibilities and the pleasant views from here make the climb worth while. The Roman fort of **Segontium (2)**, almost certainly established here in AD 78, to control the recently-conquered Ordovices tribe, is well worth visiting. Excavated in the 1920s by Sir (then Dr) Mortimer Wheeler, its ground plan and museum reveals much of the story of the Roman occupation of North Wales. The nearby **St Peblig's Church (3)** has a dark, heavily Victorianised interior, but lovers of church monuments should not miss the Vaynol Chapel with its splendid late 16th century alabaster altar-tomb.

However, the town's outstanding feature is without doubt the great **Caernarfon Castle (4)**, started here by Edward I in 1283 and only finished by his son, the first Prince of Wales, in 1327. Standing on the site of an 11th century Norman motte and bailey, at the point where the Afon Seiont and the smaller Afon Cadnant enter the Menai Strait, this was the largest of the castles built by the English king to contain the partly subjugated Welsh, and to consolidate his victory over Llywelyn, the last of the native Welsh princes. It was, however, at Conwy Castle that Edward set up his headquarters. As with most of the other castles planned by Edward, it was possible to supply both the castle, and the English town beside it, from the sea. It was twice besieged by Owain Glyndwr, but thanks to this strategy, it was able to hold out successfully. It was in the unfinished castle that the future Edward II was probably born, and it was here in 1301 that he was installed as the first Prince of Wales, at the age of 17.

Fought over in the Civil War, the castle was finally captured by a Parliamentary force in 1646. Happily most of its exterior walls have survived, although they were much restored in the 1840s by the neo-medieval architect Anthony Salvin, who is perhaps better remembered for his work on Windsor Castle and the Tower of London, and who tended, like many of his contemporaries, to take an over-romantic view of the buildings with which he was involved. Much of the interior of the castle has vanished, to be replaced by neatly trimmed lawns. However this interior has been been put to magnificent use, becoming renowned throughout the world for the colourful pageantry of the Investiture of the Princes of Wales, the most recent of which involved the present holder of this office, H.R.H. Prince Charles, who was invested here on 1st July 1969.

The finest view of the castle is to be obtained from across the Afon Seiont, the far bank of which may be reached by a footbridge, the **Pont-yr-Aber (5)**. This view is particularly attractive if the tide is in and the water calm. Beyond the bridge is the attractive **Coed Helen Recreation Grounds and Caravan Park (6)**, and it is possible to walk southwestwards from here, further along the Aber Foreshore Road.

A visit to the castle itself is essential; to stroll around its lawns, and especially to see the magnificent Eagle Tower, the Queen's Tower, and the Granary Tower, all of which provide fine views from their battlements. The Queen's Tower houses the

Regimental Museum of the Royal Welsh Fusiliers, which is also well worth visiting.

The medieval town walls to the immediate north of the castle enclose an 'old town' with attractive streets still in the grid pattern laid out by Edward I, but this only covers a small proportion of present-day Caernarfon. The old streets are full of character and the little alleys and old inns like the 'Hole in the Wall', and the 'Black Boy' have a real flavour of the past. The centre of the town is often congested, but parking is usually possible on the **Slate Quay (7)** beneath the castle walls. Climb up the steep slope from here, past the statue of David Lloyd George, MP for Caernarfon Borough from 1890 until he became an Earl a few months before his death in 1945. Then into the Square, known as **Y Maes (8)**, which is overlooked by several pleasant Georgian buildings, and which is the site of a colourful market each Saturday. There is also a **Tourist Information Centre** here *(tel: 0286 2232)*. See also the steam-dredger *Seiont II*, the main exhibit of a **Maritime Museum (9)**, based at the Doc Victoria, (Victoria Dock), a few minutes walk along the Promenade. Just beyond this are the County Archives, which open on to the quayside, and which usually have items on display. There is river and sea fishing in and around Caernarfon, but for other water sports, see Plas Menai, page 95.

Less than a mile from the town centre, on the B4366, is the **Arfon Leisure Centre (10)**, which is open 7 days a week, and which offers swimming, badminton, squash, tennis, and a variety of other activities. There is an 18-hole golf course about 1 ½ miles to the south-west of the town.

Cambrian Coast Railway This British Rail line runs from Aberystwyth northwards around the coast to Pwllheli, and is an invaluable facility for all visitors. Not only does it provide a completely different and more relaxed view of the coastlands and countryside through which it passes, but it also links with most of the 'Great Little Trains of Wales', thus opening up many further possibilities. These railway services are especially useful for walkers, who can plan expeditions starting at one station and finishing at another.

Coming from London, Birmingham and Shrewsbury is a line through Machynlleth, which joins the Cambrian Coast line at Dovey Junction Station (135) SN 98-69). From here it runs northwards through Aberdyfi, Tywyn (where it links with the Talyllyn Railway, see page 106), Fairbourne (where it links with the Fairbourne Railway, see page 62), Barmouth, Harlech, Porthmadog (where it links with the Ffestiniog Railway, see page 62; and the Welsh Highland Railway, see page 109); then on through Criccieth to its final terminus at Pwllheli. It also runs southwards from Dovey Junction to Aberystwyth, where yet another narrow gauge railway may be found, BR's own Vale of Rheidol Railway. This is, however, outside the scope of this guide. There are other stations on the Cambrian Coast Railway and for full details see BR's *Cambrian Coast Timetable*.

Capel Curig (115) (SH 72-58) *6m W Betws-y-Coed.* Standing at the junction of the A4086 and the A5, this famous fishing and climbing centre takes its name from St Curig, who was once Bishop of Dolbadarn. It is ringed by mountains, with the great peak of Moel Siabod to the immediate south, the

Snowdon from Capel Curig.

foothills of the Carneddau range to the north, and to the west, Tryfan, the Glyders and Snowdon itself. It is one of the oldest and also probably the smallest of the North Wales resorts, but it straddles the A5 for nearly 2 miles and has a number of craft shops and some good hotel accommodation. The Victorian church is not of great interest to visitors, and neither is the 'old church', which although dating from the 13th century, was restored in 1839. Plas-y-Brenin, on the A4086 just to the west of the village, is the National Centre for Mountain Activities and residential courses on climbing, canoeing, skiing and orienteering are held here regularly. (*Tel: 06904 241 for details*).

Capel Garmon (116) (SH 81-55) *2m E Betws-y-Coed.* Pleasant hamlet with a picturesque 16th century inn, The White Horse. Situated about a mile to the south is the Capel Garmon Chambered Long Cairn. This neolithic tomb is very similar to those found in the far-off Cotswolds and known there as long barrows. It has a false entrance with horns on either side formed by dry stone walling, and an actual entrance in its side — all very reminiscent of Belas Knap Long Barrow, above the little town of Winchcombe in Gloucestershire (163) (SP 01-25).

Capel Hermon (124) (SH 74-25) *7m NNE Dolgellau.* Here is a small chapel, a few houses, and a car park. Not exciting in itself, but it is situated on an adventurous road running up through the eastern fringes of the great Coed-y-Brenin Forest (see page 50), and makes a good base for a number of walks. (See also **Tour 7**, page 122).

Capel Newydd (123) (SH 28-30) *3m WSW Llanbedrog.* Located at the end of a long farm track (right of way for walkers,) it is believed to be the earliest surviving nonconformist chapel in North Wales. Dating from 1769, this is a simple barn-like structure with earth floor and box pews. When we last called here the key was available from the house on the road where the track starts.

Carmel (115,123) (SH 49-54) *5m S Caernarfon.* Large village, once prosperous from quarrying in the hills in which it nestles. There is a maze of roads and villages in this pock-marked country due south of Caernarfon. It is not part of the tourist's North Wales, but those who wish to experience every facet of the region's life and work should spend at least a short time in this area.

Carmel Head (Trwyn y Gader) (114) (SH 29-93) *5m W Cemaes.* A rocky headland forming Anglesey's north-western tip, with high cliffs, gorse-covered headlands and wind-blown pine trees. It is less than 2 miles from the nearest public road, and there are fine views north-westwards to the Skerries, and northwards to the little island of West Mouse. Combine with a visit to Hen Borth (see page 66) and Cemlyn Bay (see page 48).

Carn Fadryn (123) (SH 27-35) *7m W Pwllheli.* There is an Iron Age fort on the top of this prominent, conical-shaped hill, and a large flat stone known as Arthur's Table or the King's Table (Bwrdd y Brenin). Local legend tells of a pot of gold hidden beneath the stone, and it is also thought to have been connected with the Stone of Destiny, beneath the Coronation Chair in Westminster Abbey. Whether or not you are fascinated by legends of this type, you will enjoy the walk around the hill from Garnfadryn village. Enquire at Garnfadryn if it is in order to walk to the top, on the path that starts near the telephone box. There are fine views to be had from this summit.

The Carneddau (115) (SH 68-64 etc.) *4m NW Capel Curig.* A long and often broad mountain ridge stretching from Drum (SH 70-69) in the north-east,

47

to Carnedd Dafydd (SH 66-62) in the south-west, with the highest peak, Carnedd Llewelyn (SH 68-64), standing at 3484 feet above sea-level. With its sweeping upland expanses of grassland and only intermittent rocky outcrops, this is ideal country for experienced hillwalkers. However, distances are both deceptive and considerable, and lack of clear landmarks can make navigation difficult, especially if the weather deteriorates. Therefore, like all mountains, the Carneddau should only be tackled by properly equipped and fully experienced walkers. Thomas Pennant, in his famous *Tour in Wales* published in 1778, found these hills 'very disagreeable, of dreary bottoms or moory hills'. For further information of a more positive nature, read W. A. Poucher's *The Welsh Peaks*, or Terry Marsh's *The Mountains of Wales*.

Summertime at Castell y Bere.

Carnguwch Church (123) (SH 374-418) *6m N Pwllheli.* A small church standing alone above a small stream on the southern slopes of Mynydd Carnguwch. To reach this, the visitor will require Landranger Sheet 123, a stout pair of shoes, and the key, which should be obtainable in Llithfaen village (see page 81). The simple bell-coted building was rebuilt in 1882, but its contents include some earlier woodwork. A study of the map will show that a visit here may be made into a pleasant circular walk.

Castell y Bere (124) (SH 66-08) *11m NE Tywyn.* Dramatically sited on a great rocky outcrop rising from the broad floor of the Dysynni valley, the ruined Castell y Bere was begun by Llywelyn the Great soon after 1221, but was regrettably captured by the English in 1283. However, Edward I failed to hold it for long and after its fall in the uprising of 1294 it was finally abandoned. It is a romantic place with breathtaking views down the valley to Craig yr Aderyn, (The Birds' Rock). Castell y Bere is on our **Tour 10**, page 128, and our **Walk 16**, page 160.

Cefni Reservoir (114) (SH 44-77) *2m NW Llangefni.* A relatively small reservoir formed in the early 1950s, the surrounds of which have been planted by the Forestry Commission. There is a car park and picnic site on the B5111, at the north-eastern end, and visitors can enjoy a pleasant walk along forest tracks. Day fishing permits (for trout) may be purchased in Llangefni, and there is also a bird hide pleasantly sited amongst larches and willows a short distance from the car park.

Cemaes (114) (SH 36-93) *5m W Amlwch.* Cheerful little holiday village, which was once the main harbour on this stretch of coast, until it was overtaken by Amlwch. There are bright shops and pleasant inns, a quiet seafront, and a sandy beach backed by a convenient car park. Pleasure boat trips are available and there is good fishing for bass and pollock.

Cemlyn Bay (114) (SH 33-93) *8m W Amlwch.* A great curving bank of shingle faces the sea and protects a landlocked lagoon, the haunt of countless sea birds. The headland to the west is a sandy

Cemaes, Cemaes Bay and Wylfa

SCALE 1:25 000 or 2½ INCHES to 1 MILE

A view westwards over Cemlyn Bay.

gorse-covered waste known as Trwyn Cemlyn, with a rocky shore and a view eastwards of the vast Wylfa Power Station. This headland can be reached on foot from the car park to the west of the lagoon. There is also a car park at the eastern end of the shingle bank, with access to the beach, Traeth Cemlyn, and a path leading along the bank. Visitors are however asked not to walk along the bank during nesting time (April to June), and not to disturb the wildlife in the lagoon at any time, as it is a nature reserve. The shingle bank and Trwyn Cemlyn headland belong to the National Trust.

Centre for Alternative Technology (135) (SH 04-75) *4m N Machynlleth.* Situated in an old slate quarry near the hamlet of Pantperthog, just to the east of the A487, the Centre is a public demonstration of energy conservation, solar power, water power and wind power. There is also an organic garden, an energy conserving house, blacksmith's forge, smallholding, restaurant and large bookshop. As the Centre's interesting leaflet states — 'Alternative Technology is far more than just solar panels and windmills. It is a web that links many features of

At the Centre for Alternative Technology — 'far more than just solar panels and windmills'.

a sustainable, fulfilling society and the displays illustrate some of the ways such a society might work'. Do not miss a visit to this most interesting and thought-provoking place.

Cerrigceinwen (114,115) (SH 42-73) *3m SW Llangefni.* There is no definite village in this

sprawling, largely agricultural parish. The modest church, sitting in a small hollow down a quiet road to the west of the B4422 was rebuilt in the 19th century. However, it should be of interest to enthusiasts, as some old materials were used during the rebuilding, including a 12th century tomb slab. There is also a 12th century font and two handsome brass chandeliers.

Ceunant Mawr Waterfall (115) (SH 57-59) Walk less than a mile south of High Street, Llanberis, (see page 69) following a signpost in Church Lane to this spectacular waterfall on the Afon Hwch, which is particularly impressive when the latter is in spate after heavy rain. Follow path beyond, across the Snowdon Mountain Railway, to view smaller falls and rock pools.

Chwilog (123) (SH 43-38) *5m W Criccieth.* Small village astride the B4354, a road designed and built by the Porth Dinllaen Turnpike Trust in the 19th century, as part of William Madocks' grandiose scheme to carry traffic from London via the new crossing of the estuary at Porthmadog, across the Lleyn Peninsula to Porth Dinllaen, from whence it would cross to Ireland. It was claimed that this would have been 30 miles shorter than the Holyhead route, but it eventually came to nought. (See also Porthmadog, page 97, and Porth Dinllaen, page 96).

Clynnog-fawr (115,123) (SH 41-49) *10m SW Caernarfon.* Small coastal village sheltering beneath the northern slopes of Bwlch Mawr. It lies on the A499 Caernarfon to Pwllheli road, and has many whitewashed cottages, and a long shingle beach with patches of sand, and some boulders. The splendid late-Perpendicular church dedicated to St Beuno was built as a collegiate church in the late 15th century, on the site of a much earlier building, marking the saint's burial place. St Beuno, probably the most important Welsh saint after St David, came to Clynnog in about AD 635, towards the end of his life. He founded several monasteries, and although also noted for the miraculous restoration of the severed head of his niece, St Winefrede, he was always best known for his connections with Clynnog Fawr.

However, the richness of St Beuno's church is due not only to this saint's outstanding reputation, but also to the fact that it lay directly on the pilgrim route to Bardsey Island. Its vast interior has almost the feeling of a cathedral and contains some fine examples of wood carving in the roof timbers, rood screen and misericord seat undersides. Relics include a massive oaken strong-box known as the Chest of St Beuno, and a pair of dog tongs, used we assume by the past church wardens to carry aggressive dogs out of the church without putting themselves at risk (see also Llaneilian, page 73). The holy water of St Beuno's Well, on the side of the main road about 300 yards south-west of the church, was said to cure all ills, but only if after taking the water, the sufferer spent the night on the stone floor of the saint's original cell — a true case of kill or cure!

Just visible from the main road, and close to the sea is the Bach Wen Penarth Burial Chamber, which is still complete with a capstone on four uprights.

The Afon Eden at T'yn-y-groes, in the Coed-y-Brenin.

There is a good walk south-east from the village, up over a shoulder of the hill, through Bwlch Mawr, to join a minor road running south-eastwards and then south. Then turn right, off the road beyond a radio mast, and head westwards behind Bwlch Mawr and Gyrn Ddu, to join the coast near Trefor. From here there is no alternative but to return along the A499, unless you have friends with a car to meet you.

Cnicht (115) (SH 64-46) *4m WSW Beddgelert.* At 2265 ft, Cnicht is not one of Snowdonia's highest peaks, but it is unusually attractive in shape. Although it is in effect a long ridge, when it is viewed from the south-west its sharp-pointed profile partly justifies the over-imaginative title of 'the Matterhorn of Wales'. It is best approached from Croesor (see page 54), and although easier than many of its neighbours it should only be tackled in the company of experienced climbers.

Cochwillan Old Hall (115) (SH 60-69) *3m SE Bangor.* This fine example of medieval architecture was probably built by William ap Gruffyd, one of Henry VII's supporters at Bosworth Field. Although used as a barn for many years, the Great Hall, with its fine hammer-beam roof, now forms the core of a beautifully restored house. Open by appointment only. *Tel: 2048 364608.*

Coed-y-Brenin (The King's Forest) (124) (SH 73-26 etc.) *4m N Dolgellau.* This is a magnificent forest area stretching some 6 miles northwards from Llanelltyd into the hills that give birth to the Rivers Mawddach, Gain and Eden, all three of which spend much of their brief lives flowing through this tree-clad landscape. When the Forestry Commission started planting here in 1922, it was named after the Vaughans, the local landowners, but it was renamed Coed-y-Brenin (The King's Forest) to commemorate the Silver Jubilee of George V in 1935. The Forestry Commission publish an excellent guide map describing this forest, and this may be obtained from the Visitor Centre at Maesgwm (SH 71-27), just off to the west of the A470, 8 miles north of Dolgellau. It is anyway preferable to start your visit to Coed-y-Brenin here, as there are displays and an audio-visual programme providing an excellent introduction to the forest, and everything with which it is associated, including the famous gold mines that were once opened up in this area.

Close to the Maesgwm Centre and approached from the same general access, is the Afon Eden Trail, which starts from a car park with picnic places. This 1½ mile trail runs parallel with the Afon Eden for almost half of its length and is well described in a special leaflet. It will also provide a fitting introduction to the 50-mile network of waymarked routes shown on the guide map referred to above. These routes may be started from a number of car parks, most of which are named below.

A short distance downstream, but reached from a point on the A470 just to the north of the Maesgwm turning, is the Dôl-gefeilau car park and picnic place (SH 72-26), and this is the starting point for waymarked walks leading to viewpoints at Cefneuddwr, and to the Rhaeadr Mawddach and Pistyll Cain waterfalls (SH 73- 27) (see Pistyll Cain, page 95), close to the point where the Afon Mawddach is joined by the Afon Gain. Other car parks, some with picnic places, giving access to the forest can be found at Ganllwyd (SH 72-24), T'yn-y-groes (SH 73-23), up a minor road beside the Mawddach (SH 73-25), and at Dolfrwynog (SH 74-25) near Capel Hermon (see also page 47). There is also a 'Forest Garden', or small arboretum at Glasdir (SH 74-22) on the south-eastern fringes of the forest.

Do not miss a visit to this splendid forest area.

Colwyn Bay (116) (SH 85-78) This major seaside resort runs along a 3 mile promenade westward from Penmaen Head to Rhôs-on-Sea, and grew out

Colwyn Bay — a major seaside resort.

of the villages of *Old Colwyn (1)* and *Llandrillo-yn-Rhôs (2)* after very rapid development starting in the late 1860s. It is a lively place with a wide range of accommodation and a host of leisure activities for visitors of all ages. See especially the 50-acre *Eiras Park (3)*, with its £1.8 million *Leisure Centre*, opened in 1981, the *Welsh Mountain Zoo (4)*, which can be reached by bus from the pier, the *Pier (5)* itself, two cinemas, a puppet theatre and a theatre. Beach and promenade attractions include a miniature railway, paddling pool and donkey rides.

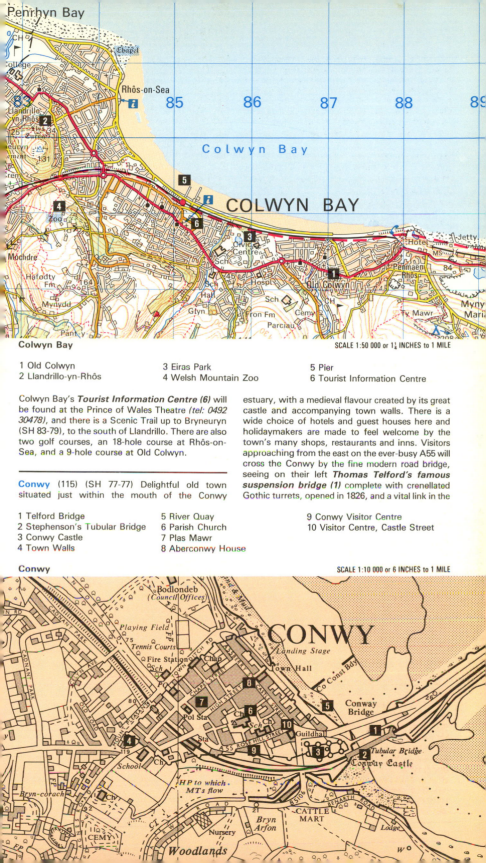

Colwyn Bay

SCALE 1:50 000 or 1¼ INCHES to 1 MILE

1 Old Colwyn
2 Llandrillo-yn-Rhôs
3 Eiras Park
4 Welsh Mountain Zoo
5 Pier
6 Tourist Information Centre

Colwyn Bay's **Tourist Information Centre (6)** will be found at the Prince of Wales Theatre *(tel: 0492 30478)*, and there is a Scenic Trail up to Bryneuryn (SH 83-79), to the south of Llandrillo. There are also two golf courses, an 18-hole course at Rhôs-on-Sea, and a 9-hole course at Old Colwyn.

Conwy (115) (SH 77-77) Delightful old town situated just within the mouth of the Conwy

1 Telford Bridge
2 Stephenson's Tubular Bridge
3 Conwy Castle
4 Town Walls
5 River Quay
6 Parish Church
7 Plas Mawr
8 Aberconwy House
9 Conwy Visitor Centre
10 Visitor Centre, Castle Street

estuary, with a medieval flavour created by its great castle and accompanying town walls. There is a wide choice of hotels and guest houses here and holidaymakers are made to feel welcome by the town's many shops, restaurants and inns. Visitors approaching from the east on the ever-busy A55 will cross the Conwy by the fine modern road bridge, seeing on their left **Thomas Telford's famous suspension bridge (1)** complete with crenellated Gothic turrets, opened in 1826, and a vital link in the

Conwy

SCALE 1:10 000 or 6 INCHES to 1 MILE

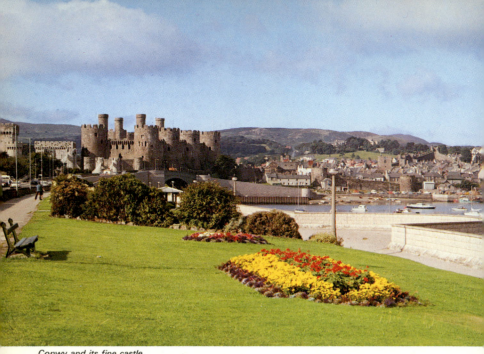

Conwy and its fine castle.

road along the north coast from Chester, and beyond it, **Robert Stephenson's tubular girder railway bridge (2)**, opened 20 years later. Telford Bridge, as the former is now known, is in the care of the National Trust, and the tollhouse which is open throughout the year incorporates an exhibition depicting the famous engineer's life and work (see also Betws-y-Coed, page 40, and Menai Bridge, page 87, but for the fascinating stories of both Telford's and Stephenson's careers, read the excellent biographies by L. T. C. Rolt, published by Penguin).

Immediately beyond the two bridges lies the great medieval **Conwy Castle (3)**. This was started by Edward I in 1283, as were Caernarfon and Harlech, but it was here that Edward established his headquarters during his campaigns against the Welsh Prince Llywelyn, and he was himself besieged here by the Welsh in 1290. This siege was successfully resisted, but just over a hundred years later the luckless Richard II had to bargain with his opponents when he was trapped here in the summer of 1399 without sufficient supplies, and within a few weeks he was forced to give up his crown. The castle was also taken by Cromwell's army in 1646, but only after a siege of 3 months, and at a time when the Royalist cause had become hopeless.

The siting of this fortress upon a narrow ledge of rock was dictated by its unusual shape. It was completed in under 5 years at a cost of £15,000, which at today's values would be about £1,500,000, making it by far the most expensive of Edward's castles. The views out over the estuary from the North-West Tower are especially fine, but all who come to Conwy should be prepared to spend time exploring this splendid castle in all its detail. The proportions of its walls and towers are unusually beautiful, and remain a tribute to the architectural skills of the Master of the King's Works in Wales, James of St George, who had already built several castles in Savoy for Edward's cousin, Count Philip, and who from 1278 onwards was responsible for the

design of all Edward's castles in North Wales. He was Constable of Harlech between 1290 and 1293, but in 1298, once his works were completed in Wales, he was moved on to Scotland.

The town itself is joined to the castle by the **town walls (4)** built by Edward I, as part of his normal plan to colonise this coast with English settlers. More than a mile in length, they still almost encircle the old town. The five gates, three original and two of later date, are still in use, and it is possible to walk along much of the wall-top with its 21 towers, and enjoy views of castle, town, river and bridges. Below the walls, with only limited access, is the **River Quay (5)**, which is still used by fishing boats. Fishing trips are available from here, and there are also excursions by boat up the Afon Conwy as far as Tal-y-cafn (a 3½ hour round trip). On the quay, and built against the town wall is the 'Smallest House in Great Britain', which is furnished as a mid-Victorian Welsh cottage.

The site of Edward's castle was occupied for about a hundred years by the Cistercian Abbey of Aberconwy, but Edward had this moved further up the valley to Maenan (SH 79-65), and the existing abbey church became **St Mary's Parish Church (6)**. Of the original building only parts of the walls and some buttresses have survived, and much of the present structure dates from the 14th century. Its contents include a Tudor font and fine 15th century screen, probably the work of the same craftsman or craftsmen who made the screen at Llanrwst (see page 79).

Near the top of the High Street stands **Plas Mawr (7)**, a rambling Elizabethan house, built in 1585 by Robert Wynn of Gwydir; it is now the headquarters of the Royal Cambrian Academy of Art, and holds regular exhibitions which are open to the public. On the corner of High Street and Castle Street is **Aberconwy House (8)**, the only surviving example in Conwy of a medieval merchant's house. This delightful building is in the care of the National Trust, and now contains an exhibition depicting life in Conwy from Roman times until the present day. There is also a pleasant National Trust shop. **The Conwy Visitor Centre (9)** will be found in Rosehill Street. This also tells the story of Conwy's past, with exhibitions, film shows and a craft shop. There is another **Visitor Centre (10)** in Castle Street *(Tel: 049263 2248)*.

Conwy is popular with sailing enthusiasts, with good anchor holding in parts of the estuary. There is pony trekking to be had from the road to the Sychnant Pass, and there is an 18-hole golf course at Morfa Conwy (SH 76-78). Opportunities for walking are largely confined to paths going westwards up into the hills, and our **Walk 3**, page 134, starts from the car park south of the castle.

Conway Falls (116) (SH 80-53) *Off A5 2m SE Conwy.* Dramatic waterfalls on the Afon Conwy, below which is the 'Fairy Glen', a beautiful walk

SCALE 1:25 000 or 2½ INCHES to 1 MILE

Conway Falls and the Fairy Glen

The Conway Falls.

beside the tree-bordered river, which here flows through a dramatic rocky defile. Do not be put off by the fashionable Victorian sentimentality of the title, it is a truly romantic place, especially if visited out of season. Just above the Conway Falls the Conwy is joined by the Afon Machno, and to visit the nearby Machno Falls, turn on to the B4406, and then turn right off it near the Penmachno Woollen Mill (see page 92). There is an attractive minor road leading first westwards, and then in a circle, passing Ty Mawr (see page 108), birthplace of Bishop Morgan, and then back to Penmachno (use Landranger Sheets 116 and 115).

Corris (124) (SH 75-07) *10m S Dolgellau.* Small slate mining and quarrying village in a valley now devoted more to forestry. Great waste tips are never far away, but mercifully many of these have now been masked by forest plantations. The village's little sloping streets have considerable character and there is also an interesting Railway Museum here. The Corris Railway Society, which is based at the museum, is in the process of restoring parts of the Corris Railway, a narrow-gauge line which once carried slate from the quarries in the Dulas Valley down to the Dyfi estuary. Founded as early as 1859 it first used horses, but these were replaced by steam locomotives in the late 1870s. There are also a number of interesting craft workshops within the Corris Craft Centre *(tel: 065 473 343)* devoted to pottery, weaving, wooden toys and even pyrography, and there is a restaurant and children's playground. At Corris Uchaf, on the A487 about a mile to the north-west, there are the Braichgoch Slate Slab Quarries, where Corris's traditional slate craft is still practised.

There are walks eastwards from Corris, up into the great Dyfi Forest, but perhaps the best base for exploring this is the Foel Friog car park near Aberllefenni, along a minor road further up the Dulas Valley (see page 63).

Craig yr Aderyn (Birds' Rock) (124) (SH 64-06) *7m NE Tywyn.* Stark rocky hill rising no less than 762 feet from the floor of the attractive Dysynni Valley (see page 61). Its unique shape is the oustanding feature of this valley, and it is the only place in inland Britain where cormorants nest.

Craig yr Ogof (The Crag of the Cave) (125) (SH 91-24) *10m S Bala.* This crag, poised dramatically over the highest of the valley farms, overhangs the little road that climbs out of Cwm Cynllwyd (see page 55), on its way from Llanuwchllyn to the high pass of Bwlch y Groes (see page 43), and provides a sense of adventure where it is perhaps less expected than in the mountains further to the north and west.

Criccieth (123,124) (SH 50-38) Small town and quiet family holiday resort at the south-eastern corner of the Lleyn Peninsula. Largely unspoilt by the type of development found in many holiday resorts, it is dominated by the ruins of **Criccieth Castle (1)** poised on a dramatic mound. To the east of the castle a gracefully curving promenade surrounds a shallow bay with a sand and shingle beach, while to the west there is a Marine Parade of hotels and guest houses. The town is centred upon the neat tree-bordered **Green (2)**, which has a

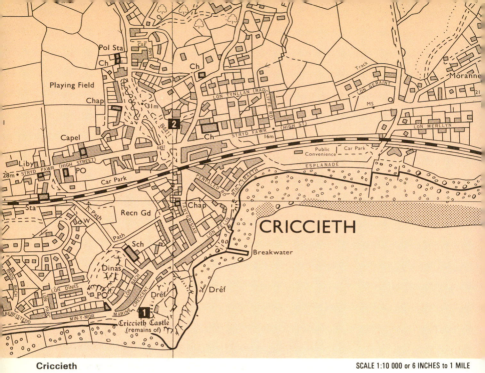

Criccieth

SCALE 1:10 000 or 6 INCHES to 1 MILE

1 Criccieth Castle   2 The Green (Tourist Information Centre here in summer)

village flavour. During the holiday season there is an Information Caravan here *(tel: 076 671 2489).*

The castle was built in the early 13th century in the time of Llywelyn the Great, and it was strengthened and extended by the English after Edward I had conquered the area in 1284 — the period when he built his magnificent new castles on the Snowdonia coast, at Beaumaris, Caernarfon, Conwy, and Harlech. The English occupation of Criccieth continued peacefully enough until the reign of Henry IV, when in spite of repairs to the castle and reinforcement of its garrison, it fell in 1404 to the Welsh during the rising inspired by Owain Glyndwr, and was sacked, burnt and left derelict. A visit to this dramatic ruin is well worthwhile, and the views from its battlements over the broad sweep of Cardigan Bay to the mountains of Snowdonia are truly breathtaking.

Criccieth from the battlements of Criccieth Castle.

Criccieth's broad expanses of beach have become popular with surfing, windsurfing, and water-skiing enthusiasts, and these activities bring further interest to family holidaymakers. Bathing is safe here at all states of the tide, and car parking space usually ample. It lies on the line of the Cambrian Coast Railway (see page 46), and this can be used to link on to the other holiday lines, 'The Great Little Trains of Wales'. There are tennis courts, a miniature golf course and a children's playground, and also a 9-hole golf course a mile to the north (SH 50-39). The best walk from Criccieth is westwards along the coast, then along the north bank of the Afon Dwyfor, and north to Llanystumdwy (see page 80). It is also possible to walk eastwards, partly parallel with the line of the Cambrian Coast Railway, and onwards to the great expanse of Black Rock Sands (see page 41).

Croesor (124) (SH 63-44) *8m NE Porthmadog.* Minute village in the lovely Croesor Valley, with a few cottages and a slate-hung chapel. There were vast slate mines deep within the sides of Moelwyn Mawr (SH 65-44), but these were never a great success commercially. However, they were used during the 39-45 War for the storage of pictures from London's National Gallery. The Croesor Tramway was started in 1860 reaching Porthmadog in 1864, and although long closed, its track provides good walking up the valley. The car park at Croesor is one of the best points from which to tackle the beautifully outlined ridge of Cnicht (see page 50) to its north-east, or the two peaks of Moelwyn Mawr and Moelwyn Bach, but these objectives are only for those with experience.

Cwm Bychan (124) (SH 64-31) *5m E Harlech.* This delightful valley lies in the hills to the east of

Cwm Bychan and the Roman Steps

SCALE 1:25 000 or 2½ INCHES to 1 MILE

Harlech, at the head of the Artro Valley and just beyond Llyn Cwm Bychan. There is a car park and a camping site near the head of the lake and this makes an excellent base for walking up the Roman Steps (see page 102). There are possibilities for moving on south-eastwards, then south and south-westward, back through the Bwlch Drws Ardudwy (SH 66-28), and down Cwm Nantcol. There is also a path north-eastwards beneath the crags of Craig Ddrwg, towards Llyn Trawsfynydd, another good

In delightful Cwm Bychan.

crossing of the Rhinog Range. However, these lengthy explorations are only for the experienced hill walker.

Cwm Cadian Forest Walks (124) (SH 75-05) *3m N Machynlleth on A487.* These start from the Forestry Commission car park and picnic site at Tan-y-Coed in the Dulas Valley between Corris and Machynlleth, and offer a choice of routes (the longest of which is only 2 miles) through that part of the Dyfi Forest lying between the Dulas Valley and Cwm Cadian. The excellent descriptive leaflet should be available at the car park, but can also be obtained at the Maesgwm Forest Visitor Centre (see Coed-y-Brenin, page 50). The Cwm is named after the well known Welsh saint, Cadfan, the founder of Bardsey Abbey.

Cwm Cynllwyd (125) (SH 90-25) *8m S Bala.* A pleasantly wide valley running south-eastwards to Bwlch y Groes (see page 43). This is unspoilt Welsh countryside at its very best, and it is good to recall that it was at the hamlet of Ty-nant (The House of the Dingle) (SH 90-26) that George Borrow stopped to talk to 'a smiling young woman', and felt himself to be 'now indeed in Wales amongst the real Welsh'.

Cwm Cywarch (124,125) (SH 86-17) *2m N Dinas Mawddwy.* There is a 'no through road' stretching 2 miles up this valley, and coming within sight of the towering rock face of Craig Cywarch (SH 84-18). This is itself a favourite with rock climbers, although there is no recognised car park near the end of the road. For access to the Arans, see page 33, and also please heed the usual warnings regarding hillwalking and climbing.

Cwm Dyffryn (The Happy Valley) (135) (SN 62-98) *4m SE Tywyn.* Cwm Dyffryn once sheltered the old coach road between Tywyn and Machynlleth, but the ever-enthusiastic Victorian visitors to Aberdyfi were soon introduced to it as 'Happy Valley', and both this and Llyn Barfog (The Bearded Lake) became an almost obligatory jaunt for those visiting the neighbourhood. Today the best approach for walkers is over the hills from Aberdyfi (see page 29), although it is also possible to incorporate it in a long circular walk south-west along the road from Tywyn, and back over the hills, returning down the Nant Braich-y-rhiw Valley (SH 62-01), a total distance of about 13 miles. A saving of 3 miles may be made by taking the Talyllyn Railway train from Rhyd-yr-onnen station, but this walk is only for hardened enthusiasts.

Cwm Dyli (115) (SH 64-54) *7m NE Beddgelert.*
Small cwm on the eastern slopes of Snowdon, at
the head of the Gwynant valley. A footpath coming
south from Pen-y-Pass (SH 64-55) runs close to the
Cwm Dyli Power Station (SH 65-54). This was one
of Snowdonia's first hydro-electric power stations,
and began operation as long ago as 1906. Water to
drive its turbines comes down a pressure pipe line
from Llyn Llydaw, which is linked to Glaslyn lake,
lying below the steep slopes of Yr Wyddfa (Snowdon) itself. The station is not open to the public, but
details of its construction and operation can be
obtained from the Central Electricity Generating
Board's very interesting booklet entitled *Hydro-
Electricity in Snowdonia*. A fine prospect of Cwm
Dyli may be obtained from the viewpoint car park
on the A498, 1 mile south of Pen-y-Gwryd (SH
65-54).

Cwm Hirnant (125) (SH 95-33 etc.) *4m SE Bala.*
An attractive minor road runs southwards from
Bala, through Rhos-y-gwaliau, up through the
thickly wooded valley of Cwm Hirnant, and then
over the hills to Llyn Efyrnwy (Lake Vyrnwy). From
here it is possible to loop westwards to Bwlch y
Groes (see page 43), and then go northwards to
return to Bala — an excellent round tour of about 25
miles. The woodlands in Cwm Hirnant are part of
the Forestry Commission's Penllyn Forest, and at
Tyn-y-cwm (SH 95-33) there is a pleasant picnic site
and car park on the banks of the Afon Hirnant. A
glance at either Landranger Sheet 125 or Outdoor
Leisure Map 18 will reveal several walking possibilities in the vicinity.

Cwm Idwal Nature Trail (115) (SH 64-59) This
trail follows an anti-clockwise route around Llyn
Idwal, and is best approached from the A5 road at
Ogwen Cottage Mountain School where there are
limited car parking facilities (SH 64-60). The area
surrounding the lake is a National Nature Reserve,
the first to be established in Wales, and the Nature
Conservancy Council's Nature Trail is well described in their excellent booklet, *Cwm Idwal Nature
Trail*. The trail is about 2 miles long, and to quote
the booklet, 'as this is a mountain reserve at over
1200 feet above sea-level, strong boots or walking
shoes and warm clothing are advisable'. There are
several small experimental enclosures within the
reserve and these of course should be left undisturbed. Fine views of the rugged faces of the
Glyders and the Idwal Slabs and the dark cliffs of
Twll Du (The Devil's Kitchen) may be obtained from
this path. With the help of the booklet anyone
taking this walk will end up with a much greater
understanding of the gigantic glacial forces that
created the mountains of Snowdonia, and of the
wildlife that has become established here since.

Thomas Pennant, in his classic travel book *Tour
In Wales*, published in 1778, was far from enthusias-
tic about Cwm Idwal and described it as 'a fit place
to inspire murderous thoughts, environed with
horrible precipices, shading a lake, lodged in its
bottom'. It can still be a sombre place, but a visit
here is well worthwhile.

It is possible to walk south-westwards from Llyn
Idwal, up below the Devil's Kitchen, over the ridge
extending from Glyder Fawr, and down to the
A4086 at the foot of the Llanberis Pass near
Gwastadnant (SH 61-57), but this is strictly for
those with wide experience of the mountains.

Cwm-mynach (The Monks' Valley) (124) (SH 68-
21) *4m W Dolgellau.* It is possible to drive almost 2
miles up this quiet valley, which was the scene of
hectic gold mining activity in the mid-19th century
and again in the early 1900s. The road is steep and
narrow and there are no adequate parking facilities
at the end of the public road, and it would be
preferable to walk up here rather than drive.
However, there is access via a public footpath
running northwards from the A496 at SH 687-191,
to Garth-gell, a 114 acre nature reserve on the west
side of the valley, owned by the Royal Society for
the Protection of Birds. Ask at the Penmaenpool
Nature Information Centre (see page 92) for further
details.

Cwm Nantcol (124) (SH 64-26 etc.) *5m SE
Harlech.* Quiet valley below the western slopes of
the Rhinogs (see page 101). There is a car park and
picnic site on the north bank of the river, at the
lower end of the valley (SH 60-27), and the Cwm
Nantcol Nature Trail starts from here, with plaques
describing the scenery of the Nantcol gorge and
waterfalls. Well to the north-west of the car park
there is a small Baptist chapel with a delightfully
unspoilt 18th century interior — Salem Chapel. This
building, with its pulpit and sloping box pews, was
the model for the sharply observed painting by S. C.
Vosper entitled *Salem*, and although the original
hangs in the Lever Art Gallery at Port Sunlight,
there is a reproduction to be seen here. Starting
from the chapel is the Cefn-Isa Farm Trail, and this
illustrates along its 2 mile course the story of Welsh
hillfarming.

At the end of the road up the valley (no parking
places) there is a farm called Maes-y-garnedd (The
Field of Stones) (SH 65-26), which was the
birthplace of John Jones, a brother-in-law of Oliver
Cromwell, and one of the judges who condemned
Charles I to death. At the Restoration twenty nine
of these judges were condemned to death, and
although only ten were finally executed, Jones was
unlucky enough to be one of their number.

To return to happier things — it is possible to
walk north-east beyond Maes-y-Garnedd, and over
the Bwlch Drws Ardudwy (see page 43) before
heading north and north-west to go down the
Roman Steps and returning south past little Gloyw
Llyn, thus encircling Rhinog Fawr. This consists of
at least 8 miles of hard going and is only for the
hardier and more experienced walker. Those wishing to take a less demanding walk should follow our
Walk 13, page 154.

Cwm Pennant (115) (SH 53-47 etc.) *8m NW
Porthmadog.* This delectable valley with oak and
ash much in evidence, stretches north into the
mountains for more than 4 miles, closely following
the Afon Dwyfor back towards its source. There are
interesting remains of old mines, but farming is the
only occupation here today. The head of the valley
is dominated on the east by lofty Moel Hebog, and
on the north and west by the Nantlle Ridge, which
incorporates the summits of Garnedd-goch, Trum y
Ddysgl and Y Garn. From the end of the public road
at Beudy'r Ddol (SH 54-49) there is a track running
north-east over the Bwlch-y-ddwy-elor, and down
through part of the Beddgelert Forest to Rhyd-Ddu
(SH 56-52), but most who come here will be
content with the tranquil charms of the valley itself.
Let us leave the last words to the much-quoted

Cwm Pennant — a delectable valley in the western mountains of Snowdonia.

Eifion Wyn — 'O God, why didst Thou make Cwm Pennant so beautiful and the life of an old shepherd so short?' Although it is possible to drive right up this valley, it would be preferable to explore it on foot, using Landranger Sheet 115, or if possible, Outdoor Leisure Map 17.

Cwm y llan (115) (SH 61-52) *5m NE Beddgelert.* This lies within the Snowdon National Nature Reserve (see page 104), and is approached by the Watkin Path. (See also our *Walk 7*, page 142.) Here will be found the ruins of old buildings connected with copper and slate working, but despite their interest, they are dangerous and should not be explored. Before setting out on a walk up here, please heed the advice given on the inside rear cover of our guide.

Cyffdy Farm Park (124,125) (SH 88-34) *3m SW Bala.* Here are a number of rare breeds and paddock animals, together with opportunities for fishing and riding, a collection of old farm machinery, a Pets' Corner and children's playground, and demonstrations of hand milking. *(Tel: 06784 271.)*

Cymmer (or Cymer) Abbey (124) (SH 72-19) *2m N Dolgellau.* Founded in 1199 by Cistercians from the abbey of Cymhir in remote country near Rhayader, the now ruined Cymmer Abbey stands close to the banks of the Afon Mawddach. Unfortunately there is a caravan and camping site close by, but the lovely lancet windows at the east end of the abbey church still give a fine impression of serenity and strength. The original plan of this church was never completed, due no doubt to the incessant conflict between the English and the Welsh in the 13th century, and the remains are what was originally intended to be merely the nave of a large cruciform building. Remains of the chapter house and day room stand in the adjoining farmyard.

Deganwy (115) (SH 77-79) *2m S Llandudno.* Now almost a suburb of Llandudno, Deganwy looks across the narrow mouth of the Conwy estuary to Conwy and the low ground to its north. The 13th century castle on its hilltop site above the town, was destroyed by Llywelyn the Great in 1260, and only fragments remain. In better shape is the stylish late 19th century church, the work of Chester architect, John Douglas.

Deiniolen (114,115) (SH 57-63) *7m E Caernarfon.* Large village which grew up to meet the needs of the vast slate quarries nearby. There are fine views southwards out over Llyn Padarn to Snowdon. The map shows no fewer than six chapels and also a church, this being built for the village in the mid-19th century by the Assheton-Smith family of Vaynol Hall (SH 53-69), owners of several quarries including the massive ones at Dinorwic (see page 58).

Dinas Dinlle (115,123) (SH 43-56) *6m SW Caernarfon.* This is a lively little beach resort with a sand and shingle shoreline stretching northwards from a small hill which is covered by the earthworks of an Iron Age settlement. There are fine views southwestwards along the Lleyn coastline to the peaks of Yr Eifl, and north-westwards to the low shores of Anglesey. The surf is strong enough to provide good sport, and fishing for bass is also a popular pastime. There are a least two large caravan and camp sites here, and to the north, beyond Morfa Dinlle, there is an airfield from which 'Snowdon

Pleasure Flights' are available from Easter to September (tel:0286 831047). At the time of writing Fort Belan (SH 44-60) (see also page 63), to the north of the airfield, is now not open to the public. This private barracks, with its own small dock, was built in the 18th century by the powerful Wynn family of nearby Glynllifon (SH 45-55) (see page 64).

Dinas Mawddwy (124,125) (SH 85-14) *10m E Dolgellau.* Pleasant village in the Upper Dyfi Valley which never seems to have fully recovered from the closure of its lead mines and slate quarries, although it now has at least one fascinating industry in addition to the usual forestry and farming. This is the Meirion Woollen Mill, which is based at the old railway yard, and which produces a variety of traditional Welsh fabrics, both plain and patterned. There is also a Coffee Shop, Art and Craft Gallery, *Tourist Information Centre (tel: 06504 311)*, a well stocked showroom and a children's play area. While visiting the mill do not miss the short walk from the car park to see the historic Pont Minllyn. This is a beautiful little twin-arched bridge built by Rev. Dr John Davies, a famous Welsh scholar who was rector of neighbouring Mallwyd from 1604 to 1644.

A study of Landranger Sheet 124 will reveal good walking possibilities in the area, including a pleasant circular walk passing close to Pen-y-graig and Hendref, both to the east of the village, beyond the Dyfi, and another walk to the west of the village, up

Dinas Mawddwy and Mallwyd

SCALE 1:25 000 or 2½ INCHES to 1 MILE

into afforested mountainside country.

George Borrow came through Dinas in 1854 and found, 'at present little more than a collection of filthy huts. But though a squalid place, I found it anything but silent and deserted. Fierce-looking red-haired banditti of old were staggering about, and sounds of drunken revelry echoed from the huts'. With the quarrymen and miners now all gone, Dinas is a quiet place once again, although on Saturday evenings in one of the local inns visitors may still catch a distant echo of times past.

Din Dryfol Burial Chamber (114) (SH 39-72) *6m SW Llangefni.* The wild and lonely site of this burial chamber is at the foot of a rocky outcrop, a short walk across fields behind Fferam Rhosydd Farm. It was probably a Neolithic burial site of the 'segmented cist' type, at least 50 feet long. The chamber has been almost completely destroyed, but its remains can be seen, with one side stone still in position, and a displaced cover stone resting on it. There is another massive stone standing about 30 feet to the east.

Dinas Gynfor (114) (SH 38-95) *5m W Amlwch.* The limestone outcrops on this exposed coastal site were turned into a fortress by Iron Age man, with its 'walls' enclosing an area of 700 x 300 yards. Owned by the National Trust, the cliff country overlooking Porth Llanlleiana is accessible by a coastal footpath east from Llanbadrig, or north from a minor road near Llanlleiana Farm.

Din Lligwy (or Llugwy) (114) (SH 49-86) *3m NW Benllech.* The remains of this ancient village, Iron Age in origin but probably much altered in the late Roman period, stand in a woodland clearing, within an impressive boundary wall enclosing more than 12 acre. The outlines of two circular and seven rectangular buildings may be traced, some with walls as much as 6 feet high in places. Not far away are the ruins of Hen Capel Lligwy, a 12th century chapel overlooking the seashore. This was partly rebuilt in the 14th century and extended in the 16th. A short distance to the south-east is the Lligwy Burial Chamber, with an enormous cover stone supported by low uprights over a natural fissure in the rock. (See also Llanallgo, page 68.)

Dinorwic (114,115) (SH 59-61) *8m E Caernarfon.* Small quarrying village to the north-west of the great Dinorwic Slate Quarries, which cover 700 acres and rise 2000 feet up the mountain side above Llyn Peris in a spectacular series of steps. These are best seen from the A4086 near Llanberis (see page 69 for The Welsh Slate Museum, which is based in the old workshops of the Dinorwic Quarries). These quarries were linked to the sea at Portdinorwic on the Menai Strait by a railway, a portion of which has been relaid as a passenger-carrying narrow-gauge line, the Llanberis Lake Railway (see page 69).

Dinorwic now has an even greater claim to fame, for here beneath the mountainside to the south-east of the village, is the vast cavern and tunnel system comprising Europe's largest pumped storage power scheme. Operated by the Central Electricity Generating Board, this power station pumps water up from Llyn Peris (SH 59-59) to the high Marchlyn Mawr Reservoir (SH 61-61) at times when demand on the National Grid is low, and then releases the stored water to generate massive amounts of power in the cheapest possible way at times of high demand. The main machine hall is some 587 feet long, 80 feet wide and no less than 200 feet deep, and is believed to be the largest man-made civil engineering excavation in Europe. Thanks to the proportion of works below the surface very little permanent damage to the environment has taken place. At the time of writing there is no regular visitor facility, but parties of not less than 10 people may apply in writing for a pre-booking, to the Station Manager, Dinorwic Power Station, Llanberis, Gwynedd.

Dolbadarn Castle (115) (SH 58-59) *To immediate SE Llanberis.* The remains of this castle, with its 40 foot high tower, stand on a rocky hillock, with fine

Dolbadarn Castle.

views of Llyn Padarn, and of Llyn Peris, with the Llanberis Pass beyond. It was built by Llywelyn the Great in the early years of the 13th century, and must have dominated this southern entry to the pass most effectively. The tower, which once had a conical roof, is traditionally the place where Owain Goch (Red Owen) was held prisoner for no less than 20 years by his far from friendly brother, the last Prince Llywelyn.

Dolbenmaen (124) (SH 50-43) *5m NW Porthmadog.* A small hamlet happily now by-passed by the busy A487, standing at the entrance to the lovely Cwm Pennant. It has a minute, largely 15th century church standing beyond an 18th century lych-gate.

Dolgarrog (115) (SH 77-67) *7m S Conwy.* This village is dominated by the large aluminium works, built here to utilise hydro-electric power generated by the waters of Llyn Eigiau and Llyn Cowlyd, large reservoirs in the hills to the south-west. The power station here was opened as long ago as 1907, only a year after the opening of North Wales's first hydro-electric station at Cwm Dyli (see page 56). It is sad to recall that no fewer than sixteen lives were lost in the village when the Llyn Eigiau dam burst in 1925 and a great tide of water swept though the village.

Dôl-gefeiliau Picnic Site (124) (SH 72-26) *7m N Dolgellau.* This car park and picnic site are delightfully situated beside the Afon Eden, in the Coed-y-Brenin Forest. Waymarked walks lead southwards to viewpoints near Cefndeuddwr, and eastwards to the waterfalls of Rhaeadr Mawddach and Pistyll Cain (see page 95).

Dolgellau (124) (SH 72-17) Beautifully sited below the northern slopes of Cadair Idris, in the broad, wooded valley of the Afon Wnion, a short distance above its confluence with the Mawddach, Dolgellau is a natural route centre and a great favourite with visitors. Until the creation of the new enlarged county of Gwynedd, it was the administrative capital of the now absorbed county of Meirionnydd (Merioneth). It is still a busy market town, with a cattle and sheep market each Friday, and it has a pleasantly vital air every day of the week. Built of lightish grey granite and slate, its buildings have a quiet dignity, especially in the area around its market square, where most of them are early 19th century in origin. Shops, inns, public buildings and hotels — all have a welcoming look, and road traffic, now happily much reduced by a bypass, is reduced to a modest pace when faced with the

1 Dolgellau Bridge   2 Tourist Information Centre   3 Parish Church

Dolgellau

SCALE 1:10 000 or 6 INCHES to 1 MILE

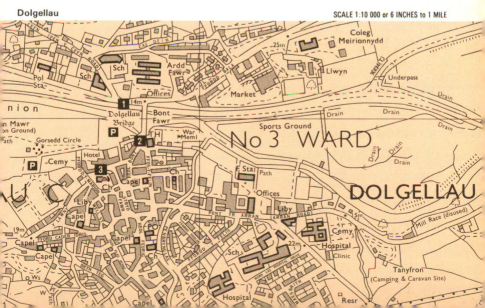

Dolgellau — lively market town below the northern slopes of Cadair Idris.

delightful irregularity of its street plan.

These narrow lanes, with their character shops and restaurants are well worth exploring, and not far to the north of the square will be found a fine **seven-arched bridge (1)** over the Afon Wnion, with a **Tourist Information Centre (2)** at its town end *(Tel: 0341 422888)*. Near the main car park in the town centre will be found Bryn Melyn Studio, where craftsmen may be seen at their work and where a wide variety of craft produce may be purchased.

The **Parish Church (3)** has a medieval tower, a broad 18th century nave, and an apsidal chancel built in the 19th century. The interior is very pleasing, with an attractively lit dome-shaped ceiling to the chancel, unusually beautiful Victorian stained glass, and the effigy of a knight below one of the windows — Meurig Ap Ynyr Fychan of Nannau (see page 89), who died in 1350.

There are facilities at Dolgellau for bowls, tennis and putting, and there is a 9-hole golf course less than a mile to the north of the town. There is a very pleasant mountain road south-west from Dolgellau, leading to Llyn Gwernan (see page 83) and Llynnau Creggenen (see page 82), and then down to Arthog (see page 33), and this road provides the best starting points for a walk up Cadair Idris (see Walk 15, page 158). For other pleasant walks near Dolgellau, see the Precipice Walk, page 99, and the Torrent Walk, page 107.

Dolgoch Falls (135) (SH 65-04) *5m NE Tywyn.* These delightful waterfalls may be reached by a 5 minute walk up a wooded valley from the B4405, or by an even shorter walk from the Dolgoch Falls

The Dolgoch Falls.

SCALE 1:25 000 or 2½ INCHES to 1 MILE

Dolgoch and Craig yr Aderyn
(see also page 53)

Station on the Tallyllyn Railway. The two higher falls may be reached by further steep paths up through the woods.

Dolwyddelan (115) (SH 73-52) *5m N Blaenau Ffestiniog.* Small village in the wooded valley of the Afon Lledr. Turn south off the A470 in the centre of the village to visit the Old Church, a beautiful little 16th century building with a slate floor, a Gothic rood-screen topped by an 18th century balustrade and several fragments of medieval glass. The old limewashed walls are enriched by several wall monuments including one to Maredudd ab Ieuan, builder of the church, and a descendant of the redoubtable Prince of Powys, who led Welsh resistance against Henry I in the 12th century. There is also a brass to Maredudd, and several other items of interest.

It is possible to walk westwards from Dolwyddelan over the course of a medieval track, up through the Bwlch y Rhediad (SH 66-52), and down into Nantgwynant. There is also a pack-horse trail eastwards over the hills to Penmachno.

Well to the west of the village are the splendidly sited ruins of Dolwyddelan Castle, which was built by the Welsh in the late 12th century. Its rectangular keep certainly dates from that time and is Norman in style, although its upper parts are now a 19th century reconstruction. The West Tower was built in the 13th century and in its wild mountain setting completes a most effective picture of impregnability. Tradition has it that Llywelyn the Great was born here, and it was certainly occupied by Llywelyn the Last during his struggles with the English. It was then abandoned following the English victories, but in the 15th century it was re-occupied by Maredudd ab Ieuan, a descendant of the Princes of Powys and ancestor of the Wynns of Gwydir Castle.

Dulas (114) (SH 47-89) *3m SE Amlwch.* Here are scattered farms, tree-shaded lanes and, hidden in woods behind Llysdulas House, the remains of the medieval church of Llanwenllwyfo (on private property). Its Victorian successor has a sharp pointed spire, and although otherwise unremarkable from the outside, contains a fine collection of late medieval Flemish glass brought here in the 1880s. To the south of here lies the almost landlocked estuary of Traeth Dulas (Dulas Sands) (see also page 107), once much used as a harbour for coastal sailing vessels and now a largely unspoilt area with wildlife in plenty.

Dwygyfylchi (115) (SH 73-77) *1m E Penmaenmawr.* This village forming a pleasant suburb of Penmaenmawr is situated in a valley below the Sychnant Pass. Beyond the 9-hole golf course, on the road towards the pass, there is a pleasant walk southwards up a valley which was named the 'Fairy Glen' by the Victorians, and which eventually leads up to bracken-covered moorlands.

Dwyran (114,115) (SH 44-65) *7m SW Llanfair P. G.* Large village to the immediate east of the little Afon Braint, and just inland from the great dune area of Newborough Warren (see page 91). It lies in the parish of Llangeinwen and the parish church of St Geinwen stands at a sharp bend in the A4080 well to the west of the village's centre. It is a spacious, largely 12th century building, restored as long ago as 1812, and its interior contains several items of interest, including a 13th century font. There was once a regular ferry service across the Menai Strait, between the pier by the old Mermaid Inn (SH 47-64) and Caernarfon, but this ceased many years ago. In the 18th century there was a ford between Abermenai Point (SH 44-61) (See also page 31) and the mainland, and some experts believe that the Roman invaders of Anglesey under Suetonius Paulinus forded the Strait at this point in AD 61. Visitors are not advised to put this theory to the test!

Dyffryn Ardudwy (124) (SH 58-23) *5m N Barmouth.* Small village astride the A496, Barmouth to Harlech road. There are two Neolithic burial chambers here, on the east side of the main road. Enthusiasts for the distant past will also wish to turn east up a side road to the south of the village, past Cors y Gedol, the house of the ancient Vaughan family. This road runs through a farmyard and then turns over open moorland, where there is another Neolithic burial chamber on the right (SH 60-22). This is known as Coetan Arthur (Arthur's Quoit). There is a track beyond here (for walkers only) over

Pont Fadog, which would make a good starting point for walking into the hills up to Llyn Irddyn (SH 62-22). It should also be possible to walk south-east over the hills to Bontddu via Bwlch y Rhiwgyr, but enquire locally if permission has to be sought.

Dyffryn (Valley) (114) (SH 29-79) *4m SE Holyhead.* It appears that the word 'Valley' was not in use until the late 1820s, and it is thought to be a description used by the great engineer Thomas Telford when he was making a cutting through a small hill, during the construction of the London to Holyhead road (see also Conwy, page 51). The village itself is not of great interest to visitors, but the great RAF airfield and the aircraft that fly from it are a feature of Anglesey that would be hard to miss. It was during excavation work on the airfield in 1943 that a number of Iron Age treasures was discovered. Known as the Llyn Cerrig Bach Hoard, this beautiful collection is to be seen at the National Museum of Wales in Cardiff. To the immediate north-west of the village is the ¾ mile long Stanley Embankment, the last great work carried out by Telford on his road to Holyhead, and named after Lord Stanley of Alderley.

Dyfi (Dovey) Forest (124,135) (SH 80-10, etc.) Large forest area situated in mountain country between Dolgellau and Machynlleth. The best bases from which to explore this are at Tan-y-Coed (124) (SH 75-05) (see Cwm Cadian, page 55), just off the A487, 4 miles north of Machynlleth, and Foel Friog (124) (SH 77-09) (see page 63), which is on a minor road running north-east from the A487 at Corris. There is also a Forest Walk from Nant Gwernol (124) (SH 68-06), at the head of the Talyllyn Railway, near Abergynolwyn. It may be

Dyfi Forest road — possibly open, but enquire locally before setting out.

possible to drive on the forest road from Aberllefenni (124) (SH 77-09) eastwards to Aberangell (SH 84-10), but there appears to be some doubt regarding this at present, and it is suggested that local enquiries be made (see page 31).

Dysynni Valley (124) (SH 64-07 etc.) The Afon Dysynni flows south-westwards from Tal-y-llyn Lake to Abergynolwyn, beyond which it turns abruptly north-west to break through a narrow defile into another parallel valley. This landscape has an odd feeling about it and is in fact a rare example in physical geography of 'an elbow of river capture', where the river has been captured by the valley with which it once ran parallel. This must have been caused by a blockage of the old valley just below Abergynolwyn. The minor road running down the 'new' Dysynni valley beyond Abergynolwyn is very attractive and is included in our **Tour 10**, page 128.

Edern (123) (SH 27-39) *8m NW Pwllheli*. Small village just to the south of Morfa Nefyn, with a trout stream flowing beside an old mill where there is a craft and coffee shop, and a modest little Victorian church.

Fairbourne (124) (SH 61-13) *7m SE Dolgellau*. This village has grown up largely in the mid-20th century, with bungalows the predominant feature, and little of architectural interest. However, there is a fascinating 2 mile long, 15'' gauge miniature railway (a horse-drawn tramway until 1916) running to the sand spit of Penrhyn Point, from whence there is a small passenger ferry across the mouth of the Mawddach estuary to Barmouth. It is also possible to drive almost as far as this, into an area of rough dunes. In summer this is a holiday place with many pleasure boats brought here for the day, and

'In steam' at Fairbourne.

glorious views up and across the broad estuary to the wooded slopes of the mountains on either side. But in winter time the mood changes, and the boats are gone, the railway ceases to run, and this becomes a wild, deserted place from which to observe a wide variety of waterfowl. There is a railway station here on the ever-useful Cambrian Coast Line (see page 46).

Fairy Glen (see Conway Falls, page 53).

Felin Faesog Museum of Old Welsh Country Life (115,123) (SH 44-50) *11m S Caernarfon, 2m E Clynnog-fawr*. A 17th century watermill on the little Afon Desach, close to the hamlet of Tai'n Lon. Its contents includes kitchen and bedroom displays and various items illustrating the old Welsh way of life. These relate to farming, blacksmithing, printing, cobbling and joinery. There are also old prams, washing machines and one of the first vacuum cleaners, and of special interest is the machinery of the old mill itself. There is a cafe and shop.

Felin Isaf (116) (SH 80-74) *6m SE Llandudno, to immediate S Llansanffraid Glan Conwy*. Although this fine watermill fell into disuse at the beginning of the century, it has been carefully restored to its 1870 condition — a time when it was operating at its peak. Much of the machinery dates back to the 18th century and flour is still ground here in the traditional manner. Mill Shop, cafe. *(Tel: 049 268 646.)*

Ffestiniog (124) (SH 70-41) *9m E Porthmadog*. Large village with stone houses in terraces on a high bluff looking south-westwards down the Vale of Ffestiniog. Just over a mile to the north-west will be found an attractive waterfall on the Afon Goedol, which may be approached from a car park on the A496 (SH 69-43). Walk south from a point near the old Ffestiniog Railway Station to visit the Rhaeadr Cynfal (waterfall), which is overlooked by a rock rising out of the Afon Cynfal known as Huw Llwyd's Pulpit. Huw was a local 17th century poet, sportsman and sometime wizard, who lived nearby at Cynfal Fawr. There is a car park and pleasant picnic site south-east of the village, on the banks of the Afon Cynfal at Bont Newydd, and it is possible to walk up the Cynfal valley from here to the waterfall of Rhaeadr y Cwm (SH 73-41) (see page 101).

Ffestiniog Railway (124) (SH 57-38 etc.) Originally built in 1836 to connect the Ffestiniog slate quarries

Fairbourne   SCALE 1:25 000 or 2½ INCHES to 1 MILE

The Vale of Ffestiniog.

with the harbour at Porthmadog, it fell into disuse by 1939, and has been revived only since 1954. From sea level at Porthmadog the line crosses the Glaslyn estuary, with splendid views of the Snowdon Range and of Harlech and the coast. It then climbs up on a ledge on the hillside giving some of the finest views obtainable from a carriage window in Britain. The full 13½ mile journey to Blaenau Ffestiniog takes approximately 65 minutes each way, and many of the services are hauled by unique steam engines. The joint Ffestiniog/British Rail Station at Blaenau Ffestiniog now provides a fine link between the North Wales coast, along the Conwy Valley, down the Ffestiniog's line, to link yet again with British Rail's Cambrian Coast Line at Porthmadog. There are gift shops at Porthmadog, Tan-y-Bwlch and Blaenau Ffestiniog, a self-service restaurant at Porthmadog and station buffets at Tan-y-Bwlch and Blaenau Ffestiniog. Journeys on the train may be combined with visits to the Llechwedd Caverns (see page 81) and the Ffestiniog Hydro-Electric Scheme (see below). *Tel: 0766 23402384 for further train details.*

Ffestiniog Hydro-Electric Scheme (124) (SH 67-44) *At Tanygrisiau, 1m W Blaenau Ffestiniog.* Opened by the Queen in 1963, this is Wales' first hydro-electric pumped storage power station. See Dinorwic, page 58, for brief account of 'pumped-storage' technique. There is an Energy Information Centre, a tour of the power station itself, and a dramatic 1000 foot climb by bus, up to the Stwlan Storage Dam, from which there are panoramic views out over the National Park. The power station is accessible by road, and is also on the doorstep of

the Ffestiniog Railway's Tanygrisiau request halt. Souvenir Shop, cafe, walks *(tel: 0766 830465).*

Foel Friog Picnic Site (124) (SH 77-09) *1m NE Corris on minor road to Aberllefenni.* There is a waymarked Forest Trail starting from this attractive car park and picnic site, which serves as a good introduction to the great Dyfi (Dovey) Forest (see page 61). It is also a good starting point for a more ambitious circular walk, heading first northwards to Aberllefenni, then south-eastwards down the valley of the Nant Esgair-neiriau, before turning south and west (See Landranger Sheet 124, or Outdoor Leisure Map 'Cadair Idris/Dovey Forest'.) Either of these maps will reveal the wealth of walking opportunities offered by Foel Friog.

Fort Belan (114,115) (SH 44-60) *3m SW Caernarfon.* This was built opposite Abermenai Point towards the end of the 18th century by the first Lord Newborough, as a 'sister' to Fort Williamsbourg (see Glynllifon, page 64). It was built here to defend the southern entry to the Menai Strait against the French and still has cannons upon its battlements. The peninsula on which it stands is not open at the time of writing, but the fort can be seen from the nearby shore.

Gaerwen (114,115) (SH 48-71) *3m W Llanfair P.G.* This village astride the A5 owes its very existence to the opening of Telford's new road to Holyhead, and there is one of the original iron milestones still standing near the church, an early Victorian building, not of great interest for visitors.

Ganllwyd (124 (SH 72-24) *6m N Dolgellau.* Small village in the Coed-y-Brenin Forest, not far from the confluence of the Gamlan and Mawddach rivers. It is possible to walk westwards from the village to visit the Rhaiadr Du waterfalls (see page 101) on the Afon Gamlan. To visit the waterfalls of Rhaeadr Mawddach and Pistyll Cain (see page 95), use the minor road heading north-eastwards from the A470 just to the north of the village, crossing the Pont ar Eden (a car park will be found at SH 73-25).

Garth Falls Walk (115) (SH 77-56) *2m W Betws-y-Coed on A5, opposite Miners' Bridge.* This Forestry Commission trail is specially designed for the handicapped and has a smooth paved path with handrails, leading through open forest beside a stream. There is a leaflet available in braille.

Glan Faenol (NT) (114,115) (SH 53-69) *3 m SW Bangor; access off A487, 1m NE Portdinorwic.* This is a 1½ mile parkland walk, with fine views out over the Menai Strait towards Plas Newydd (see page 95), and back towards the mountains of Snowdonia. *It may not be open until 1987, but tel:(0492) 74421 for details.*

Gloddfa Ganol Slate Mine (115) (SH 69-47) *1m N Blaenau Ffestiniog.* This is claimed to be 'the

At Gloddfa Ganol Slate Mine.

world's largest slate mine', and there is over ½ mile of awe-inspiring chambers and galleries on show. Many of these chambers were blasted out of the mountain by miners working by candlelight. There is a museum illustrating the history of the slate industry, and three miners' cottages depict three periods during the last 100 years. In the mill, slate blocks are processed into roofing slates, hearths and building stone, and slate goods for the adjoining shop. The massive machinery that survives is in startling contrast to the individual craftsmanship displayed. Panoramic walks. Landrover tours. Refreshments. Souvenir Shop. *(Tel: 0766 830 664.)*

The Glyders (115) (SH 65-58 etc.) *8m W Betws-y-Coed.* This splendid and most rugged of all Snowdonia's mountain ranges extends eastwards from Elidir Fawr (SH 61-61), above Llanberis, to Gallt yr Ogof (SH 68-58), not far to the west of Capel Curig. It includes such well known features as Tryfan (SH 68-59) which at 3010 ft is its dominant peak, the Idwal Slabs above Llyn Idwal, and above it, Twll Du (the Black Hole, or Devil's Kitchen), and also the two peaks from which the range takes its name, Glyder Fach and Glyder Fawr. This is climbers' country *par excellence*, and those wishing to venture onto the Glyders should refer to Poucher or Marsh for further guidance (see book list). The inexperienced are advised not to move into this range unless in the company of mountain experts.

Glynllifon (115,123) (SH 45-55) *5m SSW Caernarfon.* Formerly in the hands of the Lords Newborough, the 19th century mansion of Glynllifon (the third house on the present site) was opened as the Caernarfonshire Agricultural Institute in 1954, and the attractive gardens and grounds are now open to the public at certain times. There is an arboretum, a dingle and fountain, and a charming little stone building known as the Hermitage, which is situated above the delightfully wooded valley of the Afon Llifon. The little Fort Williamsbourg was built in about 1761, at the same time as its sister, Fort Belan (SH 43-60), which commanded the south-western entrance to the Menai Strait. Fort Belan (see also page 63) had serious military significance, but Williamsbourg was never intended to be more than a place for military practice and social gatherings — in fact its purpose was probably not far removed from that of a folly — always a popular conceit in 18th century society.

Groeslon (123,115) (SH 47-55) *4m S Caernarfon.* Not an outstandingly interesting village, but it does contain the Tudor Slateworks, which has an interesting slate showroom and (in summer) a café. *(Tel: 0286 830 242.)*

Gwalchmai (114) (SH 39-75) *10m W Llanfair P.G.* Like Gaerwen, further east, this village grew up on Telford's road to Holyhead, now known as the A5, and one of Telford's toll houses survives here (see also Llanfair P.G., page 75). The Methodist church which dates from 1780 has an ambitious interior complete with semi-circular seating, a gallery supported on iron columns and a handsomely carved pulpit.

Gwydir Castle (115) (SH 79-61) *To immediate SW Llanrwst.* This is a Tudor mansion which was lovingly restored following a fire in the 1920s. It was originally the home of the Wynn family and is now open to the public. The gardens are noted for their peacocks. *(Tel: 0492 640261.)*

Gwydir Forest (115,116) (SH 78-58 etc.) One of the great Forestry Commission developments in North Wales, this is centred upon the town of Betws-y-Coed, and the principal Information Centre relating to it is at Y Stablau (The Stables) in the centre of this town. There are leaflets describing no fewer than twelve walks, and a series of car parks and picnic sites, the location of which will be shown separately in this 'Places of Interest' section. Our own **Walks 4** and **5** explore certain areas of this forest, and our **Tours 3** and **4** also pass through it.

Gwydyr Uchaf Chapel (115) (SH 79-61) *To immediate SW Llanrwst.* Not to be confused with the Gywdir Chapel of Llanrwst Parish Church (see page 80), this was built in 1604 by Sir John Wynn of Gwydir Castle and has a painted ceiling above a wonderfully varied assortment of woodwork, most of which is contemporary with the building.

Gyffin (115) (SH 77-76) *To immediate S Conwy.* Although now a suburb of Conwy, Gyffin has a pleasantly secluded church. When this was restored in 1866 the fine 15th century chancel roof was spared, and this is painted with the figures of saints.

Happy Valley (Cwm Dyffryn) (135) (SN 62-98) *4m E Tywyn.* Cwm Dyffryn once sheltered the old coach road between Tywyn and Machynlleth, but Victorian visitors to Aberdyfi were soon being introduced to it as 'Happy Valley', and both this and Llyn Barfog (the 'Bearded Lake') became an almost obligatory visitors' jaunt. It is possible to walk up into the Happy Valley from Aberdyfi (see page 29).

Harlech (124) (SH 58-31) Built on the slopes of a steep hillside, this little town is entirely dominated by the massive 13th century castle, completed here in about 1290 by Edward I, and one of the key fortresses in his coastal chain around the mountains of North Wales (see also Beaumaris, Caernarfon, and Conwy). This plan was carried out with the help of Edward's Master of Works in Wales, James of St George, who became Constable of Harlech in 1290 (see also Conwy, page 51). The sea, now ½ mile

Harlech   SCALE 1:25 000 or 2½ INCHES to 1 MILE

away, once came right up to the base of the great promontory rock on which the castle stands, and there was a harbour here, enabling the garrison to be provisioned from the sea, an essential part of Edward's strategy for containing the Welsh. Despite this precaution, and despite the strength of Harlech's defences, it fell to Owain Glyndwr during the Welsh uprising in 1404, and according to legend he held a Welsh Parliament here. However the castle was recaptured within only 4 years, and the story of its later defence by Dafydd ab Ifan ab Einion on behalf of the Lancastrians in the Wars of the Roses, is brought to mind by the famous marching song, 'Men of Harlech'. It continued to be a place of considerable importance until the 16th century and also had a brief hour of glory in the 17th century, being the last Royalist stronghold in Britain to surrender to Parliament, as late as 1647.

Its superb overall design remains absolutely clear today, with four great towers at the corners of the curtain walls, all sited magnificently above the coastline — a perfect example of the real beauty

Edward I's splendid Harlech Castle.

that may sometimes be achieved by sheer strength of purpose. Enter through the great gateway and climb the south-east tower to begin a walk along the walls, from whence there are superb views, especially to the west and north overlooking much of the Lleyn Peninsula, the great sweep of Tremadog Bay, and the dunescape of Morfa Harlech behind its eastern shores. Beyond this dune country may be seen the mountains of Snowdonia, with Yr Wyddfa, Snowdon itself, magnificently outlined on the northern horizon. There are also views south and south-east, to the slopes of Cadair Idris, and on the clearest of days to the swelling lines of Plynlimon, over 40 miles away.

Harlech has several hotels, restaurants, and craft shops, a heated indoor swimming pool, a championship 18-hole golf course, the Royal St Davids, and splendid sweeping sands, beyond a large car park. There is a *Tourist Information Centre (tel: 0766 780658)*, and a theatre called the Ardudwy. The town is on the Cambrian Coast Railway, and this line can be used to explore southwards to Barmouth and Aberdovey, and north and west to the resorts on the southern coast of the Lleyn. The northern end of the Morfa Harlech dunes, and part of the great Traeth Bach estuary beyond, are a National Nature Reserve, and permits to visit this must be obtained from the Regional Officer of the Nature Conservancy Council at Ffordd Penrhos, Bangor, Gwynedd LL57 2LQ. At Muriau'r Gwyddelod, about a mile to the south of the town, will be found two Iron Age hut groups. Their Welsh name, 'Irishmen's Walls', implies that, like several other hut groups in North Wales, they were originally inhabited by Irish settlers, but in fact their origins are far from clear. Those without archaeological leanings might do well to pass these by. There is an attractive but very steep little road leading eastwards, up over to Llyn Cwm Bychan, the starting point for a walk to the Roman Steps (see page 102), and to the Artro valley where there are pleasantly wooded parking places, one of which has a picnic site.

Hebog Range (115) (SH 56-47 etc.) This range of mountains forms, with the Nantlle Ridge, a semicircle of mountains around the head of idyllic Cwm Pennant, although Mynydd Mawr (SH 53-54), outlying to the north of the Nantlle valley, is usually included in the group. Between Moel Hebog and Moel Lefn, at the southern end of the Beddgelert Forest, there is another cave where Owain Glyndwr and his followers are said to have taken refuge, the Ogof Owain Glyndwyr (SH 56-47) (see also Owain Glyndwr's Cave, page 92). For details of the Hebog Range's possibilities for climbers, see W. A. Poucher's *The Welsh Peaks* or Terry Marsh's *The Mountains of Wales*, but for atmosphere read William Condry's classic *The Snowdonia National Park*, in the Collins Fontana New Naturalist Series.

Hell's Mouth, Anglesey (See Porth Cynfor, page 96).

Hell's Mouth, Lleyn Peninsula (See Porth Neigwl, page 97).

Hen Borth (114) (SH 31-93) *3m W Cemaes*. Small crescent-shaped bay with shingle and some sand at low tide. Car parking space is limited where the road

is nearest, and it is probably best to park nearer Cemlyn Bay and walk westwards past little Llanrhwydrys church (see page 79).

Holyhead (114) (SH 24-82) *20m W Llanfair P.G.* This busy town is the terminus for the Irish ferry service with Dun Laoghaire, and it is situated on Holy Island at the very end of Thomas Telford's great 267-mile-long road from London, the present A5 (see Conwy, page 51). Always busy with travellers between England and Ireland, the essentially Welsh town of Holyhead has somehow survived. It is largely 19th century in feeling, despite the presence of the great alumininium smelting works to its immediate south-east.

The town is built on the site of a 3rd century Roman fort, and the church of St Cybi is within the walls of this fort, with its circular towers at the corners. Apart from the east side, the walls of Caer Gybi Fort are the actual ones built by Roman legionaries well over 1500 years ago. Despite the protection provided by these walls the original monastery church, built here by Cornish missionary St Cybi about AD 550, did not escape sacking in the year 961 by marauding Danes. The present church, large and airy, was built between the 13th and 16th centuries, and restored by Sir Gilbert Scott in the 1870s. Its contents include a massive Stanley tomb, and a window by the pre-Raphaelites, William Morris and Edward Burne-Jones. Near the south gate are the remains of the nave of a medieval chapel that served as a school in the 18th century.

The Admiralty Pier on Salt Island, now used by the car ferry, was built in 1821, and the Doric Arch, marking the end of Telford's road from London, commemorates a visit here by George IV in 1821. The building of the very long breakwater was commenced in 1845, using stone quarried from the nearby Holyhead Mountain. The story of this great harbour and of Holyhead in general is well told in the Holyhead Maritime Museum, which is housed in the former St Elbod's Church in Rhosygaer Avenue. There is a Sailing School at Holyhead, and a *Tourist Information Centre* in Marine Square, Salt Island *(tel: 0407 2622)*. It is possible to fish from the harbour walls and there is a heated indoor swimming pool on the B4545, one mile south of its junction with the A5. If a change of scene is required, it is possible to take a day excursion to Ireland, using one of the regular sailings between Holyhead and Dun Laoghaire, with a crossing time of 3½ hours. *(For details tel: 0407 4604.)*

Holyhead Mountain (114) (SH 21-82) *2m W Holyhead.* There are several paths up to this dramatic 720-foot hill, but the easiest one is up from the road to South Stack (SH 20-82). The Iron Age settlement on its summit, Caer y Twr, is an outstanding landmark, while below to the south-west, and much nearer to the car park, are the hut circles of Ty-Mawr, known here as elsewhere in this part of the world as Cytiau'r Gwyddelod (Irish Folk's Houses), remains of a farming settlement that existed here in Roman times.

Holy Island (114) (SH 23-81 etc.) Now joined to the main island of Anglesey by Four Mile Bridge and the long Stanley Embankment (see Dyffryn, page 61), Holy Island is dominated by the outline of Holyhead Mountain (see above). Its indented shore includes

Holyhead

SCALE 1:25 000 or 2½ INCHES to 1 MILE

many attractive small beaches, and apart from the Iron Age settlements on and around Holyhead Mountain itself (see above) there is also evidence of earlier Megalithic and Bronze Age occupation in the shape of standing stones at Penrhosfeilw (SH 22-80) (see page 94) and Ty-Mawr (SH 25-80) (not to be confused with the Ty-Mawr to the south-west of Holyhead Mountain), and a burial chamber at Trefignath to the south-east of Ty Mawr (SH 25-80).

Llanaber (124) (SH 60-17) *1m N Barmouth.* This village is almost an extension of Barmouth, and is not of great interest apart from its church. This is a pleasant little building above the shoreline in a churchyard crammed with monumental gravestones. Building started here in about 1200, was completed within 50 years, and has been altered very little since (the restoration of 1858 being unusually sympathetic). There is an old stone-flagged floor, stout arcading, a chancel higher than the nave, which has a beautifully-lit roof, and tall lancet windows. At high tide, standing quietly in the

church, it is possible to hear the sound of waves on the shore below — all in great contrast to the busy holiday caravan sites nearby.

Llanaelhaearn (123) (SH 38-44) *7m N Pwllheli.* Small village at the foot of Yr Eifl (The Rivals) (see page 109), with a 12th century church which probably lay on the Saints' Road to Bardsey. This cruciform building was much restored at the end of the 19th century, but it has retained its fine 15th or 16th century rood screen and its attractive box pews. Several inscribed stones, probably dating from the 6th century, were found during restoration, and provide reasonable evidence of the church's links with the pilgrimages to Bardsey.

A mile to the south-west of the village, on the B4417 road to Nefyn, there is a path leading up west and then north, to one of the three summits of Yr Eifl, this one being crowned with the remains of Tre'r Ceiri (The Town of the Giants), a native hill town occupied during the Roman period, although probably Bronze Age in origin. Here will be found a fortified camp enclosing a group of well-preserved

67

hut circles, stone-walled structures which must once have been roofed with poles and bracken. Despite these basic comforts life up on this bleak mountain-top must have been extraordinarily hard, and can only have been justified by the security against attack that its position must have provided. On a clear day the view from this mountain-top is one of the best in Wales, taking in most of the Lleyn, Anglesey and Snowdonia, with a possible glimpse of the Isle of Man when conditions are especially favourable. See also **Walk 10**, page 148.

LLanallgo (114) (SH 50-85) *1m SW Moelfre*. Here is the church of the parish in which Moelfre lies, a drastically restored building, in the churchyard of which will be found a memorial to the 140 persons drowned in the wreck of the *Royal Charter* off Moelfre (see page 88). This event, which happened on an October night in 1859 when no fewer than 114 ships were wrecked off the Welsh coast, is recalled by Charles Dickens in the *Uncommercial Traveller*, and he stayed at the nearby rectory to cover the story. The ill-fated ship was on its way home from Australia with over four hundred passengers, many of whom were gold-diggers, returning to their native land with 'an enormous quantity of gold' — so goes the tale!

To the north of the church (just to the east of the minor road) will be found the Lligwy Burial Chamber, a massive 28 ton capstone supported on smaller uprights (see also page 58). This would have once been covered with an earth mound, and excavations have revealed that no fewer than thirty people were buried here. A short way northwards, in an attractive setting to the west of the road is Din Lligwy (see also page 58), the interesting site of a native village of the Roman period, with a group of hut circles within a well-built enclosure wall. Not far distant, to the east of the road will be found the ruins of Capel Lligwy, a 12th century chapel, partly rebuilt in the 14th century and extended in the 16th.

Llanarmon (123) (SH 42-39) *4m NE Pwllheli*. Here in unspoilt country, about two miles inland from the busy coastline, is a small 15th century church. This has a pleasing arcade between its two aisles and a primitive contemporary rood screen.

Llanbabo Church (114) (SH 37-86) *6m SW Amlwch*. Delightfully situated to the west of Llyn Alaw Reservoir, this attractive little building sits in a tiny churchyard close to a stream and an old bridge. It is of partly 12th and 14th century origin and some of its roof timbers are certainly medieval. It is dedicated to St Pabo, a chief of the North Britons who led an army against the Picts, and who took refuge in Anglesey around AD 500. He is depicted in low relief as a crowned king complete with sceptre, in a fine 14th century carving, possibly by the craftsman who also created the splendid monument to St Iestyn at Llaniestyn, near Llanddona (see page 70).

Llanbadrig (114) (SH 37-94) *4m W Amlwch*. A few cottages, a farm and a church, all situated on cliffs looking westwards out across Cemaes Bay. Tragically, the largely 14th and 16th century church was gutted by fire in 1985. It had been heavily restored just over a hundred years earlier by an uncle of Bertrand Russell, Lord Stanley of Alderley. It was

he who with great caution went through four different forms of marriage with his intended bride, only to discover that the lady in question already had a husband. This highly eccentric nobleman later became a Moslem and as a result of his conversion, the interior of the church that he restored had a distinctly oriental flavour. The church is the only one in Wales dedicated to St Patrick, and this saint is supposed to have set sail from here on his great missionary journey to Ireland. The headland and most of the coast to the east of Cemaes Bay is in the care of the National Trust, and walking possibilities are considerable here.

Llanbedr (124) (SH 58-26) *3m S Harlech*. This small, neat village has sometimes been claimed to be the tidiest in Wales, and is centred upon its bridge over the Afon Artro. The early 16th century church was restored in the 1880s, and surprisingly its contents include an incised Bronze Age stone. A short distance to the north of the village are two prehistoric standing stones, while in contrast, the Maes Artro Tourist Village just to its south provides a wide variety of leisure facilities, including a sea life aquarium, a recreated old Welsh street, a model village, a Wild West Fort, and a nature trail. There are also studio workshops, a craft shop, a coffee shop and a licensed restaurant. *(Tel: 034 123 497.)*

Well to the west of the village, and reached across a causeway at low tide, is Shell Island (SH 55-26), a peninsula with camping facilities and opportunities for bathing and fishing. A wide variety of shells are to be found here, hence the name 'Shell Island' which is *Mochras* in Welsh.

There is a pleasant road running north-eastwards from Llanbedr, up the Artro Valley to Cwm Bychan (see page 54), and up the valley of the Afon Cwmnantcol (see page 56) where there is both a farm trail and a nature trail.

Llanbedrgoch (114,115) (SH 50-80) *2m SE Benllech*. Small village just inland from Red Wharf Bay, with a modest 15th and 17th century church on a small hill. 15th century bench-ends have been used in the construction of a reading desk, and one of the panels includes a carving of a mermaid complete with mirror and comb. There are two Neolithic burial chambers and a hut group at Pant-y-Saer (SH 509-824), amongst the little hills between here and pretty-sounding Tynygongl, above the busy holiday resort of Benllech.

Llanbedrog (123) (SH 32-31) *4m SW Pwllheli*. This is largely a modern seaside village. The wide sandy beach is sheltered from the prevailing south-west winds by the headland of Trwyn Llanbedrog and sands extend eastwards almost the whole way to Pwllheli (with which it was once linked by a tramcar line — see Pwllheli, page 100). There are tennis courts, miniature golf, and boats and canoes for hire.

The heavily restored medieval church stands on a wooded slope, and has a 16th century chancel divided from the nave by a substantial screen of the same age. There are a few 17th century cottages at the foot of the Mynydd Tir-y-cwmwd and it is possible to walk over this hill, from the top of which there are fine views southwards over St Tudwal's Road (bay) to St Tudwal's Islands (see page 103). On Foel Fawr (SH 30-32), well to the west of the village, is the tower of a ruined windmill, now in the care of the National Trust, and this fine viewpoint may be reached by a path up from the B4413.

Llanbedr-y-cennin (115) (SH 75-69) *6m S Conwy.* A minute village looking out eastwards across the Conwy Valley, with a delightfully simple medieval church. This has a small wooden porch and nestles amongst yew trees not far away from the hospitable 16th century Olde Bull Inn (good bar food here). On a 1200-foot hill to the west of the village stands the fine Iron Age settlement of Pen-y-gaer, complete with a number of stone walls and the remains of huts. There are fine views from here.

Llanberis (114,115) (SH 57-60) *8m E Caernarfon.* (See map on pages 84 & 85.) Standing at the south-eastern end of Llyn Padarn, and not far from the north-western end of Llyn Peris, the village of Llanberis is in the very heart of Snowdonia, and is perhaps best known as the terminus of the Snowdon Mountain Railway (for details, see page 104). There is however much more to see and do here, and although the various items of interest described below may seem to be in almost too great a profusion, their interest and variety make an early visit to Llanberis an essential part of any visitor's programme.

In view of the possible congestion it is best to park either at the northern end of the village, or perhaps preferably at the large park by the Welsh Slate Museum, near the Gilfach Ddu terminus of the Llanberis Lake Railway. This narrow gauge railway, built to carry slate, has been converted to take passengers along the shore of Llyn Padarn, a two mile run to Pen-y-llyn, with a stop at Cei Llydan, where there are lake-side and tree-shaded picnic sites. It is possible to leave the train here and join another one later in the day. There is a snack bar and souvenir shop in the terminus station at Gilfach Ddu.

This railway line runs through much of the Padarn Country Park, the central feature of which is the Llyn Padarn Walk. This circles the entire lake and is well described in a leaflet published by Gwynedd County Council. Shortly after leaving Gilfach Ddu it passes a viewing platform and beyond this will be found the Quarry Hospital Visitor Centre, which was once the hospital for employees of the Dinorwic Quarry Company and which contains much of its original equipment as well as special displays on the Country Park. For further details of this interesting walk see the leaflet referred to above.

There are two other trails starting from the car park at Gilfach Ddu — The Vivian Trails which take their name from the great Vivian Quarry just to the north. This was one of several quarries belonging to the Dinorwic Quarry Company, and was itself named after W. W. Vivian, the company's manager in the closing years of the 19th century, and whose office now forms part of the craft workshops to which we refer below. There is a Short Trail, with an alternative Top Trail for the energetic, and either will provide a most interesting insight into the workings of this vast slate quarry, especially with the help of the descriptive leaflet produced by Gwynedd County Council. Yet another trail is provided, also described in a helpful leaflet. This is a nature trail, again starting at the car park at Gilfach Ddu, and also taking in the Quarry Hospital Visitor

Centre.

Further information will be obtained by visiting the Welsh Slate Museum which is housed in the old workshops of the Quarry Company, and which contains much of the original workshop machinery, including a foundry and the well known Dinorwic water-wheel. These quarries were, until their closure in 1969, one of the largest in Britain, employing over three thousand men in their heyday. There is an interpretative gallery and films depicting life and work here are shown at regular intervals. It is also possible to take a ride into the main quarry by Landrover. *(Tel: 0286 870630.)* Not far from the Slate Museum there is a group of Craft Workshops and a Woodcraft Centre, and it is possible to watch craftspeople at work here, and to buy their products. Between the A4086 and the shore of Llyn Padarn will be found Oriel Eryri, the very interesting Welsh Environmental Centre, which provides an interpretation of the environment with a special emphasis on the countryside of Snowdonia. Tourist Information is available here. *(Tel: 0286 870 765.)*

For the nearby features of Dinorwic Pumped Storage Power Station, Dolbadarn Castle and the Ceunant Mawr Waterfall, see separate articles on pages 58, 59 and 49 respectively. Canoes, windsurfers, dinghies and bicycles may be hired in the village, and their are opportunities for pony trekking.

Llanberis, Pass of (115) (SH 62-56) *3m SE Llanberis.* The southern side of this dramatic mountain pass is bounded by the flanks of Snowdon itself, while its northern side is lined by the seemingly impassable rock faces and steep boulder-strewn buttresses which rise to the three peaks of Y Garn and the Glyders — Glyder Fawr and Glyder Fach. The car parks at Pont y Gromlech (SH 63-56) and Pen-y-Pass (SH64-55) usually fill up early in the day, but the former is a very good place from which to watch rockclimbers who can usually be seen

Llanberis Pass.

roped together on the sheer faces above. Our **Walk 6**, page 140 starts from Pen-y-pass, but it may be preferable to use the Sherpa Bus Service (see page 19) from the car park at Nant Peris (SH 60-58).

Llandanwg (124) (SH 56-28) *2m SW Harlech.* Small seaside village with a sand and shale beach (beware of currents created by the fast flowing Afon Artro, which joins the sea here), a good car park, some shops and refreshment facilities. The small church near the shore is much threatened by the movement of dunes. There is a station on the Cambrian Coast Railway here.

Llanddaniel Fab (114,115) (SH 49-70) *2m SW Llanfair P.G.* An unexceptional village in quiet country just inland from the Menai Strait, but there are three features of interest nearby — see Bryncelli Ddu Burial Chamber, page 43, Plas Newydd, page 95, and Moel-y-don, page 88.

Llanddeusant (114) (SH 34-85) *9m NE Holyhead.* This minute village in an undramatic Anglesey setting has a large and somewhat forbidding Victorian church, complete with tower and little conical spire. Llynon windmill, still standing well to the west of the village, was the last working windmill on the island of Anglesey, and is a reminder of the times when the many mills of this type were an outstanding feature of the Anglesey skyline.

Llanddona (114,115) (SH 57-79) *3m NW Beaumaris.* Large village with some old cottages amongst many more modern dwellings. The Victorian church (it cost barely £600 when built in 1873) is tucked away in the hamlet of Pentrellwyn, on the coast about a mile to the north. Steep, narrow lanes lead down to the shore, which lies at the far eastern end of Red Wharf Bay (Traeth-coch). There is a car park at SH 56-80, but this is reached by another steep, narrow lane branching off north-westwards from the lane to Pentrellwyn. Beware of possible patches of quicksand here.

Llanddwyn Bay and Island (114) (SH 38-62) *12m SW Llanfair P.G.* There is a car park and picnic site in trees on the edge of Newborough Forest, not far from the shore line. The mile long Hendai Forest Trail starts from here and the bathing on the sands of Llanddwyn Bay is excellent. It is also possible to walk from here around the bay and on to Llanddwyn Island, which may be reached on foot except at the highest tides. This charming little island has many rocky promontories punctuated by small sandy coves, but be sure to keep to the paths indicated, as this is part of the Newborough Warren Nature Reserve (see also pages 18 and 91). The lighthouse is automatic and the lifeboat station and the Caernarfon pilots who used the cottages on the islands have long since gone. The ruined 16th century church was dedicated to St Deinwen, a 5th century saint whose shrine was once a place of pilgrimage for lovers. She is commemorated by a

Llanddwyn Bay and Island.

Latin cross near the old lighthouse, while a Celtic cross remembers the victims of shipwrecks nearby, but both crosses are of comparatively recent date.

Llanddwywe (124) (SH 58-22) *4m N Barmouth.* Minute village between Tal-y-bont and Dyffryn Ardudwy, with a small, mainly Perpendicular period church. This has an attractive interior, especially the family chapel of the Vaughans of Cors y Gedol (see Dyffryn Ardudwy, page 61), which includes some unusually fine 17th and 18th century monuments.

Llanddyfnan Church (114,115) (SH 50-78) *3m NE Llangefni.* This small building is attractively sited on the northern edge of flat marshy country, with a Neolithic standing stone in a field close by. The early 16th century south doorway has interesting carvings within, but this building is usually locked. Enquire locally for the key.

Llandecwyn (124) (SH 63-37) *6m NE Harlech.* There are splendid views from little Llandecwyn church, which stands high above the estuary of Traeth Bach. It is situated in hill country some distance to the north of the little reed-bordered lake of Llyn Tecwyn Isaf, and although not itself of great interest the views from it westwards over Tremadog Bay and to the Snowdon Range in the north, make the steep climb up here well worthwhile. A glance at the Landranger Sheet 124 will reveal several walking possibilities here (see Llyn Tecwyn, page 85).

Llandegai (114,115) (SH 59-70) *2m SE Bangor.* Situated on the banks of the Afon Ogwen, at the south entrance to Penrhyn Castle, this is a 19th century estate village, built in the picturesque style by Lord Penrhyn for his workers. The medieval parish church was heavily restored at the same time, and its contents include the handsome tomb of the first Lord Penrhyn and his Lady by one of the Westmacotts, a family prolific not only in the field of sculpture, but in the number of talented offspring they produced. There are also two late medieval tombs, one of a knight and one of an archbishop — the latter being Archbishop of York, John Williams, who retired to this area after holding Conwy for King Charles in the early years of the Civil War. For Penrhyn Castle, see page 94.

Llandegfan (114,115) (SH 56-73) *2m NE Menai Bridge.* This parish between Menai Bridge and Beaumaris embraces the section of coast road along the Menai Strait sometimes known as Millionaire's Mile. The road was built by Lord Bulkeley in the early years of the 19th century, and in the years that followed many fine Victorian houses sprang up here, soon being surrounded with trees and shrubs which have thrived in the mild climate which exists here. Llandegfan church is situated well behind the coast, beyond an expanding modern residential area. The little medieval building was much restored in the 19th century and had a new tower provided by the ever-generous Lord Bulkeley in 1811. Do not overlook the effigy of a King's Messenger, Thomas Davies, who died in 1649, the same year that the monarch under whom he must have served was beheaded upon the scaffold outside Whitehall Palace. Just under a mile to the south-west of the church (SH 554-739) there is an impressive standing stone in a field to the north of the road, another of the many relics of Anglesey's prehistoric past.

Llandegwning (123) (SH 26-30) *8m SW Pwllheli.* Here, just over a mile inland from the broad expanse of Hell's Mouth, is a minute mid-19th century church, standing almost alone, with a conical spire set on a small tower which is octagonal below and round above. This delightful little building has a white-painted interior complete with box pews.

Llandrygarn Church (114) (SH 38-79) *6m NW Llangefni.* This small building stands almost alone down a long track on the edge of marshy country. It is not of great interest architecturally, but the site is full of atmosphere. Ask for location of key before leaving the road, as it will almost certainly prove to be locked.

Llandudno (115) (SH 78-81) Situated on a sweeping bay between the two limestone headlands of the Great and Little Ormes, this is the outstanding holiday resort of North Wales, having accomodation for at least 25,000 visitors. It not only has the large and lively North Shore but also the quieter 'West Shore' facing the Conwy Estuary. Development started here in the 1840s and within two decades Llandudno had already achieved the status of a major holiday town. Its fine terraces and stylish shops have survived long enough for it now to be regarded as one of Britain's most distinguished Victorian towns.

There are splendid views of the North Wales coast from the summit of the **Great Orme (1)** (now designated as a 'Country Park'), which can be reached by one of the well-known trams which have been climbing up here from the **Tram Station (10)** since 1902, or by the equally popular **Cabin Lift**

Llandudno from the Great Orme.

(11). There are all the usual seaside features for children on the North shore, together with the lively **Pier (2)** (departures by 'steamer' for the Isle of Man on certain days each week during the summer season), and the extensive **Happy Valley Gardens (3)** close by, where there is a nature trail, The Great Orme. There is a **Marine Drive (4)** enabling visitors to drive around the Orme in an anti-clockwise direction, starting from the vicinity of the Pier and the Happy Valley, and this provides impressive sea and mountain views. **The White Rabbit Memorial (5)**, on the West Shore reminds visitors of Lewis Carroll, who met the young Alice Liddell and her family while staying in Llandudno, and whose visits with her to the sand dunes nearby, helped to inspire his famous story, *Alice in Wonderland*.

The **Mostyn Art Gallery (6)** at 12, Vaughan Street holds a variety of exhibitions throughout the year and there is a **Doll Museum and Model Railway (7)** in Masonic Street. The **Canolfan Aberconwy (8)**, is a conference and leisure centre with a wealth of facilities, and there are no fewer than three 18-hole golf courses, one at Penrhyn Bay and two on the West Shore. There is also a heated indoor swimming pool, bowling greens, tennis courts and putting courses. British Rail run a service

1 Great Orme	4 Marine Drive	8 The Canolfan Aberconwy
2 Pier	5 White Rabbit Memorial	11 Cabin Lift

Llandudno (for detailed map covered by inset, see following page)   SCALE 1:50 000 or 1¼ INCHES to 1 MILE

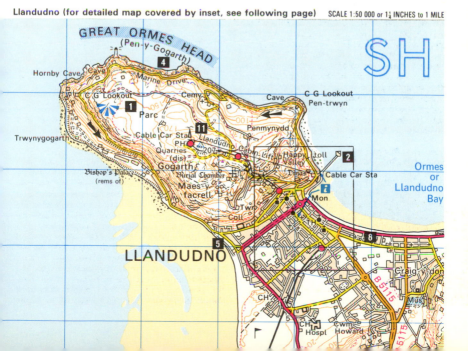

Llandudno (for general map see page 71)

SCALE 1:10 000 or 6 INCHES to 1 MILE

1 Great Orme
2 Pier
3 Happy Valley Gardens
4 Marine Drive
5 White Rabbit Memorial

6 Mostyn Art Gallery
7 Doll Museum and Model
  Railway
8 The Canolfan Aberconwy

9 Main Tourist Information
  Centre, Chapel St.
10 Tram Station
11 Cabin Lift

south through the lovely Conwy Valley and up to Blaenau Ffestiniog, where there is a connection with the privately run Ffestiniog Railway (see page 62), which itself connects with the Cambrian Coast Railway at Porthmadog. On Sundays, at the height of the holiday season, the Cambrian Coast Action Group provide an inclusive 'Sunday Shuttle' service, using these three lines, and details are available from the Tourist Information Centres. Ask also for the leaflet describing 'Day Trips from Llandudno' by bus.

The town's main **Tourist Information Centre (9)** is in Chapel Street. *(Tel: 0492 76413.)*

Llandudwen (123) (SH 27-36) *7m W Pwllheli.* Here, in unspoilt farming country beneath the northern slopes of Carn Fadryn, is a minute medieval church in a well-mown enclosure. The contents of this attractive little building, which is dedicated to St Tudwen, the great-aunt of St David, include an octagonal font probably made in the 10th century, and some early 19th century glass.

Llandwrog (115,123) (SH 45-56) *5m SW Caernarfon.* This is a Victorian estate village, and largely the creation of Lord Newborough of Glynllifon (see page 64). There is an hospitable inn, a series of stone cottages in the Gothick style, including a group of almshouses set in an attractive curve, and a small church built in 1860. This has a handsome interior, complete with stone west gallery, stalls reminiscent of an Oxford or Cambridge college, and a number of attractive 18th and 19th century monuments to members of the Wynne family in its south chapel. At Blythe Farm (SH 44-57) about a mile to the north there is a craft workshop producing models in slate and resin (tel: 0286 831050). Beyond this there is a short stretch of quiet road running beside the marshy estuary of Foryd Bay, which should provide good bird-watching opportunities in wintertime.

Llandyfrydog (114) (SH 44-85) *6m N Llangefni.* The church and old school make an attractive tree-shaded group in dark grey stone and slate. The church is largely the result of Victorian restoration, but has a 14th century chancel arch, an ancient font and some attractive old box pews. In the church-yard will be found a sundial and several interesting gravestones. The school, which once had as many as eighty pupils, was built in the 19th century by the local farming community and was one of the oldest voluntary schools in Wales; sadly it is no longer in use.

There is a rather unexciting standing stone, Carreg Leidr, in a field (private) to the east of the road about half a mile to the south of the village. However, one of the best features of Llandyfrydog is its view westwards to the slopes of Mynydd Bodafon (see page 89), which can be approached by a path which starts up a farm road opposite the church.

Llanedwen Church (See Moel-y-don, page 88).

Llanegryn (124) (SH 60-05) *4m N Tywyn.* Small village overlooking the broad Dysynni valley with an interesting little bell-coted church on high ground to its north. Its interior was restored in 1878, but by a small miracle its atmosphere has survived intact. There are elegant memorials to the Owens and the Wynnes of nearby Peniarth (SH 61-05), but inevitably the eye is drawn upwards to the exquisite rood screen — a delicately carved piece of 16th century craftsmanship, with complex carvings of vines, berries, leaves and flowers. This was possibly executed by the same group of craftsmen who created the screens at Llanbedrog and Llanengan (see pages 68 and 73), although this is by far the finest specimen of the three and may have been moved here from Cymmer Abbey (see page 57). Just over a mile to the south, on the north banks of the Afon Dysynni, there is a small mound, Domen Ddreiniog, all that remains of a 13th century wooden castle that once dominated this lowest crossing of the river.

It is possible to walk north-eastwards from Llanegryn, over the hills to Arthog, making partial use of the Ffordd Ddu (the Black Road), a distance of seven miles. This expedition is only for the hardy and experienced walker.

Llaneilian (114) (SH 47-92) *2m E Amlwch.* The parish church has a 12th century tower topped by a pyramid-shaped roof, and an interior well worth visiting. Here will be found a painted 15th century rood screen, a chancel roof supported on corbels ornamented with musicians playing assorted instruments, a massive, studded wooden chest and a pair of tongs, once used for separating aggressive dogs (dealing with dogs seems to have been an all-too-frequent duty for churchwardens to perform, not only here but in many churches throughout the land, see also Clynnog Fawr, page 49).

Beyond the village lies Porth Eilian and Point Lynas, and there are several good parking places overlooking this delightful little inlet. It is possible to walk westwards along the cliffs from Porth Eilian to Amlwch, a distance of about two miles. There is also a track to the Pilot Station and lighthouse on Point Lynas, and this makes an ideal viewing point for ships heading around this north-eastern tip of Anglesey. The lighthouse, signal and telegraph station were established here in 1835 by the Trustees of Liverpool Docks, and before the days of wireless, the imminent arrival of boats heading for the Mersey were reported either from here, or through here, from one of the points further west. The signal station, which was sited on Mynydd Eilian, well to the south of the village, has appropriately been superceded by radio masts providing up-to-date communication facilities. For further details of the old telegraph service, see Llanrhyddlad, page 79.

Llanelltyd (124) (SH 71-19) *2m NW Dolgellau.* There is a car park by the old bridge over the Mawddach at Llanelltyd, but the view from this bridge down the Mawddach estuary, which the poet Ruskin reckoned to be one of the finest in Europe, is now obscured by the modern bridge carrying the A470. However this is the best base for visiting Llanelltyd's pleasant little, long, low church, which is situated nearby in a circular churchyard with yew trees, looking out over the valley. It has a series of early 19th century round-headed windows, an attractive old north door within a small porch, an interesting monument to Sir Robert Howell Vaughan, and the story of the medieval silver gilt chalice and paten, which once belonged to Cymmer Abbey (see page 57), and which was found on a nearby mountainside. This is now to be seen in the National Museum in Cardiff. For the nearby Precipice Walk, see page 99.

Llanengan (123) (SH 29-26) *1m SW Abersoch.* Small village over the hill from Abersoch, looking south and west over the long beach of Porth Neigwl (Hell's Mouth). Lead was once mined on the hill above the village, and the remains of a few ruined engine-house chimneys are still to be seen here. The fine parish church dates from the 15th and early 16th centuries. Its three bells bear 17th century dates and are believed to have come from the abbey of St Mair on Bardsey (see page 36), with whom Llanengan was traditionally associated, and it was no doubt a port of call for Bardsey pilgrims. By some happy chance this twin-aisled building was overlooked by the over-zealous restorers of the Victorian era, and the interior retains a pleasingly unspoilt atmosphere of times past, further enhanced by two late medieval rood screens complete with loft over the southern one. Do not miss the octagonal font, nor the offertry chest carved from a single baulk of timber, and believed to have been used to receive the offerings (or tolls) of pilgrims en route to Bardsey, as well as for the storage of the much-hated papal tax, 'St Peter's Pence'.

South of the village, just under a mile beyond the Sun Hotel, there is a car park, from which a footpath leads to the south-eastern end of Porth Neigwl beach (Hell's Mouth).

Llanerchymedd (114,115) (SH 41-84) *6m S Amlwch.* Situated in undulating country to the south-east of Llyn Alaw, this sizeable village was once the market centre for the northern half of Anglesey, and still has wide streets meeting at its attractive little square. The parish church is, apart from its medieval tower, a largely mid-Victorian building, and not of great interest to visitors, but the interior of the nearby Welsh Presbyterian Church of Jerusalem is a handsome example of early 19th century architecture, with galleries around three sides. No doubt many of the town's 250 cobblers worshipped here — the town being noted in the 19th century for its boots — and also its snuff.

There is a quiet road running northwards from here to a car park and picnic site on the south-eastern shore of Llyn Alaw (see page 81).

Llaneugrad Church (114,115) (SH 49-84) *2m NW Benllech.* This little 12th and 16th century building is within the beautifully wooded Parciau Estate, and there is a fine 17th century dovecote visible from the drive to it. There is a crude but strongly executed 13th century crucifix in the north wall of the nave. Enquire locally as to rights of way up the drive.

Llanfachraeth (114) (SH 31-82) *6m E Holyhead.* An unexceptional village strung out along the A5025, Valley to Cemaes road, with several pleasant little bays not far to the west.

Llanfachreth (124) (SH 75-22) *3m NE Dolgellau.* Minute village in mountain country not far to the east of Coed-y-Brenin (The King's Forest). The interior of the largely Victorian church (rebuilt by architect E. B. Ferrey in 1873) contains a charming monument to Catherine Vaughan, the wife of the last member of the Nanney family of nearby Nannau (see page 89), who died in 1733. Do not miss the tablet on the lych-gate commemorating the death of George III, 'the people's Father and Friend'. There is a 'Forest Garden' to the west of the village, at Glasdir (SH 74-22) (see Coed-y-Brenin, page 50), and not far to the south is the best starting point for the Precipice Walk (SH 74-21) (see page 99).

Llanfaelog (114) (SH 33-73) *11m SE Holyhead.* Small village just inland from the busy holiday resort of Rhosneigr. The church was largely rebuilt in 1848, but contains an interesting tablet commemorating 'the fifty-six persons who lost their lives crossing the River Menai on the Fatal Day of December 1785', and reminding us of the considerable hazards experienced by travellers to Anglesey in the days before the opening of Telford's Menai Bridge. There is a Neolithic burial chamber called Ty Newydd in the corner of a field, on a minor road to Bryngwran, half a mile north of the church (SH 344-738). This consists of a massive capstone on three uprights.

Llanfaelrhys Church (123) (SH 21-26) *8m W Abersoch.* A delightful little elongated medieval building, not far to the north of the shore at Porth Ysgo (see page 99). There are old box pews and an air of quiet contentment here.

Llanfaes (114,115) (SH 60-77) *1m N Beaumaris.* This small village, a short distance inland from the shore of the Menai Strait, was an important commercial centre and port until Beaumaris was built. It stands on the site of a Franciscan friary, founded in 1237 by Llywelyn the Great, to house the tomb of his wife Joan, the natural daughter of King John (see Aber, page 28). No trace of this monastic house remains, apart from relics and tombs in Beaumaris and Penmynydd churches. Llanfaes parish church, which has white-painted cottages and an old smithy close by, was rebuilt in the 1840s and at the same time a spire was added to an earlier tower.

Llanfaethlu (114) (SH 31-86) *6m SW Cemaes.* Small village happily just to the west of the A5025, on ground high enough to secure good views northwards to the Skerries, and south-eastwards to Snowdonia. The church of St Maethlu stands in a windy churchyard with panoramic views of sea and farmlands, and there are one or two good memorials here and a sundial on a wooden post. The well cared-for interior has a barrel-vaulted roof and carpeted aisle, while the font is dated 1614 and there is an old box pew opposite the pulpit.

In a valley to the north-west of the village the 17th and 18th century mansion of Carreglwd is completely hidden by trees, but footpaths pass close by, one of which could be used to link on to our **Walk 2**, page 132, at Porth Swtan (Church Bay).

Llanfaglan Church (114,115) (SH 45-60) *2m SW Caernarfon.* Small medieval church standing alone in fields some distance from the road, and overlooking the sandy wastes of the Menai Strait. It is surrounded by fields, but is sheltered by trees within its churchyard wall. It was fortunate enough to escape the attentions of Victorian 'restorers', probably due to the remoteness of its setting, and retains a genuinely unspoilt character. The lintel inside the door was once a Roman tombstone and there are other re-used Roman stones in the walls — evidence of the Roman occupation of this key area opposite the southern shores of Anglesey. Study of Pathfinder Sheet SH 36/46 will reveal walking possibilities to the east of the church.

There is a car park and picnic site on the minor road running south from here, overlooking deep-set Foryd Bay, which is in effect the estuary of the Afon Gwyrfai, and this should provide good opportunities for bird-watching, especially in wintertime.

Llanfair (124) (SH 57-29) *1m S Harlech.* Small village situated just above the busy A496, with a church largely rebuilt in the mid-19th century and not of great interest to visitors. The Old Llanfair Quarry Slate Caverns, a series of caves and tunnels blasted from the hillside in the quest for slate, are open to the public. Visitors, wearing authentic safety helmets, are taken on a guided tour, and when they emerge once more into the daylight, there are fine views out over Cardigan Bay. At low tide this view includes the fourteen-mile natural causeway of Sarn Badrig, which has long been connected with the legend of the lost lands of Cantref y Gwaelod (see also Aberdyfi, page 30). On a hot summer day the contrast in temperature once inside the caverns is considerable and visitors are advised to wear something reasonably warm. There is a cafe and souvenir shop. *(Tel 0766 780247.)*

Pensarn, less than a mile south on the A496, once had a small harbour on the estuary of the Afon Artro, where sailing coasters were loaded with slate from the nearby caverns. The harbour has long since silted up, but there is still a useful station on the Cambrian Coast Railway (see page 46) here.

Llanfairfechan (115) (SH 68-74) *7m W Conwy*. A modest seaside resort with a mid-Victorian seafront and a sandy beach overlooked by the steep and much-quarried slopes of Penmaen Mawr Mountain. Near the A55 is the handsomely spired Christ Church which was built in 1855. The little church of St Mary, standing above the village, is an older foundation. It is possible to walk up here, and following the valley of the little Afon Ddu southeastwards, to eventually join the course of the Roman road running through the Bwlch y Ddeufaen (SH 71-71) (see page 43). A study of Landranger Sheet 115 will reveal several other opportunities for walking up into the mountains from Llanfairfechan, including a walk eastwards starting from Mount Road, to the Druid's Circle (SH 723-746) (see Penmaenmawr, page 92), but those in search of a shorter walk might find the interesting Llanfairfechan History Trail more suitable (enquire locally for details). There is safe bathing here and at low tide there is a wide stretch of sand, much loved by young sandcastle builders. Summer theatre takes place at the Community Centre, and there are tennis courts, bowling greens, and a putting green.

Llanfairpwllgwyngyll (114,115) (SH 53-71) *1m W Menai Bridge*. This is the correct name of the village in question, but with an early eye to tourism an enterprising 19th century village tailor expanded it to 'Llanfairpwllgwyngyllgogerychwyrndrobwllllantysiliogogogoch', meaning 'St Mary's Church in the hollow of the white hazel near the rapid whirlpool of Llandysilio of the red cave'. There are twenty two other Llanfairs (all named from churches dedicated to St Mary), and there is no doubt that the tailor succeeded in giving his own Llanfair a unique label. His enterprise should perhaps be compared with that of David Pritchard, the innkeeper at Beddgelert, who his 'legend' of the faithful hound (see page 39), for they both earned their villages a lasting reputation. For practical purposes the name is shortened to Llanfairpwll or even (as in our various cross-references) to Llanfair P.G.. Signs making use of the full title may be seen over a newsagents, a garage, and at the railway station, which was re-opened to the public in 1973. Here also is the Llanfairpwll Tourist Centre, which houses displays

of Anglesey's geology and history, and other local features.

Once on Telford's Holyhead road, which ran through the village from Menai Bridge, Llanfair P.G. is happily now by-passed. Since the re-construction of the Pont Britannia, Robert Stephenson's Britannia Bridge (see page 96), the A5 now uses this rather than Telford's Menai Bridge. However Telford's memory is preserved by one of his delightful little octagonal toll houses, which still stands in the village, complete with its list of charges, one of which reads — 'For every Horse, Mule, or other Cattle, drawing any Coach or other Carriage, with springs, the sum of — 4d'. The Holyhead Road, by then the last surviving turnpike in Britain, was freed from tolls in 1895, but happily three other of Telford's toll houses survive on Anglesey, at Gwalchmai, Caergeiliog and near the Stanley Embankment at Dyffryn.

The church was rebuilt in 1853 and is not of great interest to visitors, but there is an obelisk in the churchyard in memory of those who died during the construction of the Pont Britannia. Below the churchyard there is a path down to the shore, and here will be found a statue of Lord Nelson, erected as a navigation mark by Lord Clarence Paget, the sailor son of the first Marquess of Anglesey. It should perhaps be mentioned that the village was the first place in Britain to have a Women's Institute — an idea which was imported from Canada by a member of the Anglesey family in 1915. For the Marquess of Anglesey's Column, see page 87.

Llanfairynghornwy (114) (SH 32-90) *3m SW Cemaes*. This scattered parish covers the mainly rugged and infertile north-west corner of Anglesey, and includes the Skerries (see page 103), the rocky island two miles off Carmel Head (see page 47). The little village has an over-restored medieval church with a 16th century south chapel. Within will be found a monument to Evan Thomas, 'a most skilful Bone setter' — a reminder that this parish was once noted as the centre of the 'bonesetters of Anglesey', one of whom is said to have perfected the splint. These bonesetters were connected with the founders of the Gobowen Orthopaedic Hospital in Shropshire, which to this day continues to carry out pioneer work on modern splints. Another well-known figure in the parish was Frances Williams, wife of a 19th century rector here, who founded the 'Anglesey Association for the Preservation of Life from Shipwreck', and she was largely responsible for the establishment of the first lifeboat station in North Wales.

There are two separate standing stones and a circular earthwork to the east of the village, but the best walks in the parish are north-westwards to Carmel Head (SH 29-93) (see page 47), and west to the shore near the little island of Ynys y Fydlyn (SH 29-91) (see page 109). Use Pathfinder Sheet SH 29/39/49 to explore this pleasantly remote area, with its wild coastline, rolling country and many reminders of times past. For fine views north and

Llanfair P.G. — one of the signs resulting from 19th century enterprise.

west climb the hill Mynydd y Garn (SH 31-90), a feature which is passed on our **Walk 2**, page 132.

Llanfechell (114) (SH 36-91) *1m S Cemaes*. Situated in undramatic farming country, this tidy little village was once the site of a twice-yearly hiring fair, much used by landowners seeking agricultural labourers. Near the square where this fair was held there is a much restored medieval church which has a 16th century tower and a little spire added two centuries later. A branch of the Bulkeley family of Beaumaris and Penmon lived at Brynddu, just to the east of the village, and during the Civil War period, one of them was so passionate a Royalist that he swore to remain unshaven until the monarchy was restored, thus becoming known as Bulkeley-y-Farf (Bulkley, the bearded). He was forced to remain in hiding in a cave at Cemlyn Bay for much of the Commonwealth period, but kept his vow until the Restoration. An equally eccentric descendant, the 18th century diarist William Bulkeley, also lived at Brynddu. But this was apparently not far enough away from the church for him to be undisturbed by its bells, which he once asked to be silenced because they were, he claimed, souring his beer! It was perhaps more likely that his irritation was due to the presence of a number of grandchildren foisted on him by a daughter who had been misguided enough to marry the captain of a privateer. He was not however averse to the possible benefits of this doubtful connection, and his diary records that he 'paid a Flintshire smuggler that was come to Cemaes from Isle of Man 25s for 5 gallons of French brandy which I think is right good'.

There are two separate standing stones to the north and north-west of the village respectively, and also a burial chamber to the north-west.

Llanfflewyn (114) (SH 35-89) *3m S Cemaes*. Small church up a long track from the road, and situated beneath a bluff on the western edge of the rocky Mynydd Mechell. Its interior is full of an atmosphere of the past and its remote setting makes a visit here well worthwhile.

Llanffinan Church (114,115) (SH 49-75) *2m E Llangefni*. Small 19th century neo-Norman building, to the north-west of Plas Penmynydd, beyond the course of an old railway line and the nearby Afon Ceint, here little more than a drainage ditch. Inside will be found simple box pews and pulpit contemporary with the building, and a handsome early 18th century memorial to a child of three, John Lloyd of Hirdre-faig, a farm still standing about a mile to the south-west.

Llanfigael (114) (SH 32-82) *7m E Holyhead*. Quiet hamlet in farming country just to the north of the little Afon Alaw, with a pleasingly simple church. This has retained a flavour of the early 19th century and is complete with box and bench pews. In undramatic country well to the west (SH 342-832) will be found an impressive standing stone called Tregwehelydd. Ask locally for detailed directions.

Llanfihangel Din-Sylwy (114,115) (SH 58-81) *5m NNW Beaumaris*. The tiny church of St Michael nestles in a sloping churchyard beneath an Iron Age settlement, within sight of the sea. This early 15th century building was much restored in the mid-19th century, but it is still full of an atmosphere of the past and has a handsome Jacobean pulpit, hexagonal and beautifully carved. The settlement above is almost oval in shape and is encircled by an impressive drystone wall. Some know this as Bwrdd Arthur, and others as Din Sylwy, but it was certainly occupied by members of the native British tribe, the Ordovices, during the Roman period. There are fine views across Red Wharf Bay from here.

Llanfihangel-y-pennant (124) (SH 67-08) *9m NE Tywyn*. Here in the valley not far above Castlell y Bere, are a few farms and cottages and a delightful little church. This is a long low building with a pleasant old roof and an odd little medieval font. However, most visitors will go just to the north of the village to look at the ruined cottage at Tyn-y-ddôl, where Mary Jones once lived. A plaque recalls that in 1800, when Mary was only sixteen, she walked barefoot over the mountains to Bala, a distance of 28 miles, in order to obtain a bible from Methodist minister, Thomas Charles. He was so inspired by her enthusiasm for the scriptures that she started a campaign that was to lead eventually to the foundation of the British and Foreign Bible Society.

Llanfihangel-y-pennant is beautifully situated beneath the south-western flanks of Cadair Idris, and marks the southern end of the Pony Path. This runs north-east from here to join a minor road near Llyn Gwernan, at a point where our **Walk 15** begins. It is possible therefore to climb Cadair Idris from Llanfihangel, by using the Pony Path as far as Point B, on **Walk 15**, and then following the remaining directions (see page 158). It is also possible to join our **Walk 16** at this village.

Llanfihangel-y-traethau (124) (SH 59-35) *3m N Harlech*. Here is a small church (St Michael's on the Estuary) on a rocky hill that was an island until much of the land to the south of the Traeth Bach was drained. It was rebuilt in 1871, but there are splendid views from here, northwards to the mountains of the Snowdon Range and just across the water, to the white lighthouse of Portmeirion just across the water. This is a romantic place, especially in winter-time, when the saltings shelter oyster catchers, curlews, shelduck and teal, and low sunlight lights up the icy mudflats.

Best access to the shore is down a small track just to the north-east of Llanfihangel, to neighbouring Llechollwyn, but check that there is a right of way before driving down here.

Llanfrothen (124) (SH 62-41) *2m NE Penrhyndeudraeth*. Here, below wooded slopes on the very edge of the drained Glaslyn estuary, is a small medieval church, restored in the mid-19th century. There is a rugged rood screen and a wall monument to William Williams of Plâs Brondanw*, who 'first introduced Sea banks into this part of Wales'. He died in 1778, and thus pre-dated the great works of William Madocks (see Porthmadog, page 97) by many years.

*Plâs Brondanw is situated a mile to the north-west, and was the home of Clough Williams-Ellis, architect extraordinary and the creator of Portmeirion, (see page 99). Garreg, on the A4085 to the west of Llanfrothen was the estate village of Plas Brondanw, and happily still bears many signs of Clough Williams-Ellis's highly imaginative talents.

Llangadwaladr (114) (SH 38-69) *14m W Llanfair P.G.* Small village on the A4080 midway between the sands of Malltraeth and those of Aberffraw. The church of St Cadwaladr was used by the early Welsh princes, who had their court at nearby Aberffraw (see page 30), and a stone found in the courtyard, which is now built into the north wall, is believed to have been placed there in the 7th century by Cadwaladr, traditionally the last Briton to wear the crown before the Saxon invasion, in memory of his grandfather Cadfan. With a delightful lack of modesty, the inscription refers to him in Latin as 'Cadfan the wisest and most renowned of all Kings'.

The nave of the church was originally built in the 12th century, as shown by the blocked north door with its Norman archway, but the chancel and sanctuary are about two hundred years younger. The finest treasure here is the east window of pre-Reformation glass, depicting the Saint himself complete with royal sceptre and orb. The 17th century south chapel is dedicated to the Owens of Bodowen, a house which is now a ruin overlooking the Cefni estuary. The north chapel, which was rebuilt in 1801, belongs to the Meyrick family of Bodorgan. The house, of the same date as the chapel, is well hidden in woods except for a distant view across the broad Malltraeth Sands from the Newborough Forest shore (see page 91).

There are two paths north from the A4080, passing respectively to the east and west of delightful little Lyn Coron. Use Landranger Sheet 114 to plan a modest circular walk here.

Llangaffo (114,115) (SH 44-68) *7m SW Llanfair P.G.* An unexceptional village situated astride the straight B4421 and B4419, just above and to the east of Malltraeth Marsh. The spire of the village church, rebuilt in 1847, is a landmark for miles around. The contents of this 19th century building include a handsome brass chandelier and a 12th century font and the medieval doorway from the old church has been used as a gateway to the churchyard.

Llangeinwen Church (114) (SH 43-65) *See Dwyran, page 61.*

Llangefni (114,115) (SH 46-75) *6m NW Menai Bridge.* The Afon Cefni, on which this town stands, was once navigable at least as far as its quay. However this has long since gone, and Llangefni also ceased to be on the main road to Ireland when Telford built his new road about two miles to the south. However it remains the administrative capital of Anglesey, the island's principal market town, and a busy shopping centre. The cattle market moved from the town centre some years ago and is now held in the 'new' cattle mart. The Square, near the Bull Hotel, is however still the site of a bustling market every Thursday with colourful stalls offering a wide variety of merchandise. The town also has its own theatre — the Theatr Fach, and a sports and leisure centre — the Plas Arthur.

The parish church of St Cyngar was rebuilt in 1824 and had a new chancel added in 1898. It is well sheltered by trees beside a car park at the foot of The Dingle, a beautiful wooded valley which comes very close to the centre of the town. There is a footpath here which follows the banks of the sparkling Afon Cefni for a mile or more, and a single track railway which shares the valley for most of the way but does not spoil its peace and beauty.

Llangelynin New Church, near Conwy (115) (SH 77-73) *3m S Conwy.* This was built in 1840 and has an unusual octagonal tower, and an unspoilt interior which contains a handsome 18th century marble font. See below for the 'Old Church'.

Llangelynin Old Church, near Conwy (115) (SH 751-737) *3m SW Conwy.* This simple little medieval building is in a remote setting in the hills, and can only be reached up a narrow lane. Ask for the key at nearby Garnedd-wen Farm. The interior is delightfully unspoilt and provides a wonderful example of what so many churches must have been like in Wales before the Victorian enthusiasts got to work. The chancel has a timbered barrel-vault, and the north transept still has its earth floor. There is a 17th century communion table and altar rails, and the walls are decorated with texts in Welsh. In a corner of the churchyard will be found Ffynnon Gelynnin, a well once famed for the curing of sick children.

Llangelynnin Church, nr Tywyn (124) (SH 57-07) *7m N Tywyn.* Attractive little stone building lying just below the A493 road, and not far from the shingly sea shore. It has a small porch complete with a minute bell-cote, and a delightfully unspoilt interior with a medieval roof and early 19th century benches with the names of their original occupants still painted upon them. Some of these are labelled 'Gent', some 'Esquire' and some neither — indicating thereby the strict divisions of class that existed in the 19th century, even in a place as remote as this. There is also a Jacobean pulpit and an unusual wheel-less horse-bier with shafts at both ends, once used on the mountainous tracks in the neighbourhood. A similar specimen will be found in the church at Llangower, near Bala (see page 78). There is a halt on the Cambrian Coast Railway close to the church, but possibilities for walking from here are limited.

Llangian (123) (SH 29-28) *1m W Abersoch.* Tidy stone-built village, with trim cottages and colourful gardens overlooking a stream which eventually joins the sea at Abersoch. The simple church, dating from the 13th and 15th centuries, with some modern addition, has a particular treasure in the churchyard. This is a rough stone pillar with a Latin inscription declaring that the remains of 'Melius the doctor, son of Martinus, lie here'. This stone dates from the 5th or 6th century AD, and is the only record in Britain of an early Christian burial which mentions the profession of the deceased.

Llangoed (114,115) (SH 60-79) *2m N Beaumaris.* This large parish covers the whole eastern tip of Anglesey (see also Penmon Priory, page 93, and Puffin Island, page 99). The village straddles the closing stretch of the B5109 and at its northern end there is a small stream, the Afon Lleiniog, which flows eastwards from there to a shingle beach. There is a path part of the way to the beach beside the stream, from where it is possible to look north across it to a castle motte or mound. This was Castell Aberlleiniog, originally built in about 1090 by Hugh of Avranches, Earl of Chester, better known as Hugh the Wolf. He and his friend Hugh the Proud, Earl of Shrewsbury, were notorious for their barbarous treatment of the Welsh, but with some justice, he was later killed — like King Harold at Hastings — by an arrow in the eye, when this castle was attacked by Magnus, King of Norway. The stone bailey, the ruins of which are still visible, are of much later date, and this was held by Parliamentarian troops during the Civil War.

Llangoed's church of St Cawdraf was over-restored in the 19th century, but its contents include a handsome hexagonal pulpit and a fine candelabra.

Llangower (125) (SH 90-32) *3m SW Bala.* Hamlet on the south-eastern shore of Llyn Tegid (Bala Lake). There is a car park here and a halt on the Bala Lake Railway, together with a jetty, and lakeside picnic site. See also Bala Lake, page 34. In the lakeside church will be found a bier which was once carried by a horse at each end, recalling the days when many of the mountain tracks were too rough for wheeled vehicles. There is a similar specimen in Llangelynnin church near Tywyn (see page 109). The car park here makes a good base for walks south-eastward up the wooded valley of the little Afon Glyn, and there is an attractive road running up part of this valley as far as a ford with some stepping stones (SH 91-30).

Llangristiolus (114,115) (SH 43-73) *7m W Llanfair P.G.* A scattered agricultural parish to the immediate west of Malltraeth Marsh. The church stands well to the east of the village (SH 45-73) on a low hill overlooking the busy A5's crossing of the marsh, with a view of Llangaffo church spire on a ridge about three miles to the south. Much restored in the mid-19th century, Llangristiolus church has a fine 12th century font with strapwork and rope patterns and a 13th century chancel arch.

Llangwnnadl (123) (SH 20-33) *14m W Pwllheli.* Yet another scattered parish, this one being just behind the north coast of the Lleyn Peninsula. The church of St Gwynhoydl stands almost alone in an attractive sheltered valley running seawards. This unusual three-aisled building is still active and very well cared for. Spacious and airy, it was built in the 15th and 16th centuries on the site of a 6th century church. The sanctuary bell is a reproduction of an original 16th century bell, now in the National Museum in Cardiff. In the south wall there is a 6th century stone with an inscribed Celtic cross, said to be the headstone of St Gwynhoydl's grave. Do not miss the octagonal 16th century font.

Llangwyllog Church (114,115) (SH 43-79) *3m NW Llangefni.* This is claimed to stand at the very centre of Anglesey and is to be found down a farm track to the west of the B5111, Llangefni to Llanerchymedd road. It is in an attractive setting beside a small stream. A largely 15th century building, it was restored with surprising sympathy in 1854, and most of the 18th century woodwork, including a

combined pulpit and reading desk, have survived intact.

Llangybi (123) (SH 42-41) *6m NE Pwllheli.* Small village below a wooded hill topped by the fragmentary remains of a hill fort — Carn Bentyrch. The simple church of St Cybi occupies the site of one founded by this 6th century Cornish saint and healer of the sick. A path leads through the churchyard and over the field beyond to Fynnon Gybi (St Cybi's Well), well-known for its curative powers over the course of many centuries. Now a roofless stone structure attached to the ruins of a later cottage, this well was turned into an 18th century spa by local squire, William Price of Rhiwlas, and this appears to be the reason for the ruined buildings that remain today. The nearby almshouses were also built by Price, in 1760. There are pleasant walks around here, notably northwards to the coast and westwards to Llyn Glasfryn, but be sure to keep to the rights of way shown on Landranger Sheet 123.

Llanidan (114,115) (SH 49-66) *4m SW Llanfair P.G.* Situated between the village of Brynsiencyn (see page 43) and the Menai shoreline, the secluded, partly ruined 'old church' dates largely from the 14th century. There was an Augustinian settlement here in medieval times, but after the Dissolution it became the parish church. Most of it was demolished in 1844 to provide materials for the 'new church' which is on the A4080 at the entrance to Brynsiencyn. This has an unusually proportioned tower, with its top looking rather too large for its base, and a bright and cheerful interior, the contents of which include the 13th century font from the old church.

Llaniestyn Church, near Llanddona (114,115) (SH 585-796) *3m NW Beaumaris.* It would be easy to miss this fine 14th century church lying beyond open heathland well to the east of Llanddona. An impressive open porch leads through a doorway dated 1510, to a simple whitewashed interior. A massive beam supports the entrance to a 15th century south chapel which has a splendidly vigorous statue of St Iestyn carved in low relief, possibly the work of the same craftsman who created the monument to St Pabo in Llanbabo church (see page 68).

Llaniestyn, near Pwllheli (123) (SH 26-33) *10m W Pwllheli.* This peaceful village is situated in a wooded valley at the foot of Carn Fadryn (see page 47), and has a double-aisled medieval church which is distinguished by a pleasant musicians' gallery. It also has a good 16th century font and a number of attractive monuments including one elegant 18th century example in memory of a fellow of Jesus College, Oxford, a college noted for its Welsh connections.

Llanllechid (115) (SH 62-68) *4m SE Bangor.* An unexceptional village amongst the remains of slate quarries with fine views southwards to the mountains of the Snowdon Range. It has a solid granite neo-Norman church which is mainly of interest to those searching for 19th century architectural eccentricities.

Llanllyfni (115,123) (SH 47-51) *7m S Caernarfon.*
An unexceptional quarrying village astride the
A487, with several chapels including one, the Capel
Ebenezer, which has an unspoilt early 19th century
interior complete with box pews. To the north-east
of the village the earthworks of a defended Iron Age
settlement, Caer Engan, overlook the swift-flowing
Afon Llyfni.

Llannor (123) (SH 35-37) *2m NW Pwhelli.* This is a
rather dull village with some ugly council housing.
The medieval church has a stout tower with
stepped gables, and in the porch will be found a late
Roman tombstone. The interior was heavily restored in the 19th century, and is not of great interest
to visitors. Well to the west, and just off the A497,
is Bodvel Hall, the house where Dr Johnson's
friend, the beautiful Mrs Hester Thrale, was born in
1741. A range of farm buildings now contains a
thriving Craft Centre *(tel: 0758 613386)*, and there is
also a caravan park here.

Llanrhychwyn Church (115) (SH 775-616) *5m
NNW Betws-y-Coed.* Known traditionally as 'Llywelyn's Old Church', this may be reached up a steep
lane from Trefriw, which is on B5106 in the Conwy
Valley, but for details see our **Tour 3**, page 114. It is
approached through a little yew-shaded lych-gate
dated 1762, and has a beautifully unspoilt whitewashed interior. There is a floor of slate slabs and
the roof timbering is of oak, similar to that found in
another unspoilt church, Llangelynin, a few miles to
the north (see page 77). There is also a Jacobean
pulpit and reading desk and fragments of 15th
century glass.

Llanrhyddlad (114) (SH 33-89) *4m SW Cemaes.*
An unexceptional village just off the A5025, with a
sharp-spired church, nearly two miles to the west,
overlooking Porth Swtan (Church Bay) (see **Walk
2**, page 132). This was rebuilt in 1858 and is not of
great interest to visitors. At Craig y Gwynt, a mile to
the north-west of the village, there are the remains
of a telegraph station, Cefn du Telegraph, established here in 1841 by the Trustees of Liverpool
Docks. The telegraph system was first set up in
1810, and was used to carry news of shipping to the
ship-owners and merchants of Liverpool. This was
especially important in the days of the tea and grain
races, and it is said that during trials a signal was
once transmitted to Liverpool from Holyhead
Mountain, the most westerly station in the chain,
via Craig y Gwynt, Mynydd Eilian, Puffin Island,
Great Orme and Hilbre Island, in only a minute.
However, a time of between five and six minutes
was usually regarded as acceptable.

Llanrhwydrys Church (114) (SH 32-93) *4m W
Cemaes.* This is near Tyn Llan Farm just behind the
coast, between the cove of Hen Borth and broader
Cemlyn Bay, where there is a car park (see page
48). It is best visited during a walk along the coast
between these features (use Landranger Sheet 114
or Pathfinder Sheet SH 29/39/49). At the entrance
to the churchyard there is an archway with mounting block close by, and the simple little building
beyond has an unspoilt and well-lit interior complete
with small 18th century gallery.

Llanrug (114,115) (SH 53-63) *4m E Caernarfon.* A
largely 19th century village built for quarry workers,
with a church perched on a small hill within an
attractive churchyard. This was restored in 1856,
but the fine 15th century roof has been left
undisturbed. Less than two miles to the north-east,
there are the earthworks of an Iron Age settlement,
Dinas Dinorwig, on a hill partly covered by trees
(SH 549-653). For Bryn Bras Castle see page 42.

Llanrwst (115, 116) (SH 79-62) Pleasant, bustling
little market town in the wooded valley of the
sparkling Afon Conwy, crossed here by the **Pont
Fawr (1)**, a fine three-arched bridge built in 1636,
and just possibly designed by the great architect
Inigo Jones, whose father may have come originally
from Denbighshire. At the western end of the
bridge is **Tu-hwnt-i'r- bont (2)**, an attractive 15th
century stone building once used as a courthouse,

1 The Pont Fawr
2 Tu hwnt i'r bont
3 Gwydir Park
4 Plas Isaf (off map to north)
5 Parish Church
6 Encounter! (off plan to east)
7 Gwydir Castle
8 Gwydyr Uchaf Chapel

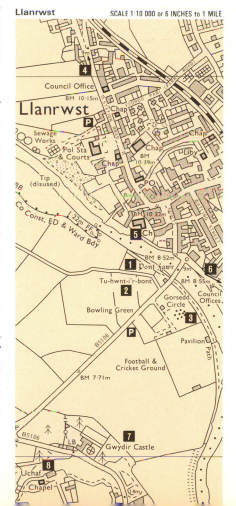

Llanrwst   SCALE 1:10 000 or 6 INCHES to 1 MILE

but later divided into two cottages. It is owned by the National Trust, but is let as a tea-room and shop. The town has lively shops, inns and hotels, and *Gwydir Park (3)* has greens for bowling and putting and a children's playground.

Near the station, are the remains of *Plas Isaf (4)*, the home of William Salisbury (*c.*1520-1599), the first translator of the New Testament into Welsh, and the compiler of the first *Dictionary in Englyshe and Welshe.* The *Parish Church (5)* was largely rebuilt in the 1880s, but its splendid rood-screen and loft, which was probably the work of the same craftsman or craftsmen who made the fine screen at Conwy, make a visit here well worthwhile. Do not miss the adjoining 17th century Gwydir Chapel (key from the verger), the contents of which include contemporary furnishings, a huge stone coffin, which probably came from Maenan Abbey (see page 52), and which was once thought to be that of Llwelyn the Great, but which is too late in date to have been his; also a handsome stone effigy of a knight and a fine series of 17th century monumental brasses.

In School Bank Road, to the east of the town, will be found *Encounter! The North Wales Museum of Wildlife (6)*, an interesting collection of natural history specimens in an old house. Visitors may wander in its grounds, meet pets, feed the ducks, and go on a nature trail. There are also refreshments and a gift shop. At the time of printing, Encounter! was temporarily closed. Enquire locally for opening details, or *tel: 0492 640664.*

Beyond the bridge, to the west of the town, is *Gwydir Castle (7)* (see page 64), and *Gwydyr Uchaf Chapel (8)* (see page 65), neither of which should be missed. The most rewarding walks from Llanrwst are westwards, and they are best started from this area.

Llansadwrn (114,115) (SH 55-75) *3m N Menai Bridge.* An unexceptional village with a heavily Victorianised church, well away from its centre. In the chancel will be found a 6th century stone inscribed in Latin 'to Saturnius and his saintly wife', while in the churchyard there is the grave of geologist A. C. Ramsay, with a fitting headstone — a glacial erratic — this being a stone which has been carried far out of its normal geological setting by glacial action. It is possible to walk north-west from here, up through the forest covering Mynydd Llwydiarth, and down to the shore of Red Wharf Bay.

Llantrisant (114) (SH 36-83) *9m E Holyhead.* Hamlet in unexciting country south of Llyn Alaw. The new church at its centre is not of great interest to visitors, but the old church, left untouched by the Victorians, could be worth finding. It lies down a farm road, at Ty-mawr well to the north-west of the hamlet (SH 34-84), and is a late 14th century building with a 17th century south chapel. Some years ago it was heading for complete decay, but when last visited its roof had been repaired and there seemed some hope that it would one day be fully restored. About a mile to the north of the new church, on the bank of the little Afon Alaw there is a burial mound, Bedd Branwen (SH 361-850), the legendary grave of the beautiful Queen Branwen. This lady was the daughter of Llyr, one of the great figures of the collection of Welsh folk tales from the Dark Ages, known as *The Mabinogion.*

Llanuwchllyn (124,125) (SH 87-30) *5m SW Bala.* A largely 19th century village just beyond the head of Llyn Tegid (Bala Lake), and the south-western terminus of the little Bala Lake Railway (see page 36). It lies between the Afon Twrch and the Afon Dyfrwy (River Dee), both of which then flow beyond into Llyn Tegid. There is an attractive statue of Sir O. M. Edwards and his son I. O. Edwards, both champions of the Welsh language and advocates for the teaching of Welsh in schools. Llanuwchllyn was also the birthplace of Michael Jones, the great Welsh Nationalist, and one of the leading initiators of the Welsh colonisation of Patagonia. The descendants of these settlers are still to be found in Patagonia, but have been increasingly absorbed into the life of Argentina.

The Old School House and the decorated, cast-iron village pump in front of it, both add a touch of character to an otherwise rather unexciting village. However there are two fine mountain roads starting from here, one southwards up to Bwlch y Groes (see page 43), and one westwards up the valley of the Afon Lliw (see page 31) and over to Trawsfynnyd.

Llanwenllwyfo Church (See Dulas, page 61.)

Llanwnda (115,123) (SH 47-58) *3m S Caernarfon.* An unexceptional village at the junction of the A487 and A499, with a neo-Norman church, the contents of which include a bucolic 17th century monument and a rather more sophisticated 18th century specimen.

Llanymawddwy (125) (SH 90-19) *5m NE Dinas Mawddwy.* An unusually pretty village sheltering in the upper Dyfi (Dovey) valley with colourful gardens, an attractive little bow-fronted shop, and a small church. This is approached beneath a neat lychgate, and contains within, a medieval font — the scalloped edges of which give it the appearance of an inverted acorn. Ask in the village for the best directions for Pistyll Gwyn (The White Waterfall), which lies about a mile and a half to the west (the path to it is shown on Landranger Sheet 125). Walk or drive north from Llanymawddwy to the splendid mountain pass of Bwlch y Groes (see page 43).

Llanystumdwy (123) (SH 47-38) *2m W Criccieth.* Its name means 'the church at the bend of the Dwy river', and the Afon Dwyfor is crossed by a narrow stone bridge in its centre. Llanystumdwy is best known for its associations with David Lloyd George, 1st Earl of Dwyfor, who spent his childhood with his widowed mother in a cottage opposite the Feathers Inn. His uncle, the village shoemaker, had his workshop next door. David Lloyd George became a solicitor and first practised in Manchester and then went into partnership with his brother in Porthmadog. He was first elected to Parliament as the Member for Caernarfon Boroughs in 1890, and retained this seat until he became an earl a few months before his death in 1945. For many years his home was a house called 'Brynawelon' at Criccieth, but his last home and his simple grave beside the river are both at Llanystumdwy.

Before looking round the village, call first at the Lloyd George Memorial Museum to learn more of the life and times of this great politician, and also to obtain a copy of the leaflet describing the Llanystumdwy Village Walk. This will take visitors past all the features of interest in the village, most of which are connected with Lloyd George. The memorial, an attractive circular composition in dark grey stone, and the entrance gates to the Museum opposite, were both designed by Clough Williams-Ellis, who had built the nearby Capel Moriah in the 1930s and who had also renovated Ty Newydd, Lloyd-George's last home, and the Bailiff's Cottage in its grounds. All these buildings bear the unmistakable stamp of this quite exceptional architect, who is perhaps best known for the creation of his Italianate village of Portmeirion (see page 99). The woods in which the memorial stands slope steeply down to the Dwyfor, crossed here by the fine four-arched Bont Fechan; and a footpath beside the river makes a beautiful walk which can be extended north-eastwards for a considerable distance, and which is known as the Llwybr Coed Trefan Walk.

There is a car park and picnic site on the edge of Cabin Wood, well to the west of the village, and a forest walk leading from it. At Rhoslan, less than two miles to the north-east there is a burial chamber situated just to the east of the B4411 (SH 483-409).

Llechwedd Slate Caverns (115) (SH 70-47) *1m N Blaenau Ffestiniog, to E of A470.* Llechwedd is the biggest working slate mine in Wales, but much of it is open to the public and there is a choice of two exciting rides into the spectacular caverns. The

Llanystumdwy   SCALE 1:25 000 or 2½ INCHES to 1 MILE

Miner's Tramway (the first ride) runs underground into 19th century slate mine workings where the original conditions have been recreated, and on returning to the surface, the mill with its ancient machinery and adjacent exhibition completes the story of the slate industry in Wales. In 1979 one of the old inclines was also opened to the public, giving access to the Deep Mine (the second ride), which contains further underground vistas and tableaux. The circular tour leads down even further until the Incline Railway is eventually joined for the return to the surface. There is also a Slate Heritage Theatre giving an audio-visual presentation, a Tramway Exhibition, a 'Harpist's Cottage', a Victorian-style pub, the Miners' Arms, and craft and gift shops. Sturdy shoes and moderately warm clothing are recommended. *(Tel: 0766 830306.)*

Lligwy (See Din Lligwy, page 58.)

Llithfaen (123) (SH 35-43) *6m N Pwllheli.* Small village on the southern slopes of Yr Eifl with no special features. Our **Walk 10**, page 148, starts from a point not far north of here. Beyond this there is a track leading to 'Vortigern's Valley'. Vortigern was the 'Great Prince' of the 5th century who summoned Hengist and Horsa to his aid, and who is supposed to have died here. Do not attempt to drive too far along here, and after ensuring that a right of way exists, visitors may wish to take the footpath through the plantation on to the high slopes overlooking the sea and a long shingle beach with the remains of an abandoned pier. Behind this beach, which is called Porth y Nant, stand the deserted ruins of quarrymen's cottages. This strange and romantic place can be reached on foot from the car park. Prominent across the valley is the sheer rock face of Craig Ddu (The Black Crag), from which rise the steep slopes of Yr Eifl, scarred with disused quarries.

Llwyngwril (124) (SH 59-09) *3m SW Fairbourne.* Tidy village astride the A493, with a small bridge over the Afon Gwril, emerging here from the mountains on its short journey to the sea. There is a useful halt on the Cambrian Coast Railway here. Access to the beach where there is sand at low tide is by a path beside an old Quaker burial ground to the north of the village. The church was built in 1843 — a pleasant little building — but not of great interest to visitors. There are the earthworks of a small Iron Age settlement, Castell y Gaer, on a hill to the south of the village, and standing stones in the hills to the north-east.

Llyn Alaw (114) (SH 38-86 etc.) *5m SW Amlwch.* This reservoir, nearly three miles long and half a mile wide, has been formed by the flooding of an area of marsh and farmland previously drained by the Afon Alaw. There is a Visitors' Centre, car park and picnic place at Bod Deiniol (SH 37-85), a subsidiary car park a short distance eastwards, beyond the dam, and a further car park and picnic place, with access to a bird hide, at Gwredog (SH 40-86) north of Llanerchymedd. The Visitors' Centre has an exhibition covering the reservoir's history and function, and it is possible to walk from here round to Drofa Point (SH 381-860). Unlike lakes and reservoirs in mountain areas, this reservoir is relatively shallow, and this fact coupled with the

Llyn Alaw

SCALE 1:50 000 or 1¼ INCHES to 1 MILE

rich inflow of nutrients has resulted in it becoming not only one of Wales' most productive brown and rainbow trout fisheries, but also an important site for wildfowl and waders. Fishing permits are obtainable from a coin-operated dispenser at the Visitors' Centre.

Llyn Celyn (124, 125) (SH 85-40 etc.) *4m NW Bala.* This most attractive sheet of water is a 'holding reservoir' established by Liverpool Corporation in the 1960s. Its impressive, grass-covered dam across the Afon Tryweryn controls this river's flow into the River Dee, which it joins just below Llyn Tegid (Lake Bala). There are no fewer than six car parks around its north and east shores, and the little granite Capel Celyn (SH 84-41) has replaced a chapel that lies buried beneath its waters. A large rough-hewn boulder further eastwards, closer to the dam (SH 87-40), touchingly recalls that Quakers met at a farmstead here in the 17th and 18th centuries, and that it was from this now-drowned valley that many of the early Quakers emigrated to Pennsylvania, to seek freedom in the New World. (See **Tour 8**, page 124, and **Walk 12**, page 152.)

Llyn Conwy (115) (SH 78-46) *5m NE Ffestiniog.* Source of the lovely River Conwy, this remote lake is set high in the treeless expanse of the Migneint. See **Tour 4**, page 116.

Llyn Cowlyd (115) (SH 72-62) *10m SSW Conwy.* Deep, dark reservoir lake in the south-eastern fringes of the Carneddau Range. It is the deepest lake in the whole of North Wales, and has steep mountain slopes on both of its long sides, a Snowdonian version of Wastwater, but gloomier. Study the configuration of streams on Landranger Sheet 115, near SH 712-609, for an apparent watershed mystery. This is caused by the (correct) marking of a contoured leat from Ffynnon Llugwy feeding into Llyn Cowlyd.

Llyn Crafnant (115) (SH 74-60) *4m NW Betws-y-Coed.* This lake is situated between the Carneddau Range and the dense woodlands of Gwydyr Forest, and is believed to contain some of the largest trout in Snowdonia. It has a monument at its northern end, like its near neighbour, Llyn Geirionydd. There is a good car park near this northern end, about two miles from Trefriw which is on the B5106, Conwy to Betws-y-Coed road. Its western shore is part of our **Walk 4**, page 136.

Llynnau Cregennen (124) (SH 66-14) *6m SW Dolgellau.* These two lakes (hence 'Llynnau' rather than 'Llyn') together with a large area of mountain plateau between Arthog and Cadair Idris, were given to the National Trust by Major C. L. Wynne-Jones in memory of his two sons, sadly both killed in the 39-45 War. The Trust has provided a good car park overlooking the lakes, and it makes an excellent base for exploring this delightful area, with its fine views of the northern flanks of Cadair Idris.

Llyn Cwellyn (115) (SH 56-54) *7m SE Caernarfon.* An impressive lake with the rock face of Mynydd

Llyn Celyn

SCALE 1:50 000 or 1¼ INCHES to 1 MILE

Mawr falling sheer into the water at the northern end, below the crags of Craig Cwmbychan. Forest plantations clad the western slopes further to the south, but even these do not detract from the grandeur of the scene. There is a good lakeside car park on the A4085 near the Snowdon Ranger Hostel (SH 56-55). Water is abstracted from here for Caernarfon's needs, but the works have been sensitively designed, and do little to offend the eye.

Llyn Cwm Bychan (See Cwm Bychan, page 54.)

Llyn Cwmdulyn (115,123) (SH 49-49) *9m S Caernarfon.* This small reservoir at the end of a rough track beyond the village of Nebo, nestles at the foot of a sheer rock face — Craig Cwmdulyn. The peak to the east, immediately behind the lake, is Garnedd-goch.

Llyn Cwmystradllyn (124) (SH 56-44) *6m N Porthmadog.* A dark reservoir sheltering in a remote setting beneath the southern slopes of Moel Hebog. There are several ruined slate mills in this quiet but rather gloomy place.

Llyn Dinas (115) (SH 61-49) *2m NE Beddgelert.* This is the smaller of the two lakes in lovely Nantgwynant (see page 90), and although it is skirted on the north side by the A498, there is a delightful path beyond its southern shore. There are fine views south-westwards to the great mass of Moel Hebog. Our **Walk 9**, page 146, has a brief encounter with the lake at its south-western end.

Llyn-y-dywarchen (115) (SH 56-53) *4m N Beddgelert.* This small lake to the immediate west of Rhyd-Ddu was noted for many centuries for its floating island. First noted by Giraldus Cambrensis in 1188, it was even visited in 1698 by the astronomer Edmond Halley, who, at the age of 42, was curious enough to swim out to it. By the time that the author of *Tour in Wales*, Thomas Pennant, came this way in the 1770s the floating island was only nine yards in length and it has now long since disappeared, the existing islet being firmly rocky, and rather unexciting.

Llyn Elsi (115) (SH 78-55) *1m SW Betws-y-Coed.* A most attractive lake in the deeply afforested hills south-west of Betws-y-Coed, complete with minute island on which gulls nest, and a monument to Lord Ancaster. This lake is included in the Gwydyr Forest Walk 1, which starts from St Mary's Church, Betws-y-Coed, and which is described in a leaflet available from the Stables Information Centre (see Betws-y-Coed, page 40).

Llyn Geirionydd (115) (SH 76-60) *4m NW Betws-y-Coed.* Its mountain flanks are densely forested, and like Llyn Crafnant, it has a monument at its northern end. This one is in honour of the great early Welsh poet, Taliesin, famous for his *Book of Taliesin*. Our **Walk 4**, page 136, starts from the pleasant car park and picnic site on its eastern shore, and in its final stages returns down the quiet west shore. There is also a short Forest Trail starting from this car park.

Llyn Glaslyn (See **Walk 7**, page 142.)

Llyn Gwernan (124) (SH 70-16) *2m SW Dolgellau.* Small mountain lake partly hidden from the road by trees, and overlooked by the pleasant Gwernan Lake Hotel. The Fox's Path up Cadair Idris starts from here, but it is dangerous, and not recommended.

Llyn Gwynant (115) (SH 64-51) *4m NE Beddgelert.* This must be one of the loveliest lakes in all Snowdonia. If possible walk up the west side of the valley known as Nantgwynant, and then around the northern end of the lake, for some of the area's finest views, with Moel Hebog providing a dramatic backdrop at the south-western end of the valley.

Llyn Hywel (124) (SH 66-26) *8m SE Harlech.* Small lake deep-set below the southern crags of Rhinog Fach, with smooth rocky glacial slabs dropping almost sheer into the water. Giraldus Cambrensis who visited this area in 1188, stated that monocular fish lived in the dark waters of this lake, but sadly this fascinating claim has never been substantiated by later visitors.

Llyn Idwal (See Cwm Idwal, page 56)

Llyn Llydlaw (See **Walk 7**, page 142.)

Llyn Morwynion (124) (SH 73-42) *2m E Ffestiniog.* There are at least two legends providing the reason for its name, 'The Lake of the Maidens'; and they both tell of a group of maidens in distress who chose drowning in the lake in preference to a life of dishonour. Situated on the western fringes of the Migneint, it provides a pleasant excuse for a walk northwards from the B4391.

Llynnau Mymbyr (115) (SH 70-57) *1m SW Capel Curig.* There is a good car park on the A4086 overlooking this long lake which is in a fine mountain setting in the Nantygwryd valley. A short distance to the west, beyond the north side of the A4086 and beneath the slopes of Gallt yr Ogof, the easternmost peak of the Glyders (see page 64), is Dyffryn Mymbyr (SH 69-57). This farm was purchased by Thomas Firbank, who subsequently immortalised it in his fine book, *I Bought a Mountain*, first published in 1940.

Llyn Nantlle Uchaf (115) (SH 51-53) *4m W Rhyd-Ddu.* There is a pleasant path along the southern shore of this lake, beneath steep mountainsides sweeping up to the Nantlle Ridge. From the western end of the lake, at the point where the B4418 crosses its outfall, there are splendid views up the Nantlle Valley to Snowdon, and it was from this point that the artist Richard Wilson painted the well-known picture that now hangs in the Walker Art Gallery in Liverpool.

Llyn Ogwen (115) (SH 66-60) *10m W Betws-y-Coed.* Dramatically set in the heart of Snowdonia, Llyn Ogwen lies just beyond the head of the rugged Nant Ffrancon Pass. It is unusually shallow by Snowdonian standards and is in fact slowly silting

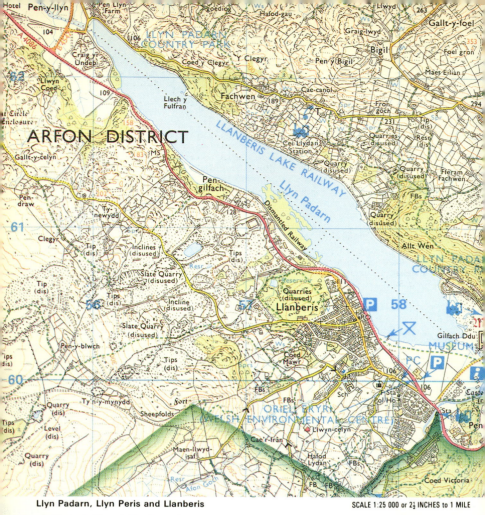

Llyn Padarn, Llyn Peris and Llanberis

SCALE 1:25 000 or 2½ INCHES to 1 MILE

up. The main A5 road skirts its southern shore and it is therefore best viewed from the path along the north side, as from here the great mass of Tryfan appears to plunge straight down into the lake. In bad weather when the mists come down, Llyn Ogwen is a wild and eerie place, a fit setting for the legend of Sir Bedivere, last of Arthur's knights, casting Excalibur into the water, only to see a pale arm 'clothed in white samite, mystic, wonderful'

Llyn Ogwen — a lake set in the very heart of Snowdonia.

rise out to grasp this magic sword. Many legendary settings have been claimed for this dramatic scene, but surely none of them could be as satisfyingly atmospheric as Llyn Ogwen.

Llyn Padarn (114,115) (SH 57-61) *5m E Caernarfon.* This is the largest and one of the most attractive of Snowdonia's lakes, but for details see Llanberis, page 69.

Llyn Peris (115) (SH 59-59) *8m E Caernarfon.* Situated to the immediate south-east of Llanberis, and only separated from Llyn Padarn by a narrow piece of land, it is best viewed from Dolbadarn Castle (see page 59), or from the car park on the A4086 at its head near Nant Peris. This lake acts as the lower reservoir of the Dinorwic Pumped Storage Power Station (see page 58), but great care has been taken to disturb it as little as possible, and its level has only been raised by two metres rather than the originally proposed nine metres. Slate workings on the mountain slopes above the lake have in the past created far greater disturbances, but this is still a lake of very considerable beauty. Salmon and trout pass through to the rivers upstream to spawn, and measures have been taken to ensure that this process is not interrupted.

Llyn Tecwyn Isaf and Llyn Tecwyn Uchaf (124) (SH 62-37 & 63- 38) *6m NE Harlech.* Two attractive lakes in the hills above the estuary of the Afon Dwyryd. Llyn Tecwyn Isaf, the small lake, is beautifully reed-bordered, in a bowl of wooded hills, while the larger lake, well to the north-east, beyond Llandecwyn church (see page 70) is in a more rugged mountain setting. It is possible to walk eastwards from here over the mountains to Llyn Trawsfynydd, to link with our **Walk 11**, page 150, and part of this journey may be accomplished on a road which ends below little Llyn Llenyrch (SH 65-37).

Llyn Tegid (See Bala Lake, page 34.)

Llyn Trawsfynydd (124) (SH 69-36) *4m S Ffestiniog.* This great artificial lake was first formed in 1928 to work the small hydro-electric station at Ivy Bridge, near Maentwrog, but it was greatly enlarged in the early 1960s to meet the needs of the Nuclear Power Station (see page 107). While great

care has been taken to minimise the impact of this great undertaking, it is bound to detract from the elemental nature of its wild mountain surroundings. The Power Station uses no less than thirty-five million gallons of water every hour for cooling purposes, and with this amount of warm water recirculating in the lake it is not surprising that the fishing here is excellent. Permits for this may be obtained from the newsagent's shop in Trawsfynydd village. There are car parks near the Power Station itself (SH 69-38), on the east shore, off the A470 (SH 70-37), and near the footbridge at the southern end (SH 70-34), which is reached by a minor road running westwards from the A470, just to the south of Trawsfynydd village. See also **Walk 11**, page 150.

Machynlleth (135) (SH 74-00) Attractive market town in the Dyfi valley, with its main streets meeting T-fashion at a splendidly ornate Victorian **Clock Tower (1)**. This was built in 1873 to commemorate the family of the Marquess of Londonderry, who then owned Plas Machynlleth (see below). Close by the clock tower is the hospitable Wynnstay Hotel, one of a series of unusually pleasant 18th and early 19th century buildings in the wide street called Maen Gwyn, which runs eastwards from the clock tower. George Borrow stayed at the Wynnstay Hotel during the great journey of 1854 recorded in his classic travel book *Wild Wales*, although it was then known as the Wynstay Arms. He was waited on by a 'brisk, buxom maid who told me that her name was Mary Evans', and on being asked if there were any books in the house, she lent him her own volume of Welsh poetry. During his stay he attended the trial of a poacher in the court being held in the town hall, or market cross, a building later to be swept away to make room for the clock tower. Borrow does tend to ramble on at times, but the account of his journeys in *Wild Wales*, is well worth reading by visitors to towns and villages like Machynlleth.

Further along the Maen Gwyn stands the **Owain Glyndwr Centre (2)**, which incorporates the remains of a building that housed Wales' first and only Parliament, established here in 1404 by the Welsh hero Glyndwr in the first heady months after his victories over the English, a triumph that was to prove to be short-lived. Here also will be found the town's **Tourist Information Centre (2)** *(tel: 0654 2401)*. Opposite the Centre are the handsome wrought-iron gates of **Plas Machynlleth (3)**, a fine 17th century house in an extensive park, given to the town by the Marquess of Londonderry just before the Second World War. The Plas houses the town's offices and the nearby grounds provide a **Public Park (4)** with tennis courts and a children's playground. There is also a bowling green near the Institute and a 9-hole golf course a short distance along the A489 road towards Newtown.

Machynlleth — town of Owain Glyndwr.

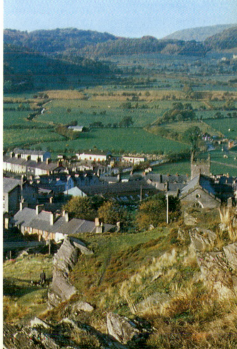

Machynlleth

SCALE 1:10 000 or 6 INCHES to 1 MILE

1 Clock Tower   2 Owain Glyndwr Centre & Tourist Information Centre   3 Plas Machynlleth   4 Park

Maentwrog (124) (SH 66-40) *7m E Porthmadog.*
Set in the beautiful Vale of Ffestiniog, this village
was built in the early 19th century by slate magnate
William Oakley, who lived at Plâs Tan-y-Bwlch (see
page 95) across the valley, and there is a lingering
'Romantic' flavour about the terraces of slate
cottages beneath wooded hillsides. The church,
with its little slate-covered spire was entirely rebuilt
in late-Victorian times and has a severe but
immaculate interior. In the yew-shaded churchyard
will be found a large stone — Maen Twrog (The
Stone of Twrog) — from which the village takes its
name. Legend has it that a giant with the splendid
name of Twrog, and a friend of St Beuno of
Clynnog-fawr, threw this stone down from the hills
above. Like the memorial stone in Llansadwrn
churchyard (see page 80) this stone is in fact a
glacial erratic, brought here by glacial action rather
than by the exertions of a giant.

The Hydro-Electric Power Station at Ivy Bridge
(SH 65-39), on the A496 about a mile to the south-
west of Maentwrog was opened in 1928, and was
the original reason for the creation of Llyn Trawsfynydd (see page 85). This was the third such station
to open in North Wales, the first two being Cwm
Dyli and Dolgarrog. The station is not open to the
public, but details of its construction and operation
can be obtained from the Central Electricity Gener-

Maentwrog, in the beautiful Vale of Ffestiniog.

ating Board's very interesting booklet entitled
Hydro-Electricity in Snowdonia. There is a steep
road climbing up from here to the village of
Gellilydan, and on the opposite (west) side of the
bridge there is a path which goes up through
woodlands, eventually linking with our **Walk 11**,
page 150, or heading westwards to Llyn Tecwyn
Uchaf (SH 64-38).

Maesgwm Visitor Centre (124) (SH 71-27) *8m N
Dolgellau.* For details of this excellent leisure facility
and the forest which it serves, see Coed-y-Brenin
Forest, page 50.

Malltraeth (114,115) (SH 40-68) *12m W Llanfair
P.G.* The correct name of the village is Malltraeth
Yard, for there was once a boatyard here. It lies at
the end of an embankment known as the Cob which
was built across the Cefni estuary in 1818 when,
with the help of the great Thomas Telford, the Afon
Cefni was canalised and the surrounding marshland
partially reclaimed. Its effectiveness was at first
mistrusted and led to a local folk- ballad which reads
in translation something like this — 'If Malltraeth
Cob breaks, my mother will drown'. The pool
between the Cob and the main A4080 road is under
the protection of the Nature Conservancy and apart
from waders and wildfowl is especially noted for its
redshank in spring and early summer. There is a car
park and picnic site close to the A4080, near the
southern end of the Cob, and from here it is
possible to look out over the vast expanse of
Malltraeth Sands (the estuary of the Afon Cefni), to
the woodlands surrounding Bodorgan. There is a
path on the embankment beside the drainage canal
stretching all the way north-eastwards from Malltraeth, first on the east bank as far as the round-
arched Pont Marquis (SH 43-69), then on the west
bank, as far as the point where it is crossed by the
A5 (SH 46-73), and this also provides a fine vantage
point, especially in winter, for spotting wildfowl in
the marshes on either side. It is no small wonder
that the famous wildlife artist, the late Charles
Tunnicliffe, made his home in this fascinating area

during the last thirty years of his life. *A Sketchbook of Birds* published in 1979, just after his death, contains a fine selection of his work, and the splendid collection of his sketches, drawings and watercolours was purchased by the Isle of Anglesey Borough Council in 1981. At the time of printing, no firm decision has been reached as to where these will be put on permanent exhibition.

The parish in which the village stands is Tref-draeth, and its church stands on higher ground overlooking the marsh (SH 40-70), about a mile to the north of Malltraeth. Built of soft grey stone, the 13th century church of St Beuno is still very much alive and stands well cared for in a tidy churchyard.

Mallwyd (124,125) (SH 86-12) *12m E Dolgellau.* George Borrow spent a pleasant evening at the Brigand's Inn in 1854 after his depressing afternoon at Dinas Mawddwy (see page 58), and the inn and its tradition of hospitality has survived to this day. Borrow described the village as 'small but pretty' and also remarked upon the size of the yew tree in the churchyard. This still stands beside the long low church 'standing on a slight elevation' above the road, with its small weather-boarded tower and its wooden framed porch dated 1641.

In the time of Queen Mary the red-headed 'banditti' of Dinas and Mallwyd had become such a menace that a certain Baron Owen was appointed judge and specially commissioned to put them down. However, despite his initial success in having no less than eight of them hanged, he was himself subsequently ambushed and murdered on his way home from Montgomery Assizes, at a bridge on the road east of Mallwyd, which is still known as Llidiart y Barwyn — the Baron's Gate (125) (SH 90-12).

Head due west from Mallwyd for a short distance to reach a pleasant minor road running down the Dyfi (Dovey) valley, to Aberangell, and beyond to Machynlleth. It may also be possible to drive across the Dyfi Forest from Aberangell (see page 29).

Machroes (formerly Marchros) (123) (SH 31-26) *2m S Abersoch.* Small steeply sited holiday village with a sheltered beach at the far end of Morfa Gors, the fine beach that stretches southwards from Abersoch. The secluded cove of Porth Bach is situated just to its east, around the headland of Penrhyn Du, and St Tudwal's Islands lie not far offshore.

Marchlyn Mawr (115) (SH 61-61) *3m NE Llanber-is.* It is possible to drive up into the hills to the east of Deiniolen, and walk beyond up rough tracks to this impressive lake which lies beneath the crags of Mynydd Perfedd, and which acts as the upper storage reservoir for the great Dinorwic Power Station (see page 58).

Marquess of Anglesey's Column (114,115) (SH 53-71) *To immediate south of Llanfair P.G., just to north of A4080.* The 1st Marquess of Anglesey was second-in-command to Wellington at Waterloo, and he led the Allied cavalry, losing a leg in the process. This earned for him the affectionate nick-name 'One-Leg', and public admiration was expressed in the building of a 90-foot-high monu-ment on the rocky hillock of Craig-y-Dinas. The bronze statue was added in 1860, some years after after his death in 1845, at the age of 86. A spiral staircase of 115 steps leads to the observation platform from which there are panoramic views of Anglesey and the Strait, with the great mass of Snowdonia beyond. See also Plas Newydd, page 95.

Menai Bridge (114,115) (SH 55-71) *2m W Bangor.* This suspension bridge was designed by the great engineer Thomas Telford, to overcome the greatest challenge presented to him in his construction of the famous London to Holyhead road, the crossing of the Menai Strait over to Anglesey. The final link in the suspension chains was driven home by Telford himself on 25th April 1825, although it was not until a stormy night in January of the following year that the bridge was finally opened to traffic. It is 1000 feet long with a central span of 579 feet, and the roadway is 100 feet above high water level, a condition imposed upon Telford by the Admiralty to avoid interference with the tall masts of sailing ships. Telford's wrought iron chains, soaked in linseed oil, were so successful that despite the strains imposed upon them by modern motor traffic, they were not replaced by steel ones until the late 1930s. The best view of this wonder of early 19th century engineering is to be had from the lay-bys on the A4080, well beyond Menai Bridge (town). Read more about the construction of this, the world's first large iron suspension bridge, in L.T.C. Rolt's fascinating biography of Thomas Telford (see Book List).

The Menai Strait and its two bridges. SCALE 1:25 000 or 2½ INCHES to 1 MILE

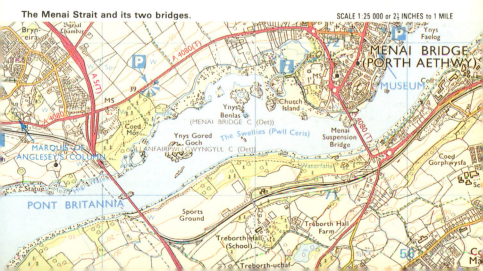

Telford's fine suspension bridge, spanning the wooded Menai Strait.

Menai Bridge (The town) (114,115) (SH 55-72) *2m W Bangor.* Telford's suspension bridge (see above) gave its name to the little Victorian market town which grew up in its shadow, in the parish of Llandysilio. While here do not miss a visit to the lively Tegfryn Art Gallery on Cadnant Road *(tel: 0248 712437)*. The old church of St Tysilio is on Church Island, easily reached by a path from the **Tourist Information Centre** *(tel: 0248 712626)* on the A4080 beyond the roundabout at the north end of the bridge. This goes through Coed Cyrnol, a dense wood of Scots pines, and over a causeway to the tiny 15th century church, from one of whose tinted windows there is a lilac-hued view westwards to the Pont Britannia (see page 96). The Belgian Promenade, built during the 1914-1918 war by Flemish refugees, and which follows the shore from the island to the suspension bridge, provides a peaceful walk with a fine view of the Strait and the Pont Britannia. The Promenade also provides the easiest pedestrian access to the town.

The Menai Strait (114,115) (SH 44-61 — SH 58-73 etc.) This attractive stretch of water between Anglesey and the mainland extends 18 miles, from Abermenai Point to Puffin Island. The outstanding features are the two fine bridges across it, Telford's Menai Bridge, and Stephenson's Pont Britannia, both built high enough, at the express command of the Admiralty, to allow tall sailing ships to pass beneath. Deep in some places and shallow in others, but always kept lively by the ever-changing tidal flows, the waters of the Menai Strait are both fascinating and dangerous. For this reason ferry crossings and attempted fordings in the days before the first bridge were often hazardous, and the Roman legions met with troubles similar to those later encountered by Edward I and his invading English forces. The shores of the Strait are often richly wooded, especially in its central section, with the parklands of Plas Newydd looking across to those of Glan Faenol (see page 64), and further colour is provided in summer by the many pleasure craft sailing to and fro.

Migneint (124,125) (SH 78-42 etc.) *5m E Ffestiniog* This literally is *The Swampy Place*, a broad moorland region, mainly 1500 feet or more above sea level, and the source of many streams. With its wide expanse of heather and marshy grasses, it is the home of snipe, grouse and curlew, and is overlooked from the east and south-east by the twin peaks of Arenig Fach and Arenig Fawr (see page 33). This is a wild, largely trackless area, and should

only be tackled by those with experience of walking in remote places.

Miners' Bridge (115) (SH 78-57) *1m W Betws-y-Coed.* A wooden bridge across the Afon Llugwy, once used by the miners of Pentre-du village heading for the lead and zinc mines in the hills beyond the river, one of which was delightfully named, 'New Pandora'. It is possible to walk to the bridge from Betws-y-Coed, along the north bank of the Llugwy. Garth Falls Walk (see page 64) starts from a nearby car park on the opposite side of the A5.

Minffordd (124) (SH 73-11) *7m S Dolgellau.* This is little more than a road junction, where the B4405 heads south-westwards from the A487 Dolgellau-Machynlleth road, to Tal-y-llyn Lake and Abergynolwyn. However, to the right of the B4405, about a quarter of a mile beyond this junction, there is a path starting through gates, which leads to Cadair Idris — known as the Minffordd Path. This is one of the most attractive ways up to Cadair Idris (see page 44), and it is well described in a leaflet available from National Park Information Centres. Also use Landranger Sheet 124, or Outdoor Leisure Map Sheet 23. Before considering this ascent, please read the advice on walking and climbing on the inside of the rear cover of our guide.

Moel Goedog (124) (SH 61-32) *3m NE Harlech.* The attractive hilly country of the Ardudwy contains many prehistoric remains, and on Moel Goedog will be found a circular fort, two cairns, and to the west of the fort, a trackway running in a SW-NE direction, with its course marked by several standing stones. This is near a minor road running behind Harlech, between Llanfair and Eisingrug, and it is possible also to walk north-eastwards from here through the northern flanks of the Rhinog Range towards Llyn Trawsfynydd, passing Bryn Cader Faner (SH 64-35), a well-defined cairn circle surrounding a central burial chamber. This expedition should only be tackled by those with hillwalking experience.

Moelfre (114) (SH 51-86) *11m N Llanfair P.G.* An attractive small holiday resort and fishing village, with a pebble beach and opportunities for sailing and water-skiing. There are good coastal walks from here, north-west around to Lligwy Bay, and south to Traeth Bychan. Porpoises are sometimes to be seen here and the small island just offshore, Ynys Moelfre, is noted for its seabirds. A lifeboat station was established here as early as 1830, and boats from it have been involved in two outstanding rescues in addition to their more routine, but often equally hazardous tasks. In October 1859 the *Royal Charter* was wrecked off Moelfre (see Llanallgo, page 68), and in October 1959 exactly a hundred years later, to the day, eight crew members of the ill-fated coaster *Hindlea* were rescued.

The Moelwyns (See Siabod Range and the Moelwyns, page 103.)

Moel-y-don (114,115) (SH 51-67) *3m S Llanfair P.G.* A quiet road leads southwards to the shore of the Menai Strait, past 16th century Plas Coch, the centre of a large caravan park, and then beyond a small turning to tall-spired Llanedwen church. This was rebuilt in 1856, but it has a reading desk which includes part of a 14th century screen. The church-yard contains a tombstone to 'gardiner', John Rowlands, which has a humbling, but less than cheerful message for all who pass this way -

Stop a foot and cast an eye
As you are now so once was I
As I am now so must you be
Prepare yourself and follow me

The landing stage at Moel-y-don, a peaceful spot with a fine view of the Strait, was once used by a busy ferry to Felinheli (Portdinorwic). It is sad to recall that it was near this now tranquil shore, in the winter of 1281-2, that some three hundred of Edward I's followers were slain by the Welsh.

Morfa Bychan (See Black Rock Sands, page 41, and Borth-y- Gest, page 42.)

Morfa Dyffryn National Nature Reserve (124) (SH 56-24) *5m S Harlech.* A large area of sand dunes and dune grassland which may be reached from either Llanbedr or Dyffryn Ardudwy. A permit is required to visit this area, and applications must be made to the Regional Officer of the Nature Conservancy Council at Ffordd Penrhos, Bangor, Gwynedd LL57 2LQ. The Council have published an interesting leaflet describing this reserve.

Morfa Nefyn (123) (SH 28-40) *7m NW Pwllheli.* Attractive holiday village behind the long curving beach of Porth Dinllaen (see page 96). Here are opportunities for fishing, boating and water-skiing, and there is a wide range of accommodation available. (See also Nefyn, page 90.)

Mynydd Bodafon (114) (SH 46-85) *6m SSE Amlwch.* Dramatic outcrop of rocky, heather-clad hills, surrounding a tranquil lake. There is a convenient car park at their foot, on the little road between Brynrefail (SH 48-86) and Maenaddwyn (SH 46-84), and from this park there is a clearly marked path to the top. It is also possible to reach Yr Arwydd summit by extending our **Walk 1**, page 130, between Point B and C. From both hill-tops it is possible to see nearly the whole of Anglesey, and to the south, many miles of the Welsh mainland, from the Great Orme to the Lleyn Peninsula, with the brooding peaks of Snowdonia in the background.

Mynydd Cilan (123) (SH 29-24) *3m S Abersoch.* Here are stretches of open moorland on a promon-tory which extends southwards to the rocky head-land of Trwyn Cilan, with the area above Trwyn y Ffosle on the western side, in the care of the National Trust. There are splendid views out over the long bay of Porth Neigwl (Hell's Mouth) from here.

Mynydd Mawr (123) (SH 13-25) *20m SW Pwllheli.* Mynydd Mawr (Big Mountain) stands above the headland Braich y Pwll, the 'Land's End' of North Wales, and most of the area is in the care of the National Trust. A concrete road zig-zags up to a car park on the summit from which the views are outstanding — Bardsey Island two miles offshore, a

panorama of the coastline of the Lleyn; and on a clear day it may also be possible to spot the distant outlines of the Wicklow Mountains of Ireland, and St David's Head across the long Cardigan Bay, in addition to the brooding peaks of Snowdonia. Footpaths lead across the rocky moorland to the cliffs, and on the eastern side of the headland it is possible, but dangerous (especially when the tide is high), to scramble down to the shore to look for the site of the ancient chapel of St Mary. It was here that pilgrims on the way to Bardsey used to pray before embarking for their final destination. They would also have drunk from the spring of St Mary's Well, which although covered by each tide, is said to always yield fresh water.

Nannau (124) (SH 74-20) *2m N Dolgellau.* Until a few years ago this small late 18th century mansion in the hills to the north of Dolgellau was the home of the Vaughan family, the most well-known of whom was Sir Robert Williames Vaughan (1768-1843). He was MP for Merioneth for many years, and the virtual creator of the Nannau estate, with its farms and cottages of rough stone relieved by Gothic detail. The Precipice Walk is on this estate, but see page 99 for details.

Nant Ffrancon (115) (SH 63-63) *8m SE Bangor.* The Afon Ogwen escapes from Llyn Ogwen at Pont Pen-y-benglog and leaps into this dramatic glac-iated valley in a series of waterfalls. The A5 road keeps to the east side, overshadowed by the rugged slopes and crags of Pen yr Ole Wen (The Summit of the Bright Sunlight) and Carnedd Dafydd. To the west, the overshadowing peaks include Y Garn, Foel Goch and Carnedd Filiast. At the foot of the valley is the minute hamlet of Ty'n-y-maes, where George Borrow drank 'tolerably good wine', after his walk down from Llyn Ogwen in the company of

Ruggedly beautiful Nant Ffrancon.

a friendly but teetotal carpenter. Thomas Pennant, writing in his *Tour in Wales* in 1778, described this road as 'the most dreadful horse path in Wales', and he had seen a few Welsh horse paths in his time!

Nant Gwernol Forest Walks (See Abergynolwyn, page 31.)

Nantgwynant (115) (SH 65-54 to SH 59-49) *To immediate NE of Beddgelert.* If coming south into this incomparable valley from Capel Curig, or south-east over the Llanberis Pass, try to stop at the viewpoint car park at SH 65-54. This is about a mile south of Pen-y-Gwryd, and almost opposite the Cwm Dyli Hydro-Electric Station. From this point it is possible to obtain some of the finest views in Snowdonia. High in front and slightly to the left, the summit of Snowdon itself — Yr Wyddfa — with the peak of Crib-goch to its right. Below them, but just hidden, lies Llyn Lydaw (see **Walk 6**, page 140), and from it can be seen the pipeline coming down the hillside to feed the Cwm Dyli Hydro-Electric Station in the valley below.

Now look left, down beautiful Nantgwynant, with wooded hills reflected in the still waters of Llyn Gwynant. Beyond rises the peak of Moel Hebog above and beyond Beddgelert, at the end of the valley. The grassy banks of the lake beside the A498 are rightly favoured as picnic places, and the few parking spaces are often full, but stop if you can to explore the hillside above, for further splendid views of the lake and the Snowdon range.

Beyond the lake is the Bethania Car Park (SH 62-50), and this is the starting point of our **Walk 7**, page 142, the Watkin Path up to Snowdon. By using a minor road to the south for a very short distance it is also possible to walk from here around the quiet southern side of Llyn Dinas, linking in with our **Walk 9**, page 146. Beyond Bethania Bridge, the A498 heads along the northern side of Llyn Dinas, and then below the small craggy hill on which stands Dinas Emrys (SH 60-49). This was an Iron Age and Roman settlement, having legendary associations with Vortigern (see also Llithfaen, page 81) and a tale involving two dragons, one red and one white, and it was also the site of a 12th century Welsh keep. This delectable valley finally ends at Beddgelert.

Nantlle Valley (115) (SH 51-53 etc) *7m S Caernarfon.* This is best approached from the A487 at Penygroes (SH 46-53), where a turn east on to B4418 is required. This road goes through dramatic slate-quarry country before passing Llyn Nantlle Uchaf and heading over the Drws-y-coed (The Wooded Pass) to join the A4085 at Rhyd-Ddu. Well to the south of the road, and approximately parallel with it, are the great peaks that make up the Nantlle Ridge, much loved by climbers (see Rhyd-Ddu, page 102, and the Hebog Range, page 66).

Nantmor (115) (SH 60-46) *2m S Beddgelert.* There is a minor mountain road that leaves the A4085 just to the south-east of Pont Aber Glaslyn. About a mile beyond the hamlet of Nantmor, turn left at Bwlchgwernog and head a short distance up the lovely Nanmor valley. Here will be found the manor house of Cae Ddafydd (SH 61-45) where there is a wood turnery and rare breeds centre. Less than a mile further on there is an attractive car park and picnic site, which is also the starting point of a forest walk. This pleasant road up the Nanmor Valley eventually joins the A498 near Pont Bethania, but for further details see **Tour 4**, page 116. Please do not forget to leave gates as you find them, which will probably be in the closed position.

Nant Peris, (or Old Llanberis) (115) (SH 60-58) *2m SE Llanberis.* This village stands at the foot of Llanberis Pass, overhung on one side by the north ridge of Snowdon, and on the other by the slopes of Elidir Fawr and Y Garn. The minute medieval church of St Peris is a typically simple building of stone and slate. It was heavily restored in 1848 and unfortunately even the early 16th century rood screen did not escape the attention of the 'improvers'. There is a useful bus service that picks up walkers and climbers from the free car park near the church, to take them to other starting points for the ascent of Snowdon – the Snowdon Sherpa. This is useful for our own **Walk 6**, page 140, which starts out for Snowdon from Pen-y-Pass. There is also a car park on the A4086 to the north-west of the village, at the head of Llyn Peris. There are fine views of this lake from here.

Nefyn (123) (SH 30-40) *7m NW Pwllheli.* Small holiday town behind the extensive beach of Porth Nefyn, which has good gently-sloping sands, a launching slipway and even beach huts for hire. In the town itself will be found a 19th century watch-tower near the 'new' church, and an 'old' church with a narrow tower upon which is a restored weather-vane in the form of a ship. Do not miss a visit to the interesting Lleyn Historical and Maritime Museum here. It should also be possible to take a boat trip to Carreg y Llam, near Penrhyn Glas (SH 33-43), a massive sea cliff where a wide variety of sea birds can be spotted (see Natural History, page 18).

Although there now does not appear to be a great deal to show for it, this town has a long and important history. In 1224 Edward I celebrated his victory over Llywelyn the Last by holding a great tournament here, and in 1355 it was designated one of the ten Royal Boroughs of Wales. It seems strange that there appears to be no trace of a medieval castle or any earthworks with which one might have been connected. Castell Mawr and Castell Bach, both well to the east of the town do not appear to have any significance, and the only hint of former glories is in the name of the field to the east of the village — Cae Iowerth (Edward's Field), which was probably used for the tournament of 1224. See also Morfa Nefyn, page 89, and Porth Dinllaen, page 96.

Newborough (Niwbwrch) (114,115) (SH 42-65) *8m SW Llanfair P. G.* Modest village with a friendly inn, a handsome chapel, the Ebenezer, and a late 19th century clock tower with half-timbered alms-houses. It was settled in about 1295 by Edward I (hence the English name 'new borough'), with villagers from Llanfaes who had been evicted at the time of the building of Beaumaris Castle, and it was soon widely known for its markets and fairs. Within a short time, due to a series of violent storms and to the clearance of trees, the nearby dunes were beginning to encroach upon the agricultural land to its south, and by the time of Elizabeth I a law was passed to encourage the conservation and spread of marram grass, a plant which has been widely used for the stabilisation of dunes for centuries, and which is still used today. The weaving of this grass soon became a thriving cottage industry in Newborough, where mats, ropes and baskets were produced in large quantities, but this craft almost died out in the 1920s. The other major occupation of the villagers was rabbit-catching, and in most years between eighty and a hundred thousand animals

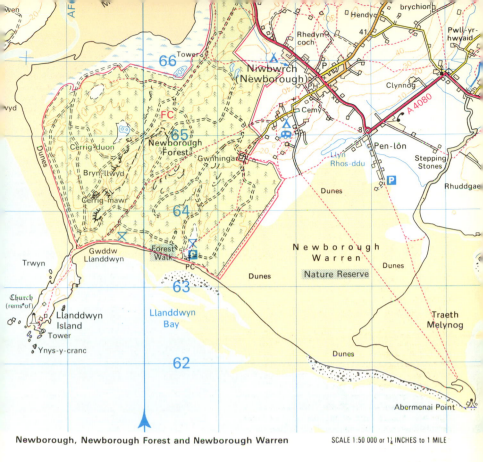

Newborough, Newborough Forest and Newborough Warren

SCALE 1:50 000 or 1¼ INCHES to 1 MILE

were trapped in Newborough Warren. However, this almost ceased with the coming of myxomatosis in the years following the first outbreak in 1954. (For Newborough Warren, see below.)

The early-14th century church of St Peter, no doubt dating from the time of Edward I's settlement, is to be found on high ground to the south of the village above the road to Llanddwyn Island, and has unusually long and narrow proportions. There are 14th century tomb slabs in the floor of the chancel, and the fine 12th century font, from an earlier church, is decorated with intricate interlacing patterns in the best Romanesque tradition.

Newborough Warren and Newborough Forest (114,115) (SH 42-63 etc.) *10m SW Llanfair P.G.*
The Warren (see above for its origins) is one of the largest expanses of sand dunes in Britain, and it is now a National Nature Reserve. This is an area of great sweeping sands, backed in parts by a large forest, and everything is on a breath-taking scale. It would be wise to first take the road past the church, and head almost two miles through Newborough Forest to the car park (SH 40-63) behind Landddwyn Bay (see page 70). During the holiday season there is an *Information Centre* here, where the aims of the Conservancy and the Forestry Commission are explained, and a series of publications are on sale including a most informative leaflet on the *Newborough Warren — Ynys Llanddwyn Nature Reserve*. If visitors already have the leaflet, the initial choice is wider, but all who come this way are strongly

advised to obtain a copy. There is a waymarked forest walk from here, known as the Hendai Trail, and this will take visitors past the remains of medieval houses which were overrun by the dunes many centuries ago.

It is also possible to walk from the car park at Pen-lôn (SH 43-64) through the dunes to the Braint estuary, and this is to be recommended in preference to the more difficult route leading from the track due south of Newborough. The dunes are the home of many birds and mammals, but for further details, see Natural History, page 18.

The planting of **Newborough Forest** was started in 1948, and this has now prevented windblown sand covering roads and growing crops in its vicinity. The forest covers about 2000 acres and consists mainly of Corsican Pine, although a small number of other conifers and broad-leaved trees have also been planted. There is a path through the forest heading south-westwards from a point near Newborough church (but not to be confused with the road, which runs parallel with it in its early stages). This path eventually arrives at delightful Llanddwyn Island (SH 38-62) (see page 70 for details). There is also a path starting from a car park and picnic site (SH 41-67) on the A4080, north-west of Newborough. This heads south above the shore of the Cefni estuary, much of it a salt marsh, and there are many wildfowl and wading birds to be seen here (see also Malltraeth, page 86).

A written permit is required to visit places away from the routes through this Nature Reserve, and for further information it is necessary to write to:

The Regional Officer, Nature Conservancy Council, Penrhos Road, Bangor, Gwynedd LL57 2LQ. For further details, see Natural History, page 18.

Niwbwrch (114,115) (SH 42-65) (See Newborough, above.)

Owain Glyndwr's Cave (Ogof Owain) (124) (SH 56-05) *6m SW Fairbourne on A493.* Here on the shoreline, some half a mile south of Cae-du Farm, is a small cave which is supposed to have once sheltered Owain Glyndwr while he was a fugitive from the English. This is not very dramatic, and cannot be visited at high tide, but it provides an excuse for a pleasant walk along the shoreline. (For another cave traditionally used by Glyndwr, see Hebog Range, page 66.) There is good camping at the farm, which can be reached from Llangelynnin Halt on the Cambrian Coast Railway.

Padarn Country Park (See Llanberis, page 69.)

Pantperthog (135) (SH 74-04) *4m N Machynlleth.* Unexceptional hamlet in the densely wooded valley of the Afon Dulas, between Machynlleth and Corris. It is in the county of Gwynedd, but across the valley which forms the boundary with Powys, will be found the interesting Alternative Technology Centre (see page 49).

Parys Mountain (114) (SH 44-90) *2m S Amlwch.* The Romans first found copper on Parys Mountain, and it was certainly worked in Elizabethan times. However, in 1768 an exceptionally rich vein was discovered, and for the following fifty years Amlwch was a true boom town, with a population estimated at five thousand and as many as a thousand ale houses. At a time when the copper coins of the realm were in very short supply, many provincial tokens were brought into circulation, and perhaps some of the finest of these were the Anglesey penny and halfpenny. Over 250 tons of Anglesey pennies were minted by the Parys Mines Company between 1878 and 1793. Eventually however, overseas competition ended the copper boom here, as it also did in South Devon and Cornwall.

Today the mountain is a fascinating site, something almost 'out of this world', with multi-coloured rocks and heaps of debris, and stagnant pools where the ore was once washed. The ruined windmill near the summit was for the powering of a mine pump. Abandoned mine shafts make the area extremely dangerous, but there are fine views from the car park on the B5111.

Penarth Fawr (123) (SH 41-37) *3m NE Pwllheli.* This well-preserved stone building in quiet country north of the A497 between Pwllheli and Criccieth was the hall of a Welsh gentleman's house of the early 15th century, and contains some fine timberwork and an impressive stone fireplace. The roof and windows are comparatively modern. In the care of the Welsh Office, it is open at all reasonable times.

Penllech Church (123) (SH 22-34) *8m NW Abersoch.* Attractive little church tucked away by a pond on the north-western slopes of Mynydd Cefnawlch,

with only a farm for company. The unspoilt early 19th century interior is well worth visiting, and the key should be available at the farmhouse.

Penllyn Forest (125) (SH 96-30, etc.) *3m SE Bala.* For details of this attractive area, see Cwm Hirnant, page 56.

Penmachno (115) (SH 79-50) *6m S Betws-y-Coed.* A small grey stone and slate quarrymen's village astride the swift flowing Afon Machno, here crossed by a rugged five-arched bridge. Baskets and chairs in cane and willow are made in the village. There is an mountain road southwards, used on our **Tour 4**, page 116, and a pleasant road west and north, up through woodlands to Ty Mawr (see page 108), the birthplace of Bishop William Morgan. Down the valley, in the direction of the Machno Falls, is Penmachno Woollen Mill, where visitors are welcome to tour the mill to see the weavers at work, weaving tweed, rugs and scarves, and to view an audio-visual presentation of 'The Story of Wool', from lambing to finished cloth. There is a Mill Wool and Craft Shop *(tel: 06902 545)*. For the Conway Falls, see page 53.

Penmaenmawr (115) (SH 71-76) *5m W Conwy.* Much loved by the redoubtable Mr Gladstone, this small holiday town shelters beneath Penmaen Mawr, the 'big stone headland' from which it takes its name, and looks across the water to north-eastern Anglesey with Puffin Island at its tip. It has a traffic-free promenade from which sailing and water-skiing can be watched and a long sandy beach backed by shingle. This is squeezed between the sea and the mountains, much scarred here by great quarries, stone from which is still shipped from its little quay in considerable quantities.

The stone from some of these slopes was also much favoured by New Stone Age man, and many stone axes, picks and adzes, mostly abandoned and incomplete specimens, have been found above the town near Graiglwyd. Perhaps more significantly, geological analysis has revealed that implements of this period, discovered in many places throughout Wales and even in Derbyshire and Wiltshire, were made in this hillside 'axe factory'. On the mountain above will be found the Druid's Circle (SH 723-746), one of the best known of Wales' stone circles or henges, and which is almost certainly of Bronze Age origin. Both axe factory and stone circle are included in an interesting History Trail, based on the town. If neither axes nor circles are your forte, despair not, for the views alone make the considerable climb worthwhile. It is also possible to walk further south over the mountains to link with the track following the course of the Roman road westwards through the Bwlch y Ddeufaen (see page 43), but treat these high, wild places with the respect they deserve. For less hazardous adventure use the minor road, eastwards over the attractive Sychnant Pass, to Conwy, which passes a 9-hole golf course (SH 73-76), beyond the turn to Dwygyfylchi.

Penmaenpool (124) (SH 69-18) *2m W Dolgellau.* This hamlet has a toll-bridge over the head of the lovely Mawddach estuary, which is overlooked by the little white-painted George III Hotel. There is also a very interesting Nature Information Centre,

Toll bridge at Penmaenpool.

which is close to the start of the Penmaenpool — Morfa Mawddach Walk. This six-mile-long 'nature trail' utilizes the course of the old railway line that ran along the southern shore of the Mawddach estuary to the old junction at Morfa Mawddach. There are fine views out over the estuary to the mountain slopes beyond, and many opportunities for bird-watching on the estuary and on the partly drained marshes at the western end of the walk. There are special facilities for disabled visitors to enjoy part of this walk from the Morffa Mawddach end. From Morffa Mawddach it is also possible to walk over the toll-bridge to Barmouth, or further along the southern shore to the dunes near Fairbourne, where there is a halt on the little Fairbourne Railway (see page 62).

Penmon Priory, etc. (114,115) (SH 63-80) *4m NE Beaumaris.* A church was founded here by St Seiriol, a 6th century recluse whose probable cell may be seen beside a well close by. The original priory was burnt down by the Danes, but a church was rebuilt here in the mid-12th century, and a century later Llywelyn the Great granted the property to the Priestholm (Puffin Island) community, who then rebuilt the priory and associated monastic buildings. At about the same time a larger chancel was added to the church, and this still serves the present parish. There are impressive carvings on the tower arches, and round-headed arcading in the south transept, where will also be found a 10th century Viking cross. Although the chancel was much restored in the 19th century, a feeling of early medieval times remains very strong in this fine church.

In the centre of a field to the west of the priory, stands the elaborately carved Penmon Cross, which dates from about AD 1000. This may be reached by a path from the car park, past St Seiriol's Well, a delightfully cool little place below a small cliff. The massive dovecote to the east of the priory was probably built in about 1600 by Sir Richard Bulkeley of Baron Hill, near Beaumaris. Beneath its impressive domed roof, pierced by a lantern through which the pigeons once came and went, there are nesting holes for almost a thousand birds. The church, priory and dovecote are open at any reasonable time. It is possible to drive north-east to Black Point, opposite Puffin Island (see page 99), and there is also a pleasant footpath heading north-west across part of the old Penmon Deer Park, and then north to the coast to the west of Trwyn Dinmor. The disused limestone quarries to the north-east of Penmon were once used by Edward I for the building of Beaumaris Castle, and much later by both Telford and Stephenson in the construction of

their two famous bridges across the Menai Strait (see pages 87 and 96). Porth Penmon beach, which is close to the road leading north to Penmon Priory is largely shingle, but there is a mixture of mud and sand at low tide.

Penmorfa (124) (SH 54-40) *2m NW Porthmadog.* Its name means *head of the marsh*, and until William Madocks (see Porthmadog, page 97) built his famous embankments, Penmorfa was indeed on the edge of marshy estuary country. It was here that Madocks first bought a small farm in 1797, and the nearby 'new town' of Tremadog was the result of his earliest reclamation activities.

Much of the small village of Penmorfa now lies on the A487, but the church will be found half a mile to the south. This attractively situated building has some 15th century glass in its west window, and also a memorial to Sir John Owen, a royalist leader in the Civil War, who was once condemned to death, but who secured a reprieve and lived to see the restoration of Charles II, the son of the monarch whose cause he had served. Close to the church there is an interesting pottery and farm museum at Tyn Llan Farm, which also has a cafe.

Penmynydd (114,115) (SH 50-74) *3m NW Menai Bridge.* Small village astride the B5420, the old road to Holyhead before Telford built his fine new road here, about two miles to the south. Lining the road well to the south-east, there is an attractive series of 17th century almshouses, which were redesigned in 1962 to provide five modern dwellings. The church dates from the 14th and 15th centuries, and has many connections with the Tudor family (see below). There is a magnificent alabaster altar tomb which is thought to have been brought from Llanfaes Priory at the Dissolution, and which commemorates an early Tudor, Gronw Fychan, and his wife, Myfanwy. Gronw had been Constable of Beaumaris Castle in 1382 and was for many years a friend of the Black Prince.

The Tudor family were especially prominent in the 14th century and lived at Plas Penmynydd (SH 49-75), well to the north-west of the village, for over three hundred years. Among their number was Owain Tudor who distinguished himself in the armies of Henry V, and who subsequently became a power at the Royal Court. On Henry's death, Owain secretly married the royal widow, Catherine de Valois, but he paid dearly for this presumptious indiscretion and eventually suffered the agonies of being hung, drawn and quartered. Despite this sad end to their union, it was not without its fruits, and Owain and Catherine's grandson, Henry Tudor, eventually became Henry VII, the founder of the great Tudor Dynasty, following his defeat of Richard III at Bosworth Field in 1485. The present farmhouse dates from the 16th century, but has been much altered, and is not open to the public.

Pennal (135) (SH 69-00) *4m W Machynlleth.* At Cefn-caer Farm, to the south-east of Pennal, there was once a Roman fort dominating what must have been the lowest crossing place of the Dyfi, but only scant evidence of this remains. There are also the mounds of a medieval motte and a Bronze Age tumulus nearer the village. In the year 1404 Owain Glyndwr summoned his parliaments in the towns, Harlech, Dolgellau, Machynlleth, and also surprisingly, in this now quiet village on the northern edge of the still marshy Dyfi (Dovey) valley. However, the only place of real interest here is the early 19th century church, situated in an angle of the often busy A493. Here will be found some pleasant 18th century monuments and a poignant Victorian brass depicting a young girl dying on a sofa, attended by the kneeling figures of her brother and sister.

There is an attractive mountain road westwards to Tywyn, forking off the A493 at Cwrt, just to the west of the village. This leads through the Happy Valley (see page 65) and passes near Llyn Barfog (The Bearded Lake). Use Outdoor Leisure Map 23 to follow several pleasant walks from Pennal, south to the banks of the Dyfi and the shores at the head of its estuary, and north into well-wooded mountain country.

Pennant Valley (See Cwm Pennant, page 56.)

Penrhos (114) (SH 27-81) *2m SE Holyhead*. Here is a great aluminium smelting works operated by Anglesey Aluminium Metal Ltd. However, a large part of the Penrhos Estate, which had previously been the home of the Stanleys of Alderley, has, with the help of the Aluminium Company and the initiative of local policeman, Ken Williams, been developed into a 450-acre Nature Reserve. The area provides a great variety of habitats for woodland, sea and wading birds, and visitors can wander largely at will. There is also a 100-acre breeding site, but access to this is restricted (for conditions of entry, *tel: 0407 2522*).

Penrhosfeilw Standing Stones (114) (SH 22-80) *2m SW Holyhead, to N of Penrhosfeilw*. Two impressive stones, each ten feet high and eleven feet apart, which date from the Bronze Age, and are believed to be the remains of a stone cist, in the centre of a stone circle. Open at any reasonable time. (See also Holy Island, page 66.)

Penrhyn Castle (N.T.) (115) (SH 60-71) *2m E Bangor*. Situated in a fine park between the mountains and the sea, this 19th century castle (1827-40), with its nine towers, barbican gateway and massive keep, is an outstanding example of neo-Norman architecture. This was a style which greatly appealed to the new, romantically inclined industrial magnates of the 19th century, and Penrhyn is the result of the ambitions of the Pennants, a family whose wealth came from the great slate quarries of Snowdonia only a few miles away. A late 18th century Gothic mansion, built by Samuel Wyatt, had to be swept away to make room

Penrhyn Castle.

for the castle, and this new building is said to have cost at least half a million pounds, a great deal of money in those days.

A visit here is well worthwhile, and the castle's interior is enriched with much carved wood and stone, and with slate from the family quarries. The furniture is on a monumental scale befitting its impressive surroundings, and there is also a museum of industrial locomotives, an exhibition of dolls, and a natural history display. There are many walks in the surrounding parkland and gardens, and views of the mountains of Snowdonia and the Menai Strait from some of the paths are outstandingly beautiful. Shop and tea room. *(Tel: 0248 353084.)*

Penrhyndeudraeth (124) (SH 61-39) *3m E Porthmadog*. Busy little town (or large village) at a meeting point of many routes, both road and rail, and situated near the head of the Dwyryd estuary, here crossed by a bridge carrying the Cambrian Coast Railway and a small toll-road. It has a station on this British Rail line (see page 46), and one on the Ffestiniog Railway (see page 62), but these are some distance apart. The Headquarters of the Snowdonia National Park is also located here, and information may be obtained by calling during normal office hours *(tel: 0766 770 274)*. Enquiries in writing should be addressed to: National Park Office, Penrhyndeudraeth, Gwynedd LL48 6LS.

Pentraeth (114,115) (SH 52-78) *5m N Llanfair P.G.* In English the name of this small village would be *head of the sands*, and at least until reclamation was carried out in the 18th and 19th centuries, it was on the edge of much larger Red Wharf Bay. The Afon Ceint, a tributary of the Afon Cefni (see Malltraeth, page 86), rises only a short distance to the south, and before the marshy areas both to the north and south of Pentraeth were reclaimed, Anglesey was almost divided by them into two islands.

There is a small road leading north-east and north from the village, across this reclaimed land to a point where the little Afon Nodwydd reaches the sea — a peaceful spot with mud flats and sandy wastes. It is also possible to walk to this point from the village beside this river via Fron Goch, and then return partly through the wooded hills of the Mynydd Llwydiarth (use Landranger Sheet 114, or Pathfinder Sheet SH 47/57).

Pentre Berw (114,115) (SH 47-72) *4m W Llanfair P.G.* Largely bypassed by Telford's A5, this village overlooks the partly drained Malltraeth Marsh. It has a well-known inn, The Holland Arms, and like so many other Anglesey villages, a ruined windmill. There is an abandoned coal mine to its south, and not far away, a 15th century house with a 17th century wing, Plas Berw.

Pentrefelin (124) (SH 52-39) *2m NE Criccieth*. This hamlet on the A497 has a simple modern church which, like the nearby rectory, was designed by Clough Williams Ellis in 1912. On the south side of the road, near the centre of the village, is a standing stone which must be one of the tallest and slimmest in all Wales. The early Victorian 'old' church of Ynyscynhaearn (SH 526-388), with its box pews and three-decker pulpit, was still standing at the end of a long farm track when we last called here, but was in a bad state of repair. We hope that it has fared better since — it certainly deserves to do so. It appears to be still possible to walk on southwards from here to the western end of Black Rock Sands (see page 41).

Pentrellwyn (114,115) (SH 57-81) *See Llanddona, page 70.*

Pen-y-bont (135) (SH 74-02) *½m N Machynlleth.* Small hamlet with a pretty row of cottages overlooking a stout old stone bridge over the Afon Dyfi (River Dovey), the lowest crossing point for vehicles. Steep woodlands run down to the hamlet from the north.

Penygroes (115,123) (SH 46-53) *7m S Caernarfon.* Small 19th century quarrying town on the western edge of Snowdonia. It has a multitude of trim looking chapels, and memories of busier times. Drive east from here on B4418, along the Nantlle Valley (see page 90).

Pili Palas, Menai Bridge (Porthaethwy) (114,115) (SH 54-72) *On B5420, Penmynydd Road, just to NW of Menai Bridge town.* Here is a delightful display of native and tropical butterflies, and a variety of other insects, all in a controlled environment through which visitors may wander. There is also a gift shop and cafe. *(Tel: 0248 712474.)*

Pistyll (123) (SH 32-42) *7m NW Pwllheli.* The simple parish church of St Beuno (see Clynnog fawr, page 49), is in a quiet setting overlooking the sea, and was almost certainly used by medieval pilgrims on their way to Bardsey Island. It is at least partly 12th century, but high up in the wall by the altar window, there is a faint inscription which is thought to be the date, 1050. Note the strong buttresses to the west front and the massive roof timbers; it was thatched until about a hundred years ago. There are also traces of wall paintings and a leper's window. The lepers would have stood outside here in order to see the Blessed Sacrament without fear of passing on their greatly feared affliction to the congregation within. The bell here was the gift of two churchwardens, and is said to ring of its own accord when there is a storm at sea. It is possible to walk north-east from here parallel with the coast to link with the start of our **Walk 10**, page 148.

Pistyll Cain and Rhaeadr Mawddach (124) (SH 73-27) *9m N Dolgellau.* (See also Coed-y-Brenin Forest, page 50.) These waterfalls are probably best approached from the car park (SH 73-25) on the minor road north-east of Ganllwyd. Beyond the end of this road, walk past a bungalow, and then take the path off to the right after about half a mile. Pistyll Cain is close to another waterfall, the Rhaeadr Mawddach, the former being on the Afon Gain and the latter on the Afon Mawddach, both just above their confluence. Pistyll Cain is on the left as walkers approach from the south, and is the tallest of the two; the Rhaeadr Mawddach is on the right, and is greater in volume and more impressive.

Between the two falls, just above the confluence of the two streams, is a tongue of land with the extensive remains of old gold workings (only discontinued in 1939), but the charm of the area lies in the falls themselves and the heavily wooded valleys in which they lie, a place of oak, beech and pine, with the aroma of thyme heavy on the still summer air. For the background to the story of mining in this area, visit the interesting Maesgwm Visitor Centre (see Coed-y-Brenin Forest, page 50).

Pitt's Head (115) (SH 57-51) *2½m N Beddgelert.* Large glacial boulder just to the west of the A4085. When seen from a certain angle this is said to resemble William Pitt's profile.

Plas Menai (114,115) (SH 50-65) *2m NE Caernarfon.* This is a fine watersports centre built by the Sports Council for Wales. The majority of its craft are sailboats, some for experts, but most are suitable for first time sailors, including dinghies, surfboards and keelboats. There are day, weekend and five-day courses for residents and non-residents, and day visitors should check in before 9 am except for swimming sessions. It has a heated indoor pool, bars, restaurant and luxurious accommodation for residents. For full details and advance bookings, *tel: 0248 670964.*

Plas Newydd (N.T.) (114,115) (SH 52-69) *1m SW Llanfair P.G.* Standing on the shore of the Menai Strait, with splendid views across the water to Snowdonia, this late 18th and early 19th century house in Gothic and neo-Classical styles was the work of James Wyatt and the less well-known Joseph Potter, a Lichfield architect. It has a Gothic Hall complete with a gallery and sumptuous plasterwork fan vaulting. The long dining room contains Plas Newydd's outstanding treasure, the magically beautiful *trompe l'oeil* mural painting by Rex Whistler, featuring a wealth of architectural fantasies worked into a highly romanticised landscape derived at least in part from the views of the Menai Strait and Snowdonia from Plas Newydd. There is also a military museum housing relics of the Battle of Waterloo, where the first Marquess of Anglesey lost his leg (see also Marquess of Anglesey's Column, page 87). These relics include the mutilated trousers worn on the fatal day and the wooden leg used by the first Marquess in the years that followed. The conversation with the Duke of Wellington following this unfortunate wounding is supposed to have run something like this: 'By God, sir, I've lost my leg' — 'By god, so you have', replied the Duke.

The gardens here are especially fine in spring, with azaleas, camelias and rhododendrons, but for the rest of the year shrubs and trees, and the terrace garden with its cypresses, are a delightful complement to the house and it setting on the shore of the Strait. In front of the house, on the edge of the lawn, there is, surprisingly, a large prehistoric burial chamber. Teas. Shop. *(Tel: 0248 714795.)*

Plâs Tan-y-Bwlch (124) (SH 65-40) *1m W Maentwrog.* This castellated country house was built by 19th century slate magnate William Oakley, who was also largely responsible for the nearby 'estate village' of Maentwrog (see page 86). Magnificently sited amidst wooded grounds which include beautiful little Llyn Mair, Plâs Tan-y-Bwlch now houses the Snowdonia National Park Study Centre.

The Centre offers a wide range of residential short courses which provide those attending with an opportunity to get out into the mountains and valleys of Snowdonia at any time of the year. A wide variety of courses range from such subjects as Mountain Walking, Houses and Gardens of North Wales, to Drovers' Roads and Landscape Photography. For further details write to: Plâs Tan-y-Bwlch, Maentwrog, Blaenau Ffestiniog, Gwynedd. LL41 3YU, or *tel: 076 685 324.*

Plas-yn-Rhiw (N.T.) (123) (SH 23-28) *5m W Abersoch.* A small 17th century manor house, with Regency alterations, looking beyond its beautiful woodland gardens across Porth Neigwl (Hell's Mouth), and out over Cardigan Bay to the distant outline of Cadair Idris and the hills of central Wales. It was given to the National Trust by the three daughters of William and Constance Keating in memory of their parents. The Misses Keating have also been generous benefactors in giving the National Trust several areas of coastline in the district. (*Tel: 075 888 219.*)

Pont Britannia (114,115) (SH 54-71) *To immediate SE of Llanfair P.G.* This was built by the great railway engineer Robert Stephenson between the years 1845 and 1850, to carry the Chester and Holyhead Railway Company's line across the Menai Strait. It was constructed of two fifteen hundred feet long rectangular box-sections, which were carried side-by-side on three massive stone piers, with stone abutments at each end. Its building captured the imagination of the public in the same way as Telford's Menai Bridge had done some twenty-five years earlier, and the raising of the long box-sections from barges below, a truly hazardous operation requiring exact calculations and great skill, was witnessed by a great crowd. Read the full story in L. T. C. Rolt's fine biography of the Stephensons. Unfortunately, the box-sections, which had been covered in a timber canopy in 1900, were burnt out by a fire in 1970, which had been started inadvertently by two boys looking for bats. The box-sections have now been replaced by double-deck platforms supported on steel girder arches, and the bridge now carries not only the railway line, but also the re-engineered A5, on its way, like the railway, to Holyhead. This has brought considerable improvements to road-traffic flow, but Stephenson would possibly not have welcomed the steel arches, and nor we feel would the relegation of the Menai Bridge to a secondary status, have met with Telford's unqualified support!

The Pont Britannia is best viewed from Llanfair P.G. churchyard (see page 75), or down the Strait from the church of St Tysilio near Menai Bridge (see page 88).

Pontllyfni (114,123) (SH43-52) *7m SW Caernarfon.* An unexceptional coastal village, at the point where the Afon Llynfni meets the sea, with shingle and rocks and small areas of sand at low tide. Half a mile inland will be found the attractive single-arch bridge that once carried the main route from Caernarfon southwards to the Lleyn — the Pont-y-Cim. It carries the date 1612 and is only seven feet between parapets — just wide enough for a car to pass. It spans the Llyfni, which is noted for its salmon and trout.

Portdinorwic (Felinheli) (114,115) (SH 52-67) *4m NE Caernarfon.* This ancient port on the Menai Strait was traditionally founded by the Norsemen, who used it as a base for their raids upon the neighbouring coasts in the 8th and 9th centuries. Its row of old greystone houses was once the home of fishermen, but in the 19th century it was developed by the Assheton-Smiths of nearby Vaynol Hall (SH 53-69) as a port through which slate could be shipped from their vast quarries at nearby Llanberis, to which it was connected by a railway specially built in 1824-5 (part of which has survived as the Llanberis Lake Railway — see page 69).

In the summer season it is now a popular sailing centre, with sailing courses and yacht hire, and during the quieter months ocean-going yachts are to be found here undergoing refits, or simply moored up for the winter. There are fine views across the Menai Strait to the old ferry point of Moel-y-don and tall-spired Llanedwen church close by (see page 89), and walks up into the hill country behind the town.

Porth Ceiriad (123) (SH 31-24) *2m S Abersoch.* A fine south-facing beach backed by high cliffs. Steep narrow paths lead down from car parks at Pantybranner Farm (SH 314-254) and Nant-y-big Farm (SH 308-251). There is a camp site at Nant-y-big.

Porth Colmon (123) (SH 19-34) *9m NW Abersoch.* Small rocky harbour beyond a caravan site, at the end of a minor road where it should be possible to park. This is at the south-western end of the long Traeth Penllech. There are good firm sands here, but do not bathe near the headland.

Porth Cwyfan (114) (SH 33-68) *1m W Aberffraw.* A remote little rocky, seaweed-covered cove. On a little island between Porth Cwyfan and neighbouring Porth China, and isolated only at high spring tides, stands the tiny 12th century church of Llangwyfan.

Porth Cynfor *(Hell's Mouth)* (114) (SH 39-95) *3m W Amlwch.* A minute cliff-girt cove best reached by the coastal path eastwards from neighbouring Porth Llanlleiana, skirting the fine Iron Age promontory fort of Dinas Gynfor, which can itself be reached by a footpath from the minor road to its south. There is also a path leading eastwards from Porth Cynfor to Porth Wen.

Porth Dafarch (114) (SH 23-79) *2m SW Holyhead.* Pleasant little sandy bay. A small alternative quay was built here in 1820, for use when winds made Holyhead dangerous for sailing craft, but Rennie's great harbour works at Holyhead soon made this redundant. Remains of the old quay may still be seen on the western side of the bay.

Porth Dinllaen (123) (SH 27-41) *8m NW Pwllheli.* Peaceful fishing village and yacht anchorage at the western end of a long beach, and sheltered by a rocky and grass-grown promontory, where there are traces of an Iron Age settlement. There is a friendly inn and a few much-sought-after cottages, and the fact that this hamlet may only be reached by walking along the beach from nearby Morfa Nefyn or by a footpath over the nearby 18-hole golf course, contributes to its very special charm. Cars may be parked in the village car park near the golf course.

William Madocks, of Porthmadog and Tremadog fame, put forward an ambitious scheme for turning Porth Dinllaen into a port for the Irish Mail, but luckily this came to nought, and the hamlet has slept more or less peacefully ever since. However one part of the scheme did materialise — the almost straight road from Pwllheli, which had been built in advance especially to carry the mail traffic to this 'port that never was'.

Porth Eilian (See Llaneilian, page 73.)

Porth Gwylan (123) (SH 21-36) *13m W Pwllheli*. Small cliff-backed cove with a beach of coarse sand.

Porth Iago (123) (SH 16-31) *4m N Aberdaron*. Small cove with a beach of golden sand between rocky headlands. It faces south-west and is a perfect sun-trap. To reach it by car turn down a side road near Tŷ-hen (SH 178-310), and then turn left on to track to Tŷ-mawr farm. Pay fee at farm for access to a car park just above this delightful beach.

Porth Llanlleiana (114) (SH 38-95) *5m W Amlwch*. Here are the remains of a minute harbour, from which locally dug clay was once shipped. The headland (N.T.) to its immediate east is the most northerly point of Wales, and here will be found the earthworks of an impressive Iron Age promontory fort, Dinas Gynfor. There is a footpath to the coast northwards from a minor road.

Porthllechog *(Bull Bay)* (114) (SH 42-94) *1m NW Amlwch*. Pleasant small resort overlooking a minute rocky bay. This was once a pilot station, and in the early 19th century it was a busy shipbuilding and fishing port. There is a good coastal path westwards to Porth Wen.

Porthmadog (124) (SH 56-38) Early in the 19th century, while already working on the creation of nearby Tremadog (see page 108), William Madocks, M.P. for Boston in Lincolnshire, gained the approval of Parliament for the building of a mile-long embankment across the mouth of the Glaslyn Estuary. This embankment, which for many years has carried both road and narrow gauge railway, and which is known as *The Cob (1)*, reclaimed nearly seven thousand acres from the sea and made Porthmadog a major port for the then rapidly growing slate industry. Boston Lodge at its eastern end was named after the M.P.'s constituency, and

Quiet moorings at Porthmadog.

the workshops of the Ffestiniog Narrow Gauge Railway are located here. The picturesque trading schooners and ketches have long since departed — all except one, the sailing ketch *Garlandstone*, now moored to the quayside as the main exhibit of Porthmadog's interesting **Maritime Museum (2)**.

The harbour is now filled with yachts and other pleasure craft, and modern houses and flats have been built on the quays. The other relic of the slate industry, and now very much alive, is the **Ffestiniog Narrow Gauge Railway (3)**, the terminus of which is close to the quays. (For details see page 62.) The **Welsh Highland Railway (4)** (see page 109) is based at Madoc Street West, at the north-western end of the town, close to the **British Rail Station (5)**, which is on the Cambrian Coast Line (see page 46).

The town itself, with its symmetrical street plan and wide tree-lined streets is a tribute to Madocks' skills as a town planner, for he not only created The Cob and drained the marshy estuary, but he also created the town itself. It was named Porthmadog, both after Madocks, and the legendary Madog, a Welsh folk hero who was supposed to have set out for the New World from here.

There is a **Tourist Information Centre (6)** in the High Street *(Tel: 0766 2981)*, and also the office where David Lloyd George (see Llanystumdwy, page 80) and his brother Dr William Lloyd George practised as solicitors. Dr William was still in practice here when he reached the age of 100, and he died two years later, as recently as 1967. Do not miss a visit to the **Porthmadog Pottery (7)** which is at the northern end of Snowdon Street. For what is perhaps the finest distant view of Snowdon, walk westwards along the cob. Despite road and narrow gauge rail traffic there is ample room for pedestrians.

The Park in the centre of the town offers tennis, putting and a children's playground. There is river and sea fishing, with boats that can be taken out to sea, and there is an 18-hole golf course at Morfa Bychan, less than two miles to the south-west.

Porth Nefyn (See Nefyn, page 90.)

Porth Neigwl *(Hell's Mouth)* (123) (SH 26-27) *3m W Abersoch*. This four mile long bay of almost deserted sand earned a grim reputation in the days of sail, when the combination of south-westerly gales and treacherous offshore currents claimed many victims. It is now popular with surfers, but bathing can be dangerous, especially in rough weather, when there is a strong undertow. The best access is from the car park to the south-west of Llanengan (SH 28-26).

Porth Nobla (114) (SH 32-71) *2m NW Aberffraw*. The southern end of a long beach, with some rock, just to the north of the headland on which stands the burial chamber of Barclodiad y Gawres (See page 36). There is good sand here at low tide and a car park on the A4080 not far to the north.

Porth Oer (123) (SH 16-30) *2m N Aberdaron*. The sand in this bay is said to produce a whistling sound if it is walked upon when dry — hence its popular name, Whistling Sands. There is a road leading down to a large car park, from whence it is only a short way down a fairly steep path to the beach.

Porthmadog

SCALE 1:10 000 or 6 INCHES to 1 MILE

1 The Cob
2 Maritime Museum
3 Ffestiniog Railway Station
4 Welsh Highland Railway
5 British Railways Station
6 Tourist Information Centre
7 Porthmadog Pottery

Porth Penrhyn-mawr (114) (SH 28-83) *9m NE Holyhead.* A sheltered, but rather muddy and shingly bay looking over towards Holyhead, with a caravan and camping site at its northern end. Good for sea-birds in wintertime.

Porth Swtan (Church Bay) (114) (SH 29-89) *6m SW Cemaes.* This rocky bay has a good sandy beach at its northern end, and there are some shops and a restaurant here. The beach is sheltered by low cliffs and it may even be possible to have a donkey ride. Our **Walk 2**, page 132 starts from here.

Porth Towyn (123) (SH 23-37) *12m W Pwllheli.* A partly sheltered and understandably popular sandy beach, which may be reached by a short path through a caravan site, from a car park at the nearby farm.

Porth Trecastell (114) (SH 33-70) *2m NW Aberffraw.* There is car park on the A4080 with easy access to this fine sandy beach which is well sheltered by headlands on either side, and which is inevitably crowded at peak holiday times. Porth Trecastell is also known as Cable Bay, as one of the undersea cables from Ireland ends here.

Porth Trefadog (114) (SH 29-86) *9m NE Holyhead.* A semi-circular beach of sand and shingle sheltered by weed-covered rocks, with the remains of an old fort on the headland to the south, and no other buildings except a delightful old farmhouse with gabled dormer windows.

Porth Trwyn (114) (SH 29-87) *7m SW Cemaes.* Sandy beach backed by dunes and a few bungalows. There is limited parking space, and it is possible to walk north from here to Porth Swtan, or south to Porth Trefadog.

Porth Tywyn-mawr (114) (SH 28-85) *9m NE Holyhead.* A fine sandy beach backed by low dunes and facing the open sea, with plenty of parking space and room for all. The swimming is safe as the beach shelves very gently.

Porth Wen (114) (SH 40-94) *3m W Amlwch.* Here is a bay backed by grassy cliffs, with a shingle beach overlooked by the ruins of an old brickworks. There is a path to Porth Wen from the minor road to its south, and fine coastal paths, both to the east and west.

Porth Ychain (123) (SH 21-36)) *9m NW Abersoch.* There is very little space for parking down the cul-de-sac road leading towards this minute rocky bay with its weed-strewn shingle beach. However, there is a pleasant path to it over a small stretch of gorse and heather-covered moorland, and a visit here is worthwhile out of season.

Porth y Nant (See Llithfaen, page 81.)

Porth Ysgaden (123) (SH 21-37) *13m W Pwllheli.* A very rough track leads off the minor road to Porth Ysgaden, known as the 'Herring Harbour' since it was once the base for a flourishing local fishing industry. At one time coal was also landed here from small coasting vessels. The harbour buildings are now in ruins, but large mooring rings can still be seen on the rocks. It is probable that a few local crab and lobster fishermen may still be found here, but the surrounding coastline is extremely rocky, and it is a wild and dangerous place in a westerly gale. Coastal footpaths lead south to Porth Gwylan, and east to Porth Ysglaig. Do not swim near the headlands.

Porth Ysgo (123) (SH 20-26) *8m W Abersoch.* Sand and shingle beach backed by sloping grassy cliffs, and completely inundated at high tide. The path to it goes down beside a small stream and past the remains of a long deserted manganese mine. Parking space at the head of the path is very limited.

Portmeirion (124) (SH 59-37) *3m E Porthmadog.* Situated on a rocky peninsula between the estuaries of the Afon Glaslyn and the Afon Dwyryd, Portmeirion is the creation of the famous architect, Sir Clough Williams Ellis. Here on a densely wooded south-facing slope amidst a wild garden of rhododendrons and azaleas, he created for us a magnificent 'folly', an Italianate village that has become one of the great showplaces of North Wales. He always intended that it should be an 'eye-opener' to awaken the visitors' sense of pleasure in architecture, and to provide an object lesson in how a very beautiful site could be developed without spoiling it, and there can be very little doubt that he achieved this aim.

His village contains an astonishing variety of romantic fantasies and detailed architectural features, some of which Williams Ellis himself rescued from buildings in course of demolition. Amongst the village's many pastel coloured buildings, there will be found a number of shops, including the Portmeirion Pottery Seconds Shop, and a restaurant. Below it and within yards of the sandy shore, is the Portmeirion Hotel, converted from a handsome early 19th century house. This has its own 'folly', a trim little sailing ship made of concrete, safely 'moored' to the quayside outside the hotel windows. There is ample parking above the village, and day visitors are welcome on payment of a fee. *(Tel: 0766 770228.)*

Portmeirion — a romantic fantasy in a Welsh setting.

Precipice Walk (124) (SH 73-20) *3m N Dolgellau.* This well-known walk starts from a point just to the west of a car park (SH 745-212) on a minor road running almost due north from Dolgellau towards the village of Llanfachreth. It is about three miles in length encircling the high ridge of Foel Cynwch and Foel Faner (Foel: a bare hill), and is all within the Nannau Estate (see page 89). Picnicking and camping are not allowed, but the walk is accessible by courtesy of the owner. By following the signs and the red waymarks you will pass through woodlands, and around the precipice itself, with magnificent views out over the Mawddach valley, to the Rhinogs and the Snowdon Range far beyond. You will then return behind the ridge and along the shores of Llyn Cynwch. As the sign at the entrance states: 'Much of the precipice section is believed to have been formed by sheep traversing the side of the mountain. Accordingly in places it is very narrow and precipitous. It is not suitable as a walk for the aged, infirm, children or any persons who suffer from fear of heights or dizziness'. However all those who are fortunate enough not to fall into any of the above categories should certainly take this splendid walk.

Presaddfed Burial Chambers (114) (SH 34-80) *To immediate NE Bodedern.* Two Neolithic burial chambers standing in the centre of a field close to the reedy bird-haunted Llyn Llywenan. The southern one has a large cover or capstone supported on four uprights, while the northern one has collapsed. No sign of any covering mounds remain, but it is reasonable to suppose that these two were once connected beneath a single 'long barrow' mound.

Puffin Island or Priestholm (Ynys Seiriol) (114,115) (SH 65- 82) *5m NE Beaumaris.* This small island lies about half a mile off Black Point (to which there is a toll road from Penmon) and it is not normally accessible to the public. The hermit, St Seriol, established a monastic settlement here as early as the 6th century, and ruins associated with this establishment are still visible. There are also the fragmentary ruins of a 12th century church.

In the 19th century a Liverpool telegraph station was operated here, one of a series linking Holy Island, near Holyhead, with the port of Liverpool (for further details, see Llanrhyddlad, page 79). The puffins for which the island was once famous have long since gone, partly due to the ravages of rats and partly due to these attractive birds once being

Puffin Island and Penmon.

SCALE 1:25 000 or 2½ INCHES to 1 MILE

regarded as a delicacy when pickled. However the island is still renowned for its other seabirds (see Natural History, page 17), and its busy cliffs are best viewed from boats which sail regularly from Beaumaris.

Pwllheli (123) (SH 37-35) This is the main town and market centre for the Lleyn Peninsula, and also the terminus of the delightful Cambrian Coast Railway (see page 46). There are one or two good buildings in the old town. The parish church was built as late as 1887 in the Decorated style, but of more character architecturally is the Penlan Chapel in Gaol Street, built some twenty years earlier. There is a *Tourist Information Centre* in Y Maes (The Field or Square) *(tel: 0758 3000)*, and close by, a

permanent fairground known as Funland. Although there are several large stores and supermarkets, there are also many shops of character, especially in the smaller side streets.

A straight road past the station entrance takes the visitor to the 'holiday town' of South Beach, a wide promenade behind a long shingle shore. For many years Pwllheli had two horse-drawn tram services, and one of these ran all the way along the coast from here to Llanbedrog. Unfortunately, part of the line was washed away in a storm in 1927 and it was never re-opened. To the east of the South Beach, beyond a council estate and a neat caravan site, is situated the harbour and a busy boatyard. Nearby stands Carreg yr Imbill (The Gimblet Rock), a still impressive mass of stone, but much reduced from its original size by quarrying. To the east of the

Pwllheli

SCALE 1:25 000 or 2½ INCHES to 1 MILE

Pwllheli Harbour.

harbour are the sands of Glan-y-don, facing on to Tremadog Bay.

Pwllheli harbour was once busy with trading vessels, but like most small ports around our coast it is now devoted to pleasure craft alone, and is full of colour. There are motor launch trips, and sailing lessons may be taken. Sea angling for bass is good from here, and for golfers there is an 18-hole course well to the west of the town. Four miles to the east will be found Butlin's Holiday Camp, and this is of interest to families looking for a fun-packed day visit, in addition to those who wish to stay for a full week. (*Tel: 0758 612112 for details.*)

Red Wharf Bay (Traeth-coch) (114,115) (SH 53-81) *6m N Menai Bridge.* At low tide the sands of Traeth-coch cover ten square miles — don't try to walk across — there are deep pools and channels that fill very quickly with the incoming tide. The quiet village on its western edge has two inns and a few shops. There was once a quarry, a shipyard and a busy quay, but only pleasure yachts are moored here now. (See also Pentraeth, page 94, and Llanddona, page 70 for other points of access.)

Rhaeadr Cynfal (See Ffestiniog, page 62)

Rhaeadr Du (124) (SH 66-38) *2m S Maentwrog.* This waterfall drops into a dark deep pool in a remote setting in the hills above Maentwrog, and presents a challenge to those who wish to find it. To do so, turn east off the A496 near the Ivy Bridge (Maentwrog) Hydro-Electric Station, and climb a minor road steeply up beside the Ceunant stream for just under a mile. Then take a path to the right, cross a small field and go down through woods. Now follow the noise of falling water and the falls will soon come into sight between the trees. Standing beside this mysterious pool, it is hard to believe that there is a Nuclear Power Station only two miles away.

Rhaeadr Mawddach (See Pistyll Cain, etc., page 95.)

Rhaeadr y Cwm (124) (SH 73-41) *2m E Ffestiniog.* These falls on the Afon Cynfal are visible from a viewpoint about 130 yards east of a small car park on B4391 (SH 735-418). The walk along the busy B4391 between car park and viewpoint is rather dangerous and children should be supervised. It is also possible to walk still further east, to take a footpath leading south-westwards beside the Afon Cynfal, past the falls, and down to Bont Newydd (see Ffestiniog, page 62).

Rhaiadr Du — a fine waterfall in steep woodlands.

Rhaiadr Du (N.T.) (124) (SH 72-24) *Nr Ganllwyd, 6m N Dolgellau.* A spectacular waterfall on the Afon Gamlan as it plunges down through the woodlands of the Dolmelynllyn Estate, the property of the National Trust. Park on the A470 at the south end of Ganllwyd, walk south a few yards and leave the road westwards by the side of a small chapel. Walk up a steep road through an oak and beech wood, and then branch off along a signed path, following the noise of falling water.

The Rhinogs (124) (SH 65-30 etc.) This rugged line of peaks runs parallel with the coast well behind Harlech, between Tremadog Bay in the north and the Mawddach estuary in the south. The highest peak in the range is Y Llethr (SH 66-25), although this only tops Diffwys (SH 66-23), which lies to its south at the end of the chain, by thirteen feet. The two peaks from whom the range derives its name, Rhinog Fawr (SH 65-29) and Rhinog Fach (SH 66-27), are in the approximate centre of the range, and between them is the pass, Bwlch Drws Ardudwy (see page 43). To the north of Rhinog Fawr another path crosses the range through Bwlch Tyddiad by way of the so-called 'Roman Steps' (see page 102). Much of the area northwards from Rhinog Fach is a National Nature Reserve, and although visitors are welcome they are of course asked to safeguard its scientific interest. The Nature Conservancy Council publish an interesting leaflet covering the geology and natural history of the area. Enquiries about the reserve should be addressed to their Regional Officer at Ffordd Penrhos, Bangor, Gwynedd LL57 2LQ.

This is hard country and should only be tackled by experienced hillwalkers, or those in their company. However our Walk 13, page 154, provides a gentle introduction to the Rhinogs in the vicinity of Cwm Nantcol.

Rhiw (123) (SH 22-27) *4m E Aberdaron.* Small village on a hilltop looking eastwards over Porth Neigwl, and south-westwards to Bardsey Island. About a mile to the north-east there is a well-preserved prehistoric burial chamber, Tan-y-Muriau (SH 238-288), but most visitors will head for the delightful 17th century manor house of Plas-yn-Rhiw (NT) (see page 96).

Rhoscolyn (114) (SH 26-75) *6m S Holyhead.* This small village was once noted for its oyster-catching, but it is now a place for modest family holidays, with two fine sandy bays and attractive cliffs. The church was largely rebuilt in the 1870s, but its 15th century font makes a visit here worthwhile. Rhoscolyn's beach has a horseshoe of firm sand between rocky headlands, the western one of which has some spectacular multi-coloured cliffs and rock formations. Above these cliffs, behind Rhoscolyn Head, will be found St Gwenfaen's Well, a spring named after the saint to whom the tiny church is dedicated. The easiest path to the well and the cliffs beyond, follows the farm road from the church, and it is possible to walk northwards above the cliffs to Trearddur Bay, passing above Bwa Du (The Black Arch) (SH 25-76), a fine piece of cliff sculpture. China clay was once quarried near Rhoscolyn, and marble from other nearby quarries was used in the building of no fewer than three English cathedrals — Peterborough, Bristol and Worcester.

Rhosgadfan (115) (SH 50-57) *4m SE Caernarfon.* Quarrying village beneath steep mountain slopes on the western confines on Snowdonia. Here will be found the shell of Kate Roberts' cottage, now restored as a tribute to this talented local writer, whose stories in Welsh are highly evocative of the surrounding countryside. *Tea in the Heather*, probably her best work, has been translated into English.

Rhoslefain (124) (SH 57-05) *5m N Tywyn.* Small village just behind the coast, with no special features apart from a minute early Victorian church with a simple interior and little diamond-paned windows.

Rhosneigr (114) (SH 31-73) *19m W Llanfair P.G.* Popular holiday village since it was 'discovered' by English family holidaymakers in the early years of this century. It is well sited on a headland between two broad sandy beaches, while just inland is the reed-fringed Llyn Maelog, and to the north, the 18-hole Anglesey Golf Course. The long beaches of Crigyll and Cymran stretching to the north, may be reached by a footbridge over the Afon Crigyll. The mouth of this little river was the haunt of the 18th century 'Wreckers of Crigyll' who were notorious for luring ships to their doom off the rocky shores nearby. They were eventually brought to justice and hanged at Beaumaris in 1741, and later became the subject of a popular local ballad.

Rhos-y-gwaliau (125) (SH 94-34) *2m SE Bala.* Attractive hamlet at the northern entry of the deeply wooded Cwm Hirnant (see page 56). Just to the north east, at Plas Rhiwaedog, there is a Youth Hostel, which apart from its usual function, serves as a residential base for sailing courses run on Bala Lake (*tel: 0678 520215* for details — YHA membership obligatory).

Rhyd-Ddu (115) (SH 56-52) *9m SE Caernarfon.* A hamlet in a deep wooded valley south of Llyn Cwellyn, at the junction of the B4418 and A4085. There is a good car park south of the village, which is the starting point of our **Walk 8**, page 144. This is also a starting point of one of the best routes up Snowdon, the early part of which is common with

our **Walk 8**. Experienced hillwalkers and climbers will also find this park useful as a starting point for a traverse of the Nantlle Ridge, a series of dramatic peaks that run south-westwards from Rhyd-Ddu. See also Hebog Range, page 66.

Roewen (115) (SH 75-71) *5m S Conwy.* A pleasant village of restored greystone and whitewashed cottages, a cheerful inn, and a stream hiding behind cottage gardens. Walk westwards from here, soon following the course of the Roman road which ran over the mountains from Canovium (Caerhun) to Segontium (Caernarfon), through the pass, Bwlch y Ddeufaen (see page 43). Half a mile beyond the Rhiw Youth Hostel, there is the Maen-y-Bard (The Bard's Stone) burial chamber (SH 740-718), and a short distance beyond, two standing stones, one of which is known as the Giant's Stick (SH 738-717). These may be the stones from which the Bwlch y Ddeufaen takes its name, 'The Pass of Two Stones'.

Roman Steps (124) (SH 65-30) *7m E Harlech.* A path leads southwards up through a wooded valley from the car park at Llyn Cwm Bychan (see page 55) to this interesting feature. The series of well-laid steps leading south-eastwards up the Bwlch Tyddiad are most unlikely to be Roman in origin, and they were probably put there in medieval times, for the use of pack-horses. They are relatively easy to ascend, and a walk to the top is well worthwhile, being the safest way to penetrate the Rhinog Range (see page 101). It is possible to climb up Rhinog Fawr from here, but only the experienced should tackle this latter stage. Those looking for a longer

The Roman Steps — in the heart of the Rhinog Range.

walk will either head south and south-west to return through the Bwlch Drws Ardudwy (see page 43), or head eastwards through forest country to the A470 just beyond Pont y Gribe (SH 70-30).

Salem (See Cwm Nantcol, page 56.)

St Mary's Chapel, Tal-y-llyn (114) (SH 367-729) *3m N Aberffraw.* Minute wayside church not far from the little Llyn Padrig, with a 12th century chancel and a 17th century south chapel. This has been beautifully restored by the 'Friends of Friendless Churches' and the County Council, and is well worth visiting.

St Tudwal's Islands (East & West) (123) (SH 33-25) *Offshore to SE Abersoch.* These two small islands are at present uninhabited, but an archaeological dig in 1959-61 revealed details of monastic settlement on St Tudwal's Island East. In the 6th century St Tudwal had a cell here, and in the 13th century there was a priory of Augustinian Canons. The Augustinians were expelled at the Dissolution, and pirates appear to have inhabited the island for some time afterwards. In the latter part of the 19th century attempts were again made to found a monastery here, but this enterprise eventually came to nought. It is possible to take a sea trip around both islands from Abersoch.

Sarn Helen (124 etc.) (SH 72-41, SH 72-32 etc.) Elen was the legendary daughter of the Welsh King Gratian, and was married to the Roman Emperor Magnus Maximus in the year 383. Tradition has it that this Elen, as Empress, henceforth became a great builder of roads, and the name Sarn Helen crops up in a number of places in Wales, although most of them must have pre-dated the lady in question. The name Sarn Helen is chiefly attached to the Roman north-south link between Segontium (near Caernarfon) and Caerhun (near Conwy) in the north, and the important fort of Muridunum, near Carmarthen, in the south. Certain stretches appear to be impossible to trace, but others are quite clearly revealed, despite the fact that the hilly nature of the country through which these roads passed largely prevented the building of the traditionally straight road. Read more about these roads in I. D. Margary's classic work, *Roman Roads in Britain*.

Sarn Meyllteyrn (123) (SH 25-32) *11m W Pwllheli.* Pleasantly sited in a wooded valley, this village stands beneath the northern end of the Mynydd Rhiw. The modest mid-19th century church with its sharply-pitched roof and little bellcote, stands well above the rest.

Segontium (See Caernarfon, page 46.)

Shell Island (See Llanbedr, page 68.)

Siabod Range and the Moelwyns (115,124)) (SH 70-54 — SH 66-43 etc.) *About 5m E Beddgelert.* This expanse of wild upland country takes its name from the mountain at its north-western extremity, Moel Siabod (115) (SH 70-54), and runs south-westwards from here, taking in the dramatic peak of Cnicht (115) (SH 64-46) (see also page 50), and ending up in the two mountains above Llyn Stwlan, Moelwyn Mawr (124) (SH 65-44) and Moelwyn Bach (124) (SH 66-43). This lonely and often boggy country is for experienced climbers and hillwalkers only.

The Skerries *(Ynysoedd y Moelrhoniaid)* (114) (SH 26-94) *8m N Holyhead, 2m NW Carmel Head.* This remote little island group, named Skerries by the Vikings, is usually visible from Carmel Head (SH 29-93), and the light that can be seen flashing from its lighthouse is the descendant of one that was set up here as early as 1716. This first consisted of a coal fire in a conical brazier which burned between eight and a hundred tons of coal per year, and in return for this service the owners were allowed to levy a

charge on all shipping that passed this way. By 1835 it was the only lighthouse still in private hands, and by then its revenues were so substantial that it was only after protracted negotiations that, in 1841, the owners were persuaded to accept a compensatory payment of no less than £444,984.11s.2d, no mean sum in the mid-19th century. Since then there has been a Trinity House lighthouse here, but it is not possible for visitors to land.

The Welsh name for the Skerries means 'seal islands', and seals and breeding birds, including puffins, are here in considerable quantities.

Snowdon *(Yr Wyddfa)* (115) (SH 61-54) *11m SE Caernarfon.* Not only the highest, but also the most impressive of all Welsh mountains, Snowdon (Yr Wyddfa) has always been looked upon by the people of Wales as a partly mystic symbol of their culture and their individual spirit. Yr Wydffa means 'the burial place', and this probably refers to the burial of a legendary giant. However, the name Snowdon, or Snawdune, is by far from a recent invention, and Thomas Pennant, in his *Tour in Wales* published in 1778, stated that it was to be found in Saxon documents. It may only be only 75 feet higher than its closest rival, Carnedd Llewelyn, some eight miles to the north-east, but its appearance to those in the valleys below and the views from its summit are both infinitely superior. These take in almost all of Snowdonia, and on occasions when the weather is exceptionally clear, Anglesey, the Isle of Man, and across the Irish Sea, the distant Wicklow Mountains.

The first recorded climb was in 1639, by botanist Thomas Johnson, who sadly was to die only five years later from a wound received during the siege of Basing House, during the Civil War. Most of the recorded climbs that followed were made by men with a scientific leaning, but by the mid-19th century tourists were already arriving at the top in considerable numbers. In 1896 the peak finally fell victim to a mountain railway, and today it is impossible to deny that it is over-visited, not only by railway passengers, but also by walkers. However, the rewards to be obtained at the summit and the special place that Snowdon has in so many hearts, will ensure that visitors will continue to come this way.

We have included three of the classic routes in our walks. **Walk 6**, page 140, makes use of the **Pig Track** and the **Miner's Track**, both of which start at Pen-y-Pass (SH 64-55). **Walk 7**, page 142, makes use of the **Watkin Path**, and starts at Pont Bethania (SH 62-50). Our **Walk 8**, page 144, follows the early stages of the **Rhyd-Ddu** or **Beddgelert Path**, which starts at Rhyd-Ddu (SH 57-52), but beyond our Point B, we leave it. Other routes up Snowdon are: **The Llanberis Path**, the longest and perhaps the easiest ascent, which runs parallel with the Snowdon Mountain Railway, starting from Llanberis (SH 58-59); and finally the **Snowdon Ranger Path**, which starts near the Youth Hostel of that name on the shores of Llyn Cwellyn (SH 56-55), and which is almost certainly the oldest route up Snowdon, being named after John Morton, the first mountain guide in the area and the landlord of the Snowdon Ranger Inn. This is not as impressive as most of the other ascents, but for this reason does have the compensation of being less crowded.

Strong and experienced mountain walkers will

also wish to follow the classic ridge walk known as the 'Snowdon Horseshoe', and this is best started at Pen-y-Pass, following above the Pig Track to Crib y Ddysgl, then round to the summit, Yr Wydffa. From here the route leads to Y Lliwedd, and then to Gallt y Wenallt, before returning to Pen-y-Pass, a total distance of seven miles. These directions are not adequate in themselves, and further reference should be made either to W. A. Poucher's *The Welsh Peaks*, or to Terry Marsh's *The Mountains of Wales*; they are both excellent.

Finally, please remember that although these routes (except the Snowdon Horseshoe) are popular and reasonably easy in good weather, they can be very dangerous if conditions deteriorate. Therefore do not be misled into thinking that no care is required. Always follow the advice given on the inside of the rear cover when leaving the road in this or any other mountain area.

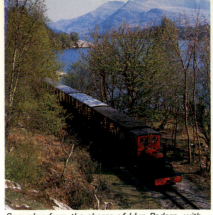

Snowdon from the shores of Llyn Padarn, with the Llanberis Lake Railway in view.

Snowdonia National Park Extending from Conwy in the north to Machynlleth and Aberdyfi in the south, and from Harlech in the west to Bala in the east, the Snowdonia National Park consists of eight hundred and forty square miles of mountains, lakes and forests, as well as three beautiful estuaries and twenty five miles of coastline. Like all National Parks it endeavours to reconcile the interests of those who live and work here, especially the farming community, with the interests of the great volume of visitors who come here each year. It is also necessary to ensure that in the achievement of this balance, the fragile nature of the area's environment is not harmed.

Inevitably there can never be a perfect balance between all the short and long term objectives, but for most readers of this book the functions of the National Parks which are most immediately relevant are the provision of certain leisure facilities, such as car parks, viewpoints, picnic areas, the Snowdon Sherpa Bus Service, and some waymarked forest paths and nature trails. In addition, information is provided that will make a visit here so much more interesting and enjoyable, and there is also a Warden Service, a detailed weather forecast *(tel: 0286 870120)*, and a regular series of guided walks and talks. Guided Walks are divided into Day Walks, Short Walks, Heritage Walks and Castle Walks, and they are listed in leaflets issued by the National Park.

We have made reference to the various Information Centres under the separate entries covering each town, but to summarise, they will be found at Aberdyfi, Bala, Betws-y-Coed, Blaenau Ffestiniog, Dolgellau, Harlech, and Llanberis. Here will be found a wealth of books, maps and leaflets providing detailed information on a bewildering number of topics. For details of residential courses see Plas Tan-y-Bwlch, page 95. To contact the Snowdonia National Park Authority *tel: 0766 770274*, write to the National Park Office, Penrhyndeudraeth, Gwynedd LL48 6LS, or call during normal office hours (closed between 12 noon and 2pm).

Snowdon (Yr Wyddfa) National Nature Reserve (115) (SH 61-54 etc.) Much of the area to the south, south-east and east of the Snowdon summit, Yr Wyddfa, is a National Nature Reserve, and it is well described in the Nature Conservancy Council's general leaflet on the Snowdon massif.

This is the largest single reserve in Wales, and covers a wide range of habitats, from oak woods near Llyn Dinas, through the sheep-walks of the lower slopes, to the arctic-alpine plant life on the exposed mountain tops. See also Cwm y llan, page 57, and our **Walk 7**, page 142.

Snowdon Mountain Railway (115) (SH 59-57 etc.) Opened to passenger traffic in 1896 on the route of the old pony track, this is Britain's only rack and pinion railway, and it is operated entirely by coal-fired, steam locomotives. Starting from Llanberis (SH 58-59) (see page 69), it climbs more than 3000 feet to the summit of Snowdon in just under five miles, a journey that takes about an hour. Weather permitting it runs from Easter to October, on every weekday and most weekends, and the first passenger train of each day is scheduled to start at 9 am. On a clear day the views from the train are most impressive, and are only surpassed by those to be had from the summit. There is a cafe and shop close to the summit, features, which, like the railway itself, inevitably dilute the elemental character of Wales' highest mountain. However, this railway does provide many thousands of people who would otherwise never have come up here with an unforgettable experience, and it must inspire at least a proportion of them to come up into the mountains again, this time on foot. (*Tel: 0286 87023.*)

South Stack Lighthouse (114) (SH 20-82) *3m W Holyhead*. This was first built in 1808 on a small island, on the western shore of Holy Island, itself an appendage of Anglesey. There is a zig-zag path leading to a bridge linking the lighthouse to the shore beyond the end of the minor road, but the best car park is a little further to the south-east. The cliffs here are the home of thousands of sea-birds, and grey seals breed in the caves below. The Royal Society for the Protection of Birds have a reserve here, and there are excellent bird-watching facilities, with an interesting descriptive leaflet being available. At Ellen's Tower (SH 20-81), on the cliffs to the west of the main car park and to the south of South Stack itself, there is a R.S.P.B. Visitor Centre which has an interesting series of displays. See also Holyhead Mountain, page 66, and Natural History, page 17.

Stwlan Dam (See Ffestiniog Hydro-Electric Scheme, page 63.)

The Swallow Falls and Ty-hyll

Swallow Falls (115) (SH 76-57) *2m W Betws-y-Coed.* These falls on the Afon Llugwy are just to the north of the A5 (where there is a car park), and have been a popular port of call for visitors since the early 19th century. George Borrow came here in 1854 during the epic journey recorded in *'Wild Wales'*, and summmed them up thus — 'The Fall of the Swallow is not a majestic single fall, but a succession of small ones'. Before leaving he felt impelled to give the local woman guide sixpence, a generous reward in those days.

The Afon Llugwy, split into several streams, falls some thirty feet into a deep pool, from which it continues as a single foaming torrent; very spectacular when the river is in spate after heavy rain. Less than half a mile to the west, along the A5, there is another car park complete with picnic area, and from here there is a forest walk through the Cae'n-y-coed Arboretum. But for the best forest walk including the Swallow Falls, turn north off the A5 at Ty-hyll (Ugly House), park at SH 758578 and follow the Summerhouse Crag and Swallow Falls Walk. This is *Gwydyr Forest Walk 11* (see Gwydyr Forest, page 64).

Sychnant Pass (115) (SH 75-77) *2m W Conwy.* The old coach road between Conwy and Bangor passed through the hills this way to avoid the coastal route around the foot of Penmeaen-bach Point, which was extremely hazardous in the days before the tunnel was built. There is an attractive

rocky gorge at the top of the pass, and there are fine views of the Great Orme and Anglesey from the ramparts of the hill fort on Alltwen to its north (see **Walk 3**, page 134, which passes this way). Although this pass provided coach travellers with an alternative to the terrors of Penmaen-bach, there was no way of avoiding the equally hazardous Penmaen Mawr headland further to the west, and here coaches had to be taken to pieces and carried for some way. There is no doubt that the Romans were far more logical in taking their road over the pass in the hills much further south, the Bwlch y Ddeufaen (see page 43).

Talsarnau (124) (SH 61-35) *4m NE Harlech.* Modest village astride the A496, Maentwrog to Harlech road, with a wide variety of accommodation including a motel, and a useful station on the Cambrian Coast Railway. There are fine views across the sands of Traeth Bach to the white buildings of Portmeirion, and excellent bird-watching opportunities from the embankments at the edge of the marshy Glastraeth. Talsarnau is also a good starting point for walks via Soar or Eisingrug, up into the moorland country of the Ardudwy and the northern end of the Rhinogs.

Tal-y-bont (124) (SH 58-21) *4m N Barmouth.* Attractive hamlet with an old bridge over the Afon Ysgethin, and not far away, the Old Country Life Museum. Walk up into the hills from here past the oval-shaped hill settlement of Pen y Dinas (SH 607-209), the two long burial cairns of Carneddau Hengwm (SH 614-205), and over the Bwlch y Rhiwgyr (SH 62-20) to Barmouth. There are stations on the Cambrian Coast Railway at both Tal-y-bont and Barmouth.

Tal-y-Bont (115) (SH 76-68) *6m S Conwy.* An unexceptional hamlet on the B5106, with a bridge over the Afon Dulyn. This fast-flowing stream drops down towards Tal-y-Bont through a deep tree-shaded ravine, and about half a mile to the west of the hamlet there is an impressive waterfall, not far below a small road which climbs steeply up towards Llyn Eigiau.

Tal-y-llyn (124) (SH 71-09) *10m S Dolgellau.* A beautiful lake set in a deep valley below Cadair Idris,

Tal-y-llyn — a view from the south-western end.

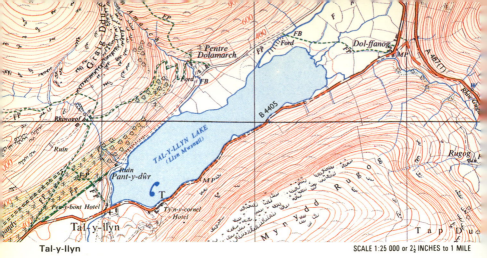

Tal-y-llyn

SCALE 1:25 000 or 2½ INCHES to 1 MILE

with great sweeping mountain sides dropping down to its shores. In winter swans and ducks will be found here and trout are plentiful in the clear waters beneath. Overlooking the south-western end of the lake, not far from the attractive Tyn-y-Cornel Hotel, is an interesting little church, with a pleasantly unspoilt interior which includes early 17th century carved panels in its chancel ceiling. It is near the church that the Afon Dysynni has its outflow from the lake, as it starts on its far from normal course to the sea (see page 61).

Talyllyn Railway (135,124) (SH 58-00 — SH 68-06)
The oldest 2 foot gauge railway in the world, the Talyllyn has been in continuous service since 1867, and it was the first railway in Britain to be saved by volunteers. It runs 7¼ miles inland from Tywyn through magnificent scenery including the Dolgoch Falls (see page 60), to its upper terminus at Nant Gwernol where there are extensive forest walks (see Abergynolwyn, page 31). The original purpose of the railway was for the transport of slate to the main line at Tywyn, but from its inception passengers were also carried. Two of its locomotives are over a hundred years old, and there is a Narrow Gauge Museum and Railway Shop at Wharf Station, Tywyn. Duration of the full journey from Tywyn to Nant Gwernol is 55 minutes. It is possible to link on to this line from the nearby Cambrian Coast Railway's station at Tywyn. For details of services tel: 0654 710472.

Tal y Waen Farm Trail (124) (SH 69-17) *2m W Dolgellau.* Here beneath the crags of Craig y Castell is an interesting 2 mile walk around a working hill farm, with spectacular views out over the Mawddach estuary to the peaks of Diffwys and the Rhinogs. There is also a covered licensed barbecue, a Welsh tea and craft shop, a video depicting the farm trail story, and various attractions for children. (*Tel: 0341 422580.*)

Tan-y-bwlch (124) (SH 65-40) *To immediate W Maentwrog.* (See also Plâs Tan-y-Bwlch, page 95.) This hamlet is beautifully situated in the Vale of Ffestiniog, and has a number of interesting Nature Reserves in the woodlands, both to its east and west (see Landranger Sheet 124). Take the B4410 for a short distance north-westwards to arrive at the shores of lovely Llyn Mair, where there is a car park at the start of the Coed Llyn Mair Nature Trail, (well

described in a Nature Conservancy Council leaflet). A little further on is Tan-y-Bwlch Station on the Ffestiniog Railway (see page 62), with regular services to Porthmadog and Blaenau Ffestiniog. Just beyond the turn to the station there is a minor road heading up through woodlands to Croesor (see

Mountain country above Tan-y-bwlch.

page 54). This is steep in places and there may be several gates to be opened (please close them after passing), but the wild mountain scenery makes it all worthwhile, with the rugged slopes of Moelwyn Bach and Moelwyn Mawr up to the east, and to the south, the great expanse of Traeth Bach with Tremadog Bay beyond. See **Tour 4**, page 116.

Tanygrisiau (115) (SH 68-45) *1m W Blaenau Ffestiniog.* This mountain village is now very much a tourist centre, and has a station on the Ffestiniog Railway (see page 62), and an Energy Information Centre providing information and visitor facilities relating to the Ffestiniog Hydro-Electric Scheme (see page 63), which includes a bus journey up to the Stwlan Storage Dam. Moelwyn Mill, a restored 18th century water-powered fulling mill, is situated close to the station. For those who prefer to walk away from the crowds it is also possible to walk north-westwards up Cwmorthin to Llyn Cwmorthin, past slate-tips and ruined quarrymen's cottages.

Tomen-y-mur (124) (SH 70-38) *3m SE Maentwrog.* This mound, a Norman motte, possibly built by William Rufus, lies within the earthworks of a Roman station built in the 1st century AD. This stands at a point where the Roman road, Sarn

Helen (see page 103) is crossed by another Roman road running from Caer Gai (see page 44) near Lake Bala, north-west to Segontium, the Roman fort near Caernarfon. This must have been occupied for some time, as there are extensive remains associated with it, including two practice works well to the east, and a small amphitheatre just to the north. All these remains are on private ground, but there are splendid views out over Llyn Trawsfynydd, and good picnic possibilities on the hillside beyond a nearby wood. (See also **Walk 11**, page 150.)

The Torrent Walk (124) (SH 75-18) *2m E Dolgellau.* Turn north off the A470, on to the B4416, to reach a car park at the south-eastern end of this famous footpath. It lies within the bounds of the Caerynwch Estate, but is open to the public by permission of the owners. The 'walk', under a mile in length, follows the south-western side of the fast flowing Afon Clywedog, which is boulder-strewn and tree-shaded for its entire length. Here, on a sunny day in summer, are deep pools, with shafts of sunlight upon a seemingly endless series of falls, but after heavy rains the force of the torrent is deafening, and spray hangs in the air beneath dripping trees. A leaflet describing this walk is available at the National Park Information Centre in Dolgellau.

Traeth Bychan (114, 115) (SH 51-84) *2m N Benllech.* A wide, but sheltered sandy beach ('traeth' is the Welsh word for strand, beach or shore), with views of Puffin Island and the Great Orme. This is popular with dinghy sailors and here will be found the headquarters of the Red Wharf Bay Sailing Club. There is a good car park at the northern end of the beach. Walk north to Moelfre, or south to Benllech.

It was here in 1939 that the submarine *Thetis* was finally grounded, after she had failed to surface during trials and 99 men were lost. She was later refitted as *HMS Thunderbolt*, and served in World War II.

Traeth-coch (See Red Wharf Bay, page 101.)

Traeth Dulas (114) (SH 48-88) *4m SE Amlwch.* This long, landlocked estuary, was once used as a harbour for coastal sailing vessels bringing fuel for the long-abandoned brickworks, and shipbuilding and lime-burning were also carried on here. It is now a largely unspoilt area providing shelter for a wide variety of wildlife. The tower on Ynys Dulas (SH 50-90), well to the north-east, was used not only as a seamark, but also as a refuge for shipwrecked sailors, with emergency supplies of food and water being stored away here.

Traeth Lligwy (114) (SH 49-87) *4m N Benllech.* A large and popular sandy bay, backed by low dunes, a caravan site and two car parks. The tide goes out for almost half a mile leaving a wide expanse of firm sand. It is possible to walk eastwards along low cliffs to Moelfre, or north to Traeth yr Ora. See also our **Walk 1**, page 130.

Traeth Penllech (123) (SH 20-34) *9m NW Abersoch.* A fine stretch of sand with a path leading

down from the cliffs, above which is a car park less than half a mile from the shore. If swimming here, keep away from the headlands. See also Porth Colmon, page 96.

Traeth yr Ora (114) (SH 49-88) *5m SE Amlwch.* Small curved sandy beach backed by dunes, and situated just to the south of Dulas Bay, the entrance to Traeth Dulas. See also our **Walk 1**, page 130.

Trawsfynydd (124) (SH 70-35) *5m S Ffestiniog.* A long stone village happily bypassed by the often busy A470, the road whose forerunner may have provided Trawsfynydd's name — 'That Which Spans the Mountain'. Here is remembered the local shepherd, Ellis Humphrey Evans, one of whose poems won him the Bardic Chair at the National Eisteddfod in 1917, just five weeks after his death in France. A bronze statue of 'Hedd Wyn', Evans' bardic name, stands in the main street.

Trawsfynydd Nuclear Power Station (124) (SH 69-38) *3m S Ffestiniog.* This impressive group of buildings stands on the northern shore of Llyn Trawsfynydd (see page 85), an artificial lake created in the late 1920s to supply water to Maentwrog Hydro-Electric Scheme. The buildings were designed by Sir Basil Spence, perhaps best known for his creation of Coventry Cathedral, and the site was carefully landscaped in the hope that it would harmonise with its wild mountain and lakeside setting. Readers may judge for themselves on the effectiveness of this exercise.

Trawsfynydd began to supply power to the national grid in January 1965 and was the first nuclear station to be built inland and the first to use a lake for the supply of cooling water. There is a car park with information provided and a nature trail nearby. See also our **Walk 11**, page 150. Pre-booked parties may visit this station all the year (no children under 14). Write to: C.E.G.B., Trawsfynydd, Blaenau Ffestiniog, Gwynedd LL41 4DT.

Trearddur (114) (SH 25-79) *2m S Holyhead.* A well-loved holiday resort with a flavour of the 1930s. It has a wide variety of accommodation, a series of attractive little sandy bays, including Trearddur Bay itself, and there is a fine 18-hole golf course, 'The Holyhead', just to its north. Towyn Lodge, the Georgian house on the south side of the bay, was used by civil engineer Thomas Telford, when he was building the last sections of his famous London

Trearddur Bay   SCALE 1:25 000 or 2½ INCHES TO 1 MILE

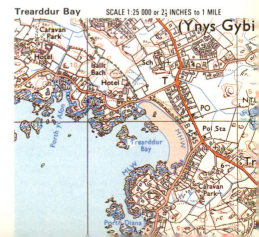

to Holyhead road. Four Mile Bridge on the B4545 was used at high tide by coach travellers to Holyhead, in the days before Telford constructed the Stanley Embankment (see Dyffryn, page 61).

Trefdraeth (See Malltraeth, page 86.)

Trefor (123) *(SH 37-46) 9m N Pwllheli.* A small quarrying village on the northern slopes of Yr Eifl, with a quiet shingle beach just to its north, protected by a little quay wall and pier. On the slopes above the village are vast granite quarries, which were once the largest source of granite paving slabs in the world, and the village takes its name from one of the 19th century quarry managers, a certain Mr Trefor Jones. There is a pottery on the mountain road behind the village — the Cwm Pottery *(tel: 028 685 545).* Walk south from Trefor to Llithfaen over the little Bwlch yr Eifl, or link on to our **Walk 10**, page 148.

Trefriw (115) *(SH 78-63) 2m NW Llanrwst.* A large village beneath wooded hillsides on the western side of the Vale of Conwy. This grew up largely as a result of two nearby springs, and efforts are now being made to revive the village's 'spa status'. The church was heavily restored by the Victorians, but has retained its fine 17th century pulpit.

The fast flowing Afon Crafnant powers the hydro-electric generators that in turn drive the Trefriw Woollen Mills. Visitors are welcome to walk round here and view all the processes in the manufacture of tapestries and tweeds, and there is a large shop selling the mill's products — bedspreads, blankets, rugs, tweeds, knitting wools, etc. There is also a cafe. (*Tel: 0492 640462.*)

Drive up the Crafnant valley to Llyn Crafnant, or by a more circuitous route, to Llanrhychwyn church (see page 79) and Llyn Geirionydd. Our **Walk 4**, page 136, starts from the latter.

Tregaian (114,115) *(SH 45-79) 3m N Llangefni.* Minute hamlet with small bell-coted church in quiet country to the north of Cefni Reservoir. It is worth recalling that in the 16th century a man once lived here to the age of 105, and that his funeral was attended by no fewer than 300 of his descendants. The extraordinary number of his offspring is accounted for by his having been married three times, in addition to his having had at least two mistresses. At his death, his eldest son was 85 and his youngest no more than 2½. He was apparently 'never troubled with Cholick, Gout or stone' and 'had his Senses perfect to the last'. If there had been a a spa here, it would no doubt have continued in popularity to this very day!

Tremadog (124) *(SH 56-40) 1m N Porthmadog.* This little town was developed by William Madocks M.P., between 1805 and 1812, on a relatively small area of land reclaimed from the marshes of Traeth Mawr. He had originally bought a small property at Penmorfa (see page 93) in 1797, but the development of Tremadog was the first stage of an ambitious project to make Porth Dinllaen on the north coast of the Lleyn, the port for a new mail route to Ireland. The buildings facing Tremadog's open square have an attractive unity of design, and are a good example of early town planning.

Madocks also built a small neo-Gothic church and a solidly classical chapel, and the street names 'London' and 'Dublin' remind the visitor of Madocks' ambition to make Tremadog the final inland staging post on his new route to Ireland.

High in the woods to the east of the town there once stood a fine Regency house, Tan-yr-allt, built by Madocks, and rented by him to the poet Shelley in the years 1812-13. T. E. Lawrence, the Lawrence of Arabia, was born at Tremadog in 1888, and his birthplace is now in use as a Christian Mountain Centre.

Tudweiliog (123) *(SH 23-36) 11m W Pwllheli.* Exposed village astride the B4417, with a pleasant inn and a Victorian church of minimal interest to visitors, rebuilt by Sir Gilbert Scott in 1850. There is a large burial chamber or cromlech, popularly known as Arthur's Quoit, on the slopes of Mynydd Cefnamwlch, about 1½ miles SSW of the village (SH 229-346). Tradition has it that this burial chamber was once dug up by a local farmer, but that his cattle made such a noisy and continuous protest, he was forced to replace it. See also Porth Towyn, page 98.

Ty-hyll (Ugly House) (115) *(SH 75-57) 3m W Betws-y-Coed.* This well-loved feature is situated at a point where the A5 crosses the Afon Llugwy, about half a mile west of the Swallow Falls. It is built of great rough blocks of unmortared stone, and is said to date from the late 15th century. Its origins are believed to be the result of the law stating that any freeman could gain freehold rights on common land by building a hearth and chimney, and having smoke rising from it, between dawn and dusk on the same day. The minor road northwards from the A5 at this point heads for some fine forest and lake country, some of which is covered in our **Tour 3**, page 114.

Ty Mawr (N.T.) (115) *(SH 77-52) 4m SW Betws-y-Coed.* Here in the remote valley of the Afon Wybrnant is a late-medieval farmhouse, the birthplace of Bishop William Morgan, who made the first complete translation of the Bible into Welsh. His family were tenants of the Gwydir Estate and he was born between 1540 and 1545, and was fortunate enough to attract the attention of the Wynns of Gwydir Castle, with whom he was educated, and by whom he was sent to St John's College, Cambridge. He completed his translation in 1588, and his Welsh Bible was finally published ten years later. It should be noted however that William Salisbury (see Llanrwst, page 79) had translated the New Testament into Welsh some years earlier, probably in 1563.

The National Trust and the Forestry Commission have jointly organised a 'Bishop Morgan Trail' starting from the Ty Mawr Car Park, and heading for ¾ mile through forest country, before returning to the farmhouse itself. Do not miss a visit here. *Tel: 06903 213.*

Tyn-y-groes (124) *(SH 73-23) 6m N Dolgellau.* Turn east off the A470 just north of the Tyn-y-groes Hotel, at Ganllwyd, and cross the Afon Mawddach to arrive at this car park and picnic site. Here is a grass sward shaded by splendid Douglas firs on the banks of the Mawddach. It is also the starting point for waymarked walks to some fine viewpoints on the hill above, or northwards along a forest road to the waterfall, Rhaeadr Mawddach (see page 95). (See also Coed-y-Brenin, page 50.)

Tywyn (135) (SH 58-00) *4m N Aberdyfi.* The rugged arcading of St Cadfan's church reveals that its history dates back as least to early medieval times. In the church will also be found a 7th century inscribed stone, which was subsequently used as a gatepost until rescued. This has for many years been known as St Cadfan's Stone, but its connections with that saint appear to be somewhat tenuous. There is no doubt, however, that St Cadfan founded a teaching cell here in the 6th century, and it appears to have remained a centre of learning until the time of Henry VIII.

Tywyn's early popularity as a seaside resort was due to the activity of a wealthy Droitwich salt baron, John Corbett. He was responsible for the Marine Terrace, the Market Hall, and the quaint and colourful Assembly Rooms beside the church. The handsome Corbett Arms Hotel was built in the early 19th century, and was originally called the Corbet Arms, following the purchase by John Corbett of the local estate from a family with almost the same name as his own.

See also the excellent modern design of the Roman Catholic church with its attendant sculpture in green slate; the fascinating Narrow Gauge Museum, which is part of the Wharf Station Terminus of the Talyllyn Railway (see page 106); and of course, the line of beautiful sands along the front. It is normally possible to walk south through the dunes to Aberdyfi, but this may also be reached by the ever-useful Cambrian Coast Railway, which passes through both towns. There is tennis and putting near the promenade, paddling pools, cafes, plenty of shops, and an indoor heated swimming pool. The *Tourist Information Centre* is in the High Street *(tel: 0654 710070).*

Ugly House (See Ty-hyll, opposite page.)

Vortigern's Valley (See Llithfaen, page 81.)

Welsh Highland Railway (124) (SH 57-39) *Terminus opposite Queens Hotel, Porthmadog.* The original Welsh Highland Railway ran for a distance of 22 miles from Porthmadog to Dinas Junction near Caernarfon, and was the longest narrow gauge railway in Wales. Unfortunately, this was closed in 1937, and the present line which was re-opened in 1980 only runs as far as Pen-y-Mount, a distance of ¾ mile. It is hoped however that this line will eventually be re-opened as far as Beddgelert. (*Tel: 0766 3402.*)

Wylfa Nuclear Power Station (114) (SH 35-93) *At Cemaes Bay, 6m W Amlwch.* First commissioned in 1971, this is the largest of its kind in the world, and although not everyone approves of its setting on Anglesey's rugged and largely unspoilt northern coast, it is a striking example of industrial architecture. The C.E.G.B. have provided an observation tower giving visitors a good view of the buildings and a display of photographs and charts. The open space at Wylfa Head has been given to the public, and a nature trail from the car park is described in an

excellent booklet. There is also a picnic site. Tours of the station itself are possible without prior booking between June and mid-September, and with pre-booking, all the year. (*Tel: 0407 710471.*)

Ynys y Fydlyn (114) (SH 29-91) *5m W Cemaes.* This minute rocky island, split into two and fissured with caves, provides shelter for a minute shingle bay. It may be reached on foot from the minor road to the west of Llanfairyghornwy, by a footpath following the south side of a conifer plantation. Do not miss this very pleasant little expedition.

Yr Eifl (The Rivals) (123) (SH 36-44) *7m N Pwllheli.* (See also Llanaelhearn, page 67, and our **Walk 10**, page 148) These three peaks are a prominent landmark, with their height somewhat exaggerated by the proximity of the sea and the low ground to their south. Properly their Welsh name means 'The Forks', and 'The Rivals' is only a fancy name thought up by the English. The central peak is the highest at 564m (1850 ft), and the one nearest the sea, the lowest at 444m (1458 ft), its slopes ending

The three peaks of Yr Eifl — 'The Rivals'.

in the rugged headland of Trwyn y Gorlech above Porth y Nant. The eastern peak above Llanaelhearn at 485m (1591 ft) is crowned by an ancient settlement — Tre'r Ceiri — to which there is a fairly easy footpath from the B4417 (see Llanaelhearn, page 67, and **Walk 10**, page 148).

Yr Wyddfa (See Snowdon, page 103.)

Ysbyty Ifan (116) (SH 84-48) *7m SE Betws-y-Coed.* This small village in the upper valley of the Conwy is the centre of the National Trust's great Penrhyn Estate, here a fine stretch of sheep country. It derives its name from the 'Hospice of St John of Jerusalem', which, until the abolition of this order of medieval knights, provided shelter in this wild mountain area, both against marauding bands of thieves and the dangers of the elements. The vacuum that resulted from the closure of this order appears to have made this area a haven for wrongdoers of every type, but all is now peaceful again at Ysbyty. The church was rebuilt in 1861 but its contents include three medieval effigies, one of which is believed to represent Rhys ap Meredydd, a standard bearer to the Henry Tudor at Bosworth Field, who became Henry VII soon after his famous victory over Richard III in 1485.

Motor and Cycle Tours

Tour 1

Countryside and Coastlands of Eastern Anglesey

50 miles. Reasonable for cyclists, although there are a few steep little hills in the later coastal section.

Our route moves northwards from the shores of the Menai Strait, across the gently undulating countryside of Anglesey, to pass the fine National Trust property of Plas Newydd, a prehistoric burial chamber and two attractive reservoirs, before reaching the north coast at Amlwch. From here we turn southwards to follow the eastern coast, never far away from a succession of beautifully-sheltered sandy bays. Skirting the broad sands of Red Wharf Bay, we head eastwards to Penmon and Black Point, before heading through Beaumaris with its splendid castle, to end our journey just beyond Menai Bridge.

This tour starts from **Llanfairpwll**, the famous little town with the long name (see page 75). Assuming that you have just crossed the Menai Strait into Anglesey on the A5 over the **Pont Britannia**, bear left and turn left, on to A4080, and pass **the Marquess of Anglesey's Column** on right. Now turn left, keeping on A4080, and soon pass entrance to splendid National Trust property of **Plas Newydd** on left. Turn right off A4080 at first X-rds (sign — Llanddaniel Fab). Park on right by gate of Bryncelli Ddu Farm, for a ½ mile walk to right, to interesting **Bryncelli Ddu Burial Chamber**.

Bear right, and then left in **Llanddaniel Fab**. Under railway bridge and immediately fork right, keeping on wider road. Now turn left into Gaerwen, straight, not right, and then turn left on to A5 with great care. Turn right with care in **Pentre Berw**, off A5, and head up long straight road with views of marshy valley over to left. After 2m, turn left onto B5420, the old coach road to Holyhead before Telford built the new road that was to become the A5, and almost immediately turn right off B5420. Keep straight, not right twice, and then straight, not left at entry to Talwrn. Beyond village, turn left at X-rds onto B5109. (But turn right if you wish to visit the **Bodeilio Weaving Centre**, over to right after ¼ m.)

Now head down B5109 into **Llangefni**, Anglesey's administrative centre and prin-

cipal market town. Beyond entrance to town, turn right onto B5420, and turn right again near the Square, onto B5111. Church and entrance to the attractively wooded valley known as The Dingle on left (see page 77). Fork left keeping on B5111, which we shall keep on until reaching **Amlwch**, 12m ahead; therefore the briefest of route directions until then. 2m beyond Llangefni, car park for **Cefni Reservoir** on left. Picnic site, birdwatching and fishing. Through **Llanerchymedd**, once noted for its boots and snuff, on B5111. (But go straight ahead by church and almost immediately fork right, if you wish to visit **Llyn Alaw**, 2m ahead at Gwredog. Car park, picnic site, bird-watching. Visitor Centre at SW end of lake visited on Tour 2.)

Head north from Llanerchymedd on B5111, through Rhosybol, and over the western slopes of **Parys Mountain**. Car park with viewpoint, signs of long deserted copper mines. Over roundabout at entry to **Amlwch**, crossing A5025. A boom-town in the late 18th and early 19th century, Amlwch is still a lively place and has a harbour and a fine new Leisure Centre. Bear right twice near the end of the town, but turn left if you wish to visit Amlwch Port.

Turn left (Sign — Porth Eilian), and enter **Llaneilian** (interesting church on left). Straight, not left beyond church, but turn left if you wish to visit Porth Eilian and Point Lynas (see page 73). Turn sharp left at X-rds in centre of Pengorffwysfa hamlet and up narrow road with care. Bear left at next junction and follow around Mynydd Eilian, a hill with radio masts, where there was once a signal station on the Holyhead to Liverpool Telegraph (see page 73). Keep straight at next two junctions, and then turn right by woodlands of Llysdulas House. Straight, not left at next junction, but turn sharp left if you wish to visit Llanwenllwyfo New Church (see Dulas, page 61).

Turn left at next junction and then turn left with great care on to A5025. Keep on A5025 at small X-rds, but turn left if you wish to visit the shoreline of **Traeth Dulas**. Keep on A5025 through City Dulas. Then Pilot Boat Inn on left, and Morris Memorial on hill to left, just beyond (see Brynrefail, page 43). Keep on A5025 through **Brynrefail**, but turn left if you wish to visit **Traeth Dulas**, **Traeth Ora** or **Traeth Lligwy**. Note also that our **Walk 1**, page 130, starts from this village. Bear left off A5025 ½m beyond **Brynrefail**. Turn right at X-rds, but turn left if you wish to visit **Traeth Lligwy**. After ¼ m, path on right to the ruined 12th century Hen Capel (see page 58) and the Iron Age and Roman village of **Din Lligwy**. After ¼ m Lligwy Burial Chamber on right (see page 58).

Over roundabout on to A5025. But turn left if you wish to visit **Moelfre**. Over X-rds, but turn left if you wish to visit **Traeth Bychan**. Over main X-rds in Benllech (but turn left for beach car park). Keep on A5025 (but take one of two turns to left if you wish to visit **Red Wharf Bay**). Turn left off A5025 in **Pentraeth** onto B5109, and bear right keeping on B5109 unless you wish to fork left for the shore of Red Wharf Bay. After 2½ m turn left off B5109 (Sign — Llanddona), and after 1½ m turn right at entry to **Llanddona**. (But turn left for another narrow lane down to the shores of **Red Wharf Bay**.)

Turn left beyond entry to **Llanddona**, and turn right at end of village. Bear left on to wider road, but fork right across open heathland if you wish to visit interesting **Llaniestyn Church**. Straight, not left, just beyond TV mast. After ½ m, straight not left. But turn left if you visit the tiny church of **Llanfihangel Din-Sylwy** beneath the earthworks of Bwrdd Arthur (see Natural History,

page 76). Fine views ahead of Puffin Island and the Great Orme.

Take the next few junctions carefully, the route is rather involved here. Turn left in Mariandyrys hamlet, bear left at next junction, then straight at next two junctions. Now down steep hill, bear right, turn left, and straight, not right. You should now be on a road leading northwards parallel with the shore, to head past **Penmon Priory**, to Black Point, opposite **Puffin Island**. Now return from Black Point, again parallel with the shore, turning left at T-junction beyond shingly beach, and eventually turning left at X-rds onto B5109. Follow B5109 into **Beaumaris**, a pleasant town with a castle and a series of other interesting features.

Leave Beaumaris on A545, with frequent glimpses of the Menai Strait to left before reaching **Menai Bridge (town)**. Pass Tegfryn Art Gallery on right. Keep straight over X-rds in town centre and continue past church with unusual spire, heading **initially** towards the **Menai Bridge**. Before reaching bridge, follow roundabout to right heading back on the A4080. *Tourist Information Centre* on left. Park here to visit church and to use the Belgian Promenade (see page 88). Use A4080 to link on to the start of this tour immediately beyond the Pont Britannia by going under A5, or bear left with care on to A5 to return to the mainland, thus completing Tour 1.

SCALE 1:190 080 or 3 MILES to 1 INCH

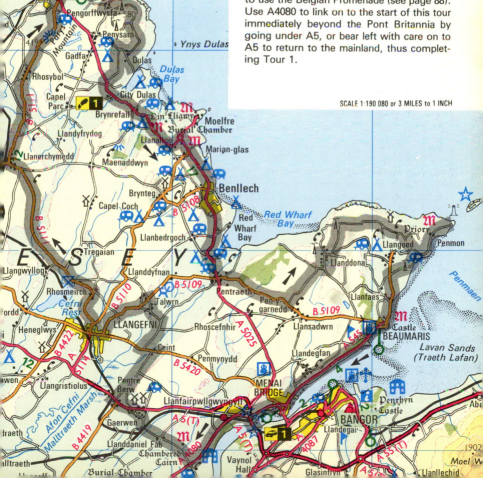

Tour 2

North-west Anglesey and Holy Island

45 miles. An easy and rewarding run for cyclists, with quiet roads and very few hills.

This route sets out from Holyhead on Holy Island, and after crossing the Stanley Embankment, it heads northwards behind the sandy coves of Anglesey's west coast. It changes direction just inland from the rugged Carmel Head, and follows the rocky northern coast almost as far as Amlwch, where it is possible to link on to our Tour 1. Our route now runs south-westwards, passing the shores of two attractive lakes, before making use of a short stretch of Telford's London to Holyhead road (now the A5), as far as Dyffryn (Valley). From here we pass over to Holy Island, to explore much of its delightful coastline, its ancient monuments, and the rugged little Holyhead Mountain, before returning to Holyhead itself.

Start from the busy ferry and holiday town of **Holyhead** and head south-eastwards on the A5 road, soon passing the great aluminium smelting works on the right, and the **Penrhos Nature Reserve** on the left. Now cross the water between Holy Island and Anglesey

on the Stanley Embankment, the last challenge presented to the great civil engineer Thomas Telford in his construction of the London to Holyhead road.

Turn left in **Dyffryn (Valley)**, onto A5025 and keep on this until turning left beyond **Llanfachraeth** (Sign — Llanfwrog). Keep straight through Llanfwrog, but beyond church turn second left if you wish to visit **Porth Penrhyn-mawr**, and/or **Porth Tywyn-mawr**. At entry to **Llanfaethlu**, turn left if you wish to visit **Porth Trefadog**. Turn left in **Llanfaethlu** (Sign — Porth Swtan) and then, after taking in sweeping views of Anglesey's western coast, sharp right in Borthwen hamlet, and pass turning on left to **Porth Trwyn**. After 1m pass turning on left to **Porth Swtan** (which is starting point of **Walk 2**).

Up hill, keeping straight, not right, by St Rhyddlad church, then bear left onto wider road, and fork left. After 1m, path to **Ynys y Fydlyn** on left. Turn right (Sign — Llanfair-ynghornwy). Probable access for walkers down farm road leading to path to **Carmel Head**. Turn sharp left in **Llanfairyghornwy** (Sign — Cemlyn) (but go straight ahead if you wish to visit church). After 1¼m turn right (access for walkers to left leading to **Carmel Head**). After ¼m path to small rocky bay of **Hen Borth**. Also possible to reach **Llanrhwydrys Church** from here.

Straight, not left (but turn left for 1st car park for **Cemlyn Bay**). Left at T-junction,

SCALE 1:190 080 or 3 MILES to 1 INCH

Calm waters at Porth Cynfor (Hell's Mouth).

and then fork right (but fork left for 2nd car park for **Cemlyn Bay**). Turn left onto A5025 in Tregele, and after ¼m, a turn to left for **Wylfa Nuclear Power Station**. Keep through **Cemaes** on A5025, but turn left at roundabout to visit shore. Beyond **Cemaes** turn left, off A5025. Fork right twice in **Llanbadrig**, but take second left if you wish to visit ruined church and headland. At ¾m beyond Llanbadrig, a path on left to **Porth Llanlleiana**, **Dinas Gynfor** and **Porth Cynfor** (Hell's Mouth). After ¾m, a path on left to **Porth Wen**.

Turn left, rejoining A5025, and after 1m, turn right off A5025 (but go straight ahead on A5025 if you wish to visit **Bull Bay** or **Amlwch**, or link on to **Tour 1**). After 1m bear left at Y-junction; then straight not left, and turn right at X-rds just beyond railway bridge. Over X-rds at Four Crosses, and through Rhosgoch. Now straight, not left and straight not right (Signs — Llyn Alaw), and **Llyn Alaw** is soon visible over to left. Straight, not right, and after 1¾m left at Y-junction. **Llanbabo** Church on left, is worth visiting. Soon go straight, not right (Sign — Llyn Alaw), and after ¾m, entrance to **Llyn Alaw Visitor Centre** on left.

Turn right near **Llantrisant New Church**, and after ¼m, left at Y-junction. Bear right at next T-junction, and through Pen-Llyn hamlet. Now skirting northern edge of reedy, bird-haunted Llyn Llywenan, and bear left twice. Now turn right (at this point it is possible to go left to visit **Presaddfed Burial Chambers**), and then turn right onto B5109.

Turn left, off B5109 in **Bodedern**, and go straight not left twice, before turning right with care, onto A5. Keep on A5 through **Caergeiliog**, and then turn left at traffic lights at entry to **Dyffryn (Valley)** onto B4545. Keep on B4545 for 3m, having crossed over Four Mile Bridge onto Holy Island, and then turn left in Trearddur (Sign — South Stack). Now skirting coast of Holy Island. Straight, not right (Porth-y-post down to left). Straight, not right at **Porth Dafarch**.

Straight, not right (but turn right if you wish to visit **Penrhosfeilw Standing Stones**). After 1m straight, not left (but turn left if you wish to visit **South Stack** and **Holyhead Mountain**, good car park ahead). Now follow into **Holyhead**, thus completing Tour 2.

Tour 3

The Conwy Valley, and Around the Carneddau Range

65 miles. Mostly reasonable for cyclists, especially if the diversions up from the Conwy Valley are ignored, and more of B5106 is used (but don't miss Bodnant). Be prepared for one long climb — up from Capel Curig to Ogwen Cottage, although the Nant Ffrancon descent provides a splendid reward for this effort.

Our route sets out from Conwy and soon heads down the Conwy Valley, visiting the lovely Bodnant Garden, and making several diversions into the foothills of the lofty Carneddau Range. We then drive through part of the Gwydyr Forest before turning westwards near Betws-y-Coed to follow up the beautiful Llugwy Valley, past Miners' Bridge, the Swallow Falls and Capel Curig. From here we climb into the mountains, past Llyn Ogwen, and then down the dramatic Nant Ffrancon (valley), through Bethesda, to visit the splendid Penrhyn Castle. We now head along the dramatic north coast and up over the Sychnant Pass, before arriving back at Conwy.

Leave the lovely old town of **Conwy**, with its fine castle and town walls and wealth of other interesting features (it is also the start of our **Walk 3**, page 134). First head eastwards on the A55, crossing the Conwy Estuary by road bridge which runs parallel with the earlier bridges built by Telford and Stephenson (see page 51). Beyond bridge, bear right at roundabout, keeping on A55 (if coming from Llandudno, it would be easy to join the route here). Now watch for possible road layout changes ahead, but bear round to right at roundabout onto A470 heading southwards near estuary shore.

Beyond Llansanffraid Glan Conwy, pass the beautifully restored watermill of **Felin Isaf**. After about 1m, bear left off A470, and soon pass entrance to lovely **Bodnant Garden (NT)** on right. Turn right at X-rds in Graig hamlet, and drop steeply down to cross Afon Conwy beyond Tal-y-cafn. Bear right onto smaller road immediately beyond bridge and head northwards, with pleasant views over estuary. Turn left with care onto B5106, and almost immediately turn right off B5106. **Llangelynin New Church** on right (see page 77 for location of **Llangelynin Old Church**).

The Swallow Falls.

Head straight for pretty village of **Roewen** by turning right at first X-rds. Straight, not right, at end of village and head steeply up mountain slopes. Turn left at T-junction (SH 738-710) (but turn right if you wish to drive further towards the **Bwlch y Ddeufaen** — no through road). Now head down slopes towards **Llanbedr-y-cennin**, and through this village, with its attractive 16th century Olde Bull Inn.

Now turn right onto B5106 (but turn left if you wish to visit **Caerhun**, with its Roman earthworks and medieval church). Keep on B5106 through **Tal-y-Bont** and **Dolgarrog**, running between wooded hills and the Conwy Valley. In **Trefriw**, with its interesting woollen mill, take second right off B5106 and then turn left at end of village (but go straight on here if you wish to divert up to lovely **Llyn Crafnant** — no through road). After about ¾m, turn right at small X-rds, and after about ¼m **Llanrhychwyn Church** on left. Pass Llyn Geirionydd on right, car park here is the start of our **Walk 4**, page 136.

Now head south-east into part of **Gwydyr Forest**, and after 1m turn left, passing car park with picnic site and start of nature trail. Llyn Sarnau on right, this is on our **Walk 5**, page 138. After 1½m bear right, and then bear right rejoining B5106 (but go straight over if you wish to visit **Llanrwst**). **Gwydyr Castle** on left, and **Gwydyr Uchaf Chapel** beyond on right. Now head southwards on B5106, and after passing the Pont-y-Pair car park, which is the start of our **Walk 5**, page 138, cross the Afon Llugwy and turn right with care onto A5 (but turn left if you wish to visit **Betws-y-Coed** — it is also possible to link with Tour 4, which starts there).

Our tour now follows the A5 road for about 18m, so route directions will be kept to a minimum on this section. Pass car park on left, giving access to **Miners' Bridge** (opposite) and the **Garth Falls Walk** (to left). After

1m car park on left for **Swallow Falls** (opposite). After ½m, car park on left, with picnic site and trail giving access to **Cae'n-y-coed Forest Garden**. Over bridge crossing Afon Llugwy, and **Ty-hyll (Ugly House)** on right.

Bear right in Capel Curig, keeping on A5. The crags of Galt yr Ogof up to left. **Llyn Ogwen** to right (car park on right). The rugged peak of Tryfan up to left. Ogwen Cottage (Outdoor Pursuits Centre and Mountain Rescue Post) at end of lake. Car park on left gives access to **Cwm Idwal Nature Trail**. Outfall of lake is marked by modern road bridge, the Pont-y-benglog, beneath which may be seen remains of 18th century packhorse bridge, popularly known as the 'Roman Bridge'.

Now start descent into the splendid **Nant Ffrancon** (valley), in the footsteps of Pennant and Borrow (see page 89). Through Ty'n-y-maes and 19th century slate-quarrying town of **Bethesda**. Over dual carriageway and join A5122 (Sign – Bangor), and within 1m turn right into pleasant estate village of **Llandegai**. Do not miss a visit to the splendid

19th century neo-Norman **Penrhyn Castle (N.T.)**; entrance on left, by the Grand Lodge.

Fork left at end of Llandegai, over small X-rds. Then over bridge crossing dual carriageway of A55, and immediately turn left, to run parallel with it. Follow this road eastwards to **Aber**, and turn right with care onto A55. Turn right, up valley to Bont Newydd for walk to the beautiful **Aber Falls**, and then return to the A55, and head north-eastwards through **Llanfairfechan** on A55 (but at central X-rds, turn left for beach or right for church, Druid's Circle access etc.). The A55 now runs close between shore and steep slopes of Penmaen Mawr, and under archways cut in the rock. Over X-rds in centre of **Penmaenmawr**, and after ¼m fork right off A55. Continue ahead up hill bearing right at first, and after ¾m bear right at edge of **Dwygyfylchi**. Then straight not left, and after ¾m, bear left past Fairy Glen Hotel. Now straight not left, and through the beautiful **Sychnant Pass** (our **Walk 3** crosses the road here, at its Point E). Fine views from here. Now drop down into **Conwy**, thus completing Tour 3.

SCALE 1:190 080 or 3 MILES to 1 INCH

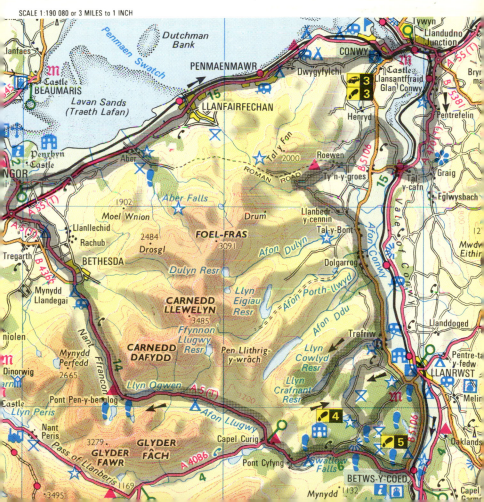

Tour 4

Betws-y-Coed, the Ffestiniogs and Snowdon's Southern Flanks

45 miles. This is a challenging route for cyclists. The mountain section starting near Tan-y-bwlch Station could be avoided by using more of the B4410, although this is also very hilly in places. The steep climb out of the Nanmor Valley and the long pull up Nantgwynant are both hard work, but many will consider that the scenic rewards justify these exertions.

This route starts from Betws-y-Coed, and after passing some spectacular waterfalls, heads up through a long wooded valley onto the bleak moorland country of the Migneint. We then drop down into gentler country before briefly turning northwards to explore the past glories of Snowdonia's slate industry, including the famous Ffestiniog Railway, and also the present marvels of hydro-electric power. Now we go southwards down the lovely Vale of Ffestiniog

before climbing up into the hills below Cnicht, the 'Matterhorn of Snowdonia'. We drop down once again before heading up the Nanmor Valley and down into the outstandingly beautiful Nantgwynant. From here we climb to Pen-y-Gwryd and then down past Capel Curig and the Swallow Falls, to journey's end at Betws-y-Coed.

Leave the greystone village of **Betws-y-Coed** southwards on A5, soon crossing the Afon Conwy on Telford's fine cast-iron Waterloo Bridge, reminding us that this was part of his great London to Holyhead road. Keep on A5 for almost 2 miles noting fine views up LLedr Valley to distant Moel Siabod to right. Turn right onto B4406 near restaurant car park for **Conway Falls** (Sign — Penmachno). Over X-rds by the interesting **Penmachno** Woollen Mill, but turn right if you wish to visit the Machno Falls and the Fairy Glen (see Conway Falls, page 53). (It is also possible to continue on this diversion in an anti-clockwise direction, past the Fairy Glen, up part of the Lledr Valley and past **Ty Mawr (N.T.)**, the birthplace of Bishop Morgan, and to link up with the main route at **Penmachno**.)

Head up the B4406, and turn right and then left in **Penmachno** and on minor road southwestwards up the wooded Machno Valley. Straight, not right at Carrog hamlet (Sign —

SCALE 1:190 080 or 3 MILES to 1 INCH

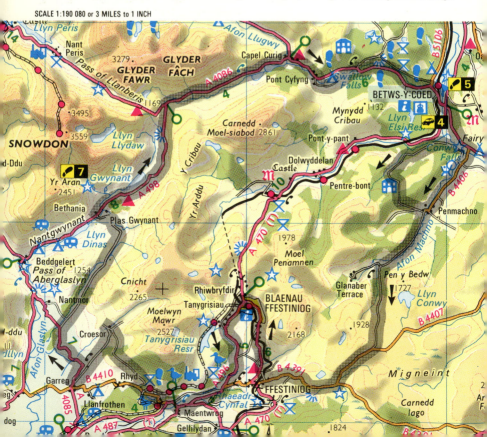

Llyn Gwynant from the south.

Ffestiniog). Steeply up through forest plantations, and then on to open moorland of the **Migneint**. After ½ m, path on left leading up to **Llyn Conwy**, starting near Hafodyredwydd, an isolated house on right. Bear right onto B4407. After 1½ m **Llyn Morwynion** visible over to right.

Turn right onto B4391 (Sign — Ffestiniog). Viewpoint car park on left for **Rhaeadr y Cwm**. Follow B4391 into **Ffestiniog**, turn right onto A470, and head north to **Blaenau Ffestiniog**. Beyond here turn left onto A496 (but go ahead on A470 for short distance if you wish to visit the **Llechwedd Slate Caverns** (to right) and/or the **Gloddfa Ganol Slate Mine** (to left)).

Go straight, not left if you wish to visit **Tanygrisiau**, the **Ffestiniog Hydro-Electric Scheme**, or take a trip on the **Ffestiniog Railway**. Otherwise head south from Ffestiniog down the beautifully wooded Vale of Ffestiniog, on A496 almost as far as **Maentwrog**, but then bear right on A487, over the Afon Dwyryd. Now turn right with care onto B4410 (Sign — Rhyd) at **Tan-y-bwlch**. After ½ m Llyn Mair (see **Tan-y-bwlch**, page 106) on left, car park on right. Tan-y-bwlch Station (on the **Ffestiniog Railway**) up to right. Almost immediately turn sharp right with great care, onto attractive mountain road. There are several gates across this road, please close them after passing. This is partly afforested, but dramatic view of **Cnicht** ahead. Turn sharp left at X-rds. **Croesor** car park, just beyond, is a good base for **Cnicht**.

Fine views ahead of Traeth Mawr, the drained Glaslyn Estuary (see **Porthmadog**,

page 97). On right, pass Plâs Brondanw, home of the late Clough Williams Ellis (see **Llanfrothen**, page 76), and sharp right with care onto A4085. After 2¼ m, turn right at small X-rds and head up the attractive Nanmor Valley. Straight not left at Bwlchgwernog hamlet, and after ¼ m, Cae Ddafydd Rare Breeds Centre and Wood Turnery on left (see **Nantmor**, page 90). After 1m Picnic Area on right with Forest Walk. Head up Nanmor Valley and beyond small pass, drop down into **Nantgwynant** (fine views).

Over bridge and turn right with care onto A498. After ¼ m, pass Bethania Bridge Car Park. This is start of our **Walk 7**, page 142, making use of the Watkin Path to Snowdon. **Llyn Gwynant** on left. Good car park well beyond on left gives good views of **Nantgwynant**, **Cwm Dyli**, and of **Snowdon** itself (but see Nantgwynant, page 90). Bear right onto A4086 at Pen-y-Gwryd. After 2½ m Dyffryn Mymbyr visible over to left beneath **the Glyders**. This farm was immortalised by Thomas Firbank in *I Bought a Mountain* (see Llynnau Mymbyr, page 83). **Llynnau Mymbyr** on right — good car park.

Turn right in **Capel Curig**, onto A5. After less than 1m turn right with care, and cross the Afon Llugwy by the Pont Cyfyng. After ¾ m, site of **Caer Llugwy** (Roman fort) on left. Bear right with great care onto A5. **Cae'n-y-coed Picnic Site** on right, with forest garden. **Swallow Falls** on left - car park on right. After 1m **Miners' Bridge** on left — car park opposite, on right — **Garth Falls Walk** starts from here. Now follow A5 into **Betws-y-Coed**, thus completing Tour 4.

Tour 5

Around the Snowdon Massif and down to Lloyd George Country

60 miles. With the Llanberis Pass to be tackled, this is not always an easy route for cyclists, but the run down Nantgwynant from Pen-y-Gwryd would be hard to beat — a gentle descent through idyllic countryside. To the north-east of Llanystumdwy, use the A487 and A498 to avoid some steep and narrow mountain roads.

Our route sets out from Caernarfon, through fascinating Llanberis, terminus of the Snowdon Mountain Railway, and climbs over the Llanberis Pass into the very heart of Snowdonia. (In the encirclement of the Snowdon massif, this route passes the start of two walks leading to Snowdon's summit, and two further walks in the surrounding area.) We then run down lovely Nantgwynant to Beddgelert before heading through the Aberglaslyn Pass and down to the coast at Porthmadog. After visiting Llanystumdwy, the village always associated with Lloyd George, we turn north-eastwards to return over quiet roads to the Aberglaslyn Pass and Beddgelert, with an option to explore the beautiful Cwm Pennant. From Beddgelert we head northwards, passing Beddgelert Forest and Llyn Cwellyn, before returning to Caernarfon.

Start from **Caernarfon**, busy market and holiday town, and administrative capital of Gwynedd. Leave eastwards on A4086, passing through Pont-rug and quarry village of **Llanrug**. Beyond here keep on A4086 (but turn right if you wish to visit **Bryn Bras Castle**). **Llyn Padarn** soon on left. Now through the village of **Llanberis** which is full of interest. Park near entry, or by turning left in village for car park near the fascinating Welsh Slate Museum, the Llanberis Slate Railway Station and the Llyn Padarn Country Park. Terminus of **Snowdon Mountain Railway** to right of A4086. But for all details, including the Welsh Environmental Centre, see Llanberis, page 69.

Keep on A4086 beyond village. Footpath to **Dolbadarn Castle** to left. Views of **Llyn Peris** to left, note stepped quarry workings above. Car park near head of lake. Through village of **Nant Peris (Old Llanberis)**, where it is possible to park and make use of the Snowdon Sherpa Bus Service (see page 19).

Start to climb **Llanberis Pass** — climbers often visible from the crowded car parks on this road. Over summit of pass at Pen-y-Pass, the starting point of our **Walk 6** to the summit of Snowdon. If no parking space, return to Nant Peris and use bus (see above).

Turn right at Pen-y-Gwryd, onto A498 (Sign — Beddgelert), and head down the lovely **Nantgwynant**. Car park after 1m has fine views (for details see Nantgwynant, page 90, and Cwm Dyli, page 56). Now descend to level of **Llyn Gwynant**, soon visible on right. Pass Bethania Bridge car park, the starting point of our **Walk 7**, making use of the Watkin Path to **Snowdon**. At ¼m beyond, small road to left heads up over the mountain to the Nanmor Valley (but this is best tackled on Tour 4). **Llyn Dinas** soon on left, and beyond on right, the hill fort of Dinas Emrys (see Nantgwynant, page 90).

Turn left in ever-popular **Beddgelert**, keeping on A498 (but turn right if you wish to return to Caernarfon — see below for route details). Beddgelert is the starting point of our **Walk 9**, page 146. In less than 2m beyond the **Aberglaslyn Pass**, turn left at Pont Aber Glaslyn, onto A4085. Follow this road southwards beside the Traeth Mawr (the reclaimed Glaslyn Estuary) to **Penrhyndeudraeth**, which has stations on both the **Ffestiniog Railway** and the **Cambrian Coast Railway**. Now turn right onto A487, and after about 1m, entrance to **Portmeirion** on left. Dont miss this.

Pass Boston Lodge, station and depot for the **Ffestiniog Railway**, and over the Cob, the embankment built by William Madocks to drain the Glaslyn Estuary, to the full-of-flavour town of **Porthmadog**. Turn left at X-rds by Post Office (Sign — Borth-y-Gest), and after ¼m, fork right (but fork left if you wish to visit attractive **Borth-y-Gest**). Through northern edge of Morfa Bychan. Turn right at X-rds, but keep straight ahead if you wish to visit **Black Rock Sands**. Now up small road generally northwards and after 2m turn left with care onto A497 and under railway bridge. Keep on A497 through the attractive family resort town of **Criccieth**, and after 1½m, fork right into attractive village of **Llanystumdwy**, with its connections with David Lloyd George.

After exploring **Llanystumdwy** leave north-eastwards by taking road to immediate south of bridge, and after 1½m, turn left onto B4411. Take first turn to right beyond caravan and camp site, off B4411, and almost immediately fork left. After 2m, over X-rds crossing A487, and bear right at next two Y-junctions, passing Golan hamlet (but turn left at second Y-junction, through Golan, if you wish to explore up lovely **Cwm Pennant** — a diversion of 8m in all, but well worth the effort).

SCALE 1:190 080 or 3 MILES to 1 INCH

Brynkir Woollen Mill on left. Turn left onto smaller road, and after 1m, fork right (but fork left if you wish to visit **Llyn Cwmystradllyn**). Now drive slowly and carefully over little-used mountain road before dropping steeply down through woods and turning left with care onto A498. Now head up beside the Afon Glaslyn to Pont Aber Glaslyn, keeping on A498 through the **Aberglaslyn Pass** and turning left onto A4085 in **Beddgelert**.

From Beddgelert move northwards on A4085, with **Beddgelert Forest** on left. Forest caravan site on left. Picnic site and forest walk on left. Second picnic site and forest walk on left. **Pitt's Head** Rock on left.

Llyn y Gader on left. At entry to Rhyd-Ddu, car park on right. This is start of our **Walk 8**, page 144, and also the start of the Rhyd-Ddu Path up Snowdon (see page 103). Bear right in **Rhyd-Ddu**, keeping on A4085. Impressive **Llyn Cwellyn** on left. Snowdon Ranger Youth Hostel on right. Nearby car park is starting point of Snowdon Ranger Path up Snowdon (see page 103). Pass entrance to Hafoty House Gardens on left, before reaching **Betws Garmon**. Now follow A4085 into Caernarfon, pausing to visit Segontium Roman Fort (see Caernarfon, page 46), which is on right just beyond entrance to town. Arrive at Caernarfon centre, thus completing Tour 5.

Tour 6

The Glorious Coastal Country of the Lleyn Peninsula

45 miles. Although there are a few steep little hills to be tackled from time to time, and road traffic can be rather heavy at peak holiday times, this route is ideal for cyclists. If some of the coast roads become too busy, use Landranger Sheet 123, and head further inland. There's a wealth of unspoilt countryside to be explored here.

Our route starts from Pwllheli, and heads south-westwards on a clockwise exploration of the beautiful coves, bays, beaches and cliffs of the Lleyn coast. *It passes through such well-known villages as Abersoch and Aberdaron, but also follows a quiet trail over many miles of often narrow roads along the coast. During this coastal exploration it also visits the National Trust property of Plas-yn-Rhiw, and passes beneath the dramatic Iron Age hill town of Tre'r Ceiri, before eventually heading back from the north coast on quiet inland roads to Pwllheli, to complete its circuit.*

Leave the busy market centre and holiday town of **Pwllheli** south-westwards on A499, and keep on this through the attractive seaside village of **Llanbedrog**, to its conclusion at the bright and cheerful sailing centre and holiday resort of **Abersoch**. Keep straight on main road south-westwards out of Abersoch, having visited its beach and harbour. After ½m fork right off main road (but keep straight ahead for **Porth Ceiriad**

SCALE 1:190 080 or 3 MILES to 1 INCH

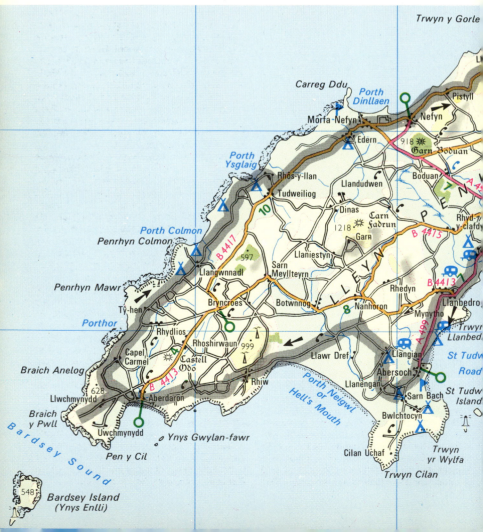

and **Mynydd Cilan**). Left at T-junction, and right at small X-rds, and then over X-rds by **Llanengan** church (but turn left if you wish to arrive at car park at eastern end of **Porth Neigwl (Hell's Mouth)**).

Right at T-junction (Sign — Llangian), and then left in trim little village of **Llangian**. Left at next X-rds (Sign — Rhiw). Bear left at T-junction (Sign — Aberdaron) (but turn right to visit **Llandegwning** church), and immediately bear round to right. Straight, not right, just beyond caravan and camping site, and up steep hill. Over X-rds in Rhiw (but take three turns right if you wish to visit **Plas-yn-Rhiw (N.T.)**). Bear left, then sharp left at

Y-junction, and **Llanfaelrhys Church** on right. Path from farm on left leads to **Porth Ysgo**.

Turn left at X-rds, and go direct to pleasant little fishing and holiday village of **Aberdaron**. Turn right past Ship Hotel, over hump-backed bridge, and bear left up hill (Sign — Uwchmynydd). Straight up hill beyond car park (Sign — Ffynnon Fair).

Bear right onto major road and at once fork left into narrow lane (Sign — Anelog) (but turn left for **Mynydd Mawr** (N.T.) and its views of **Bardsey Island**). Through Anelog hamlet and turn left at T-junction at Capel Carmel. Car park down to left for **Porth Oer**

(Whistling Sands). Left at T-junction in Methlem hamlet. After ¾m, road on left leads to Porth Iago (pay car park at Tŷ-mawr Farm). Left at Y-junction just beyond Tŷ-hen).

Now keep straight for 2¼m, and then turn right at T-junction opposite Pen-y-graig chapel (Sign — Tudweiliog) (but turn left to visit **Porth Colmon**). Almost immediately turn left at X-rds, and after ¾m, car park for **Traeth Penllech** on left (walk ¼m to this fine beach). After 1¾m, bear right onto wider road (but keep straight ahead to visit **Porth Ychain**, parking space limited here).

Bear left at Y-junction at end of Tyddyn hamlet, and after ½m turn right at T-junction (track to left is to **Porth Ysgaden**). Almost immediately turn left, and after ½m, car park for **Porth Towyn** on right. Bear right, into Rhôs-y-llan hamlet, and turn left onto B4417. Keep on B4417, through **Edern** and **Morfa Nefyn**, but turn left in the latter to visit **Porth Dinllaen** (partly on foot, but well worth the effort).

Turn left in **Nefyn**, keeping on B4417. Take second turn left in **Pistyll** if you wish to visit the interesting church. Now keep on B4417, with view of Moel Gwynus ahead. Over X-rds in **Lithfaen** (but turn left for road to 'Vortigern's Valley', and start of our **Walk 10**, page 148). Our road now running beneath southern slopes of **Yr Eifl (The Rivals)**. Path on left leads to Iron Age hill town of Tre'r Ceiri (see Llanaelhaearn, page 67). Over X-rds in centre of Llanaelhaearn, and bear left at end of village onto A499.

Turn left, off A499 (Sign — Trefor). Good views of Yr Eifl and quarries to left. Bear right twice in attractive holiday village of **Trefor**, and then turn right onto A499, and follow this southwards past the turns to Llanaelhaearn, for a total of almost 3m. Now turn left, off A499 (Sign — Pencaenewydd). Over first X-rds, and turn left at second X-rds (Sign — Llangybi). Now turn right at Y-junction in **Llangybi** (but turn left to visit church and St Cybi's Well).

Turn right (Sign — Llanarmon), bear right at Y-junction, and over offset X-rds by **Llanarmon** church (Sign — Y Ffor). Over X-rd crossing B4354, then straight, not right, and turn right at T-junction. Almost immediately, straight, not right, and then bear left round farm. Medieval **Penarth Fawr** is just beyond on left (open to the public). Turn right with care onto A497 (but turn left if you wish to visit Butlin's Holiday Camp — day visits possible — which is less than 1m away, on right). After 1¼m, fork right, off A497 (Sign — Abererch). Through pleasant little village of **Abererch**. Fork right at end of village, and almost immediately straight, not right. Now bear left on to A499 and return to **Pwllheli**, thus completing our Tour 6.

Tour 7

Coastlands of the Ardudwy, and beyond to the Rhinogs and mighty Coed-y-Brenin

55 miles. In this encirclement of the Rhinogs, cyclists could easily avoid the most hilly sections by using nothing but the A496 and A470, but it would be a pity to miss gems like Cwm Nantcol, the Artro Valley and Coed-y-Brenin.

Our route heads northwards up the Ardudwy coastal country before turning inland to the delectable cwms of Nantcol, Artro and Bychan, all within the shadows of the craggy Rhinog Range. After visiting the splendid Harlech Castle, we turn north again, up a beautifully wooded valley to lonely Llandecwyn church, just beyond Llyn Tecwyn Isaf. Now on main roads for a time, we pass a small hydro-electric power station, and then in contrast, the massive nuclear station at Trawsfynydd. After glimpses across the haunting Llyn Trawsfynydd, we head south-eastwards over open mountain country before turning south through the great Coed-y-Brenin, the King's Forest. Beyond this forest we pass the start of the Precipice Walk, and the ruins of lovely Cymmer Abbey, before crossing over the Mawddach Estuary, to return to Barmouth along its heavily wooded northern shore.

This tour starts from the lively seaside town of **Barmouth**, which is beautifully situated at the mouth of the Mawddach Estuary. Head northwards on the A496. After 1½m, **Llanaber** church on left. After 1¼m, path on right to Carneddau Hengwm burial cairns (see Tal-y-bont, page 105). Keep on A496 through **Tal-y-bont**. Small museum here, and opportunities for walking up into the hills. Over offset X-rds, keeping on A496, near the interesting **Llanddwywe** church.

Enter **Dyffryn Ardudwy** and after short distance, burial chambers on right. Straight, not right by chapel, and after ¼m, fork right at X-rds off A496 (Sign — Cwm Nantcol — watch for this with care). Straight, not left, then Rhinog Fawr visible ahead, and over offset X-rds (Sign — Cwm Nantcol). After 1m, small car park with fine views. Our **Walk 13** leaves road here (Point F), you could follow it from here. Now turn left at T-junction (Sign — Llanbedr). It is possible to drive ahead up to Maes-y-garnedd — see Cwm Nantcol, page 56, but lack of parking

space makes a walk preferable.

Now cross Afon Cwmnantcol, and after 1m, riverside car park down to left. This is start of our **Walk 13**, page 154, and of the Cwm Nantcol Nature Trail (for this and other details below, see Cwm Nantcol, page 56). Salem Chapel on right; Cefn-Isa Farm Trail starts from here. Turn right, over bridge, and turn right again (Sign — Cwm Bychan). We are now heading up the beautifully wooded **Artro Valley**, with streamside picnic possibilities. Fork right, keeping in Artro Valley. After 1m, fork left out of valley (but go straight ahead to explore up **Cwm Bychan** to Llyn Cwm Bychan (just over 2m), and the famous **Roman Steps**.

Climb steeply out of the Artro Valley, and after 2m turn left at T-junction (but turn right if you have already visited Harlech and rejoin route at junction marked 'Eisingrug' on map — refer to **Moel Goedog**, page 88, for details of this area). Turn right at X-rds (Sign — Harlech) and then turn right with care onto B4573 in **Harlech** (but go straight over to visit the splendid castle).

Head north-eastwards on B4573, and after 3m, turn right off B4573. Bear left at top of hill (Sign — Llandecwyn). (This is junction marked 'Eisingrug' on map.) Road to Maes y Neuadd Hotel to right. Down steep hill into pleasant valley. Straight, not left, and after ¼m, turn left by phone box (but turn right if you wish to visit **Llyn Tecwyn Isaf** and **Llandecwyn** church).

Turn right with care onto A496 in Cilfor hamlet. Good views of Dwyryd Estuary to left. Straight, not right near **Maentwrog** Power Station on right (but turn right to visit **Rhaeadr Du** waterfalls). Straight, not right in attractive village of **Maentwrog**. Turn right, keeping on A496, and beyond village, straight, not left, onto A487 (Sign — Dolgellau). Straight, not left at major T-junction, joining A470. After short distance, straight not left (but turn left to observe earthworks of **Tomen-y-mur** etc, although better visited on our **Walk 11**, page 150, which starts from car park on right in Utica, not far beyond on A470). **Trawfynydd Nuclear Power Station** on right, entrance to public car park beyond on right. **Llyn Trawfynydd** now visible to right.

Straight, not right twice, keeping on A470 (unless you wish to visit **Trawsfynydd** village). Straight, not left, at major T-junction, keeping on A470. Over bridge, over small X-rds and almost immediately turn left off A470 (watch for this with care). (If you wish to explore along the road running the southern side of Llyn Trawsfynydd, keep on A470 for short distance and then turn right.) After about 2m, course of Roman road (**Sarn Helen**) runs to left, parallel with road. Keep left, bear left and immediately straight, not

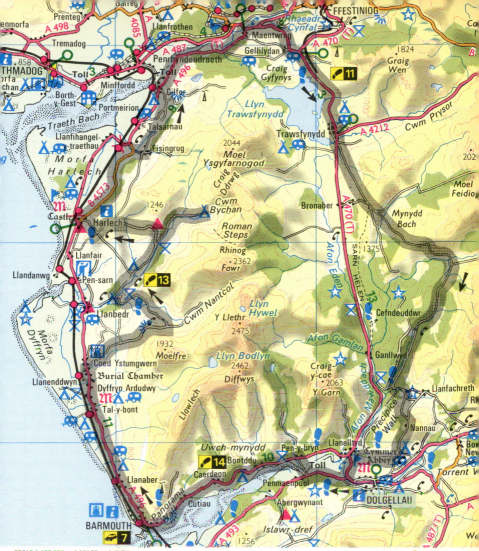

SCALE 1:190 080 or 3 MILES to 1 INCH

right, and then turn right on steep hill, to drop down into valley. Llech Idris, possible prehistoric standing stone, well over to right.

Now cross **Afon Gain**, and over fine stretch of mountain country. Splendid views westwards to the **Rhinogs** and northwards to the **Moelwyns**. Drop steeply down into valley and over the Pont Aber-Geirw crossing the Afon Mawddach. Now after ¼ m, bear right at Y-junction and soon enter the woodlands of **Coed-y-Brenin (The King's Forest)**. Fork right at Y-junction, and then fork left over bridge after passing Capel Hermon chapel (but fork right for car park if you wish to explore forest from here). Now follow down valley of the little Afon Wen. Then bear left out of valley, and over diagonal X-rds (but bear left if you wish to visit **Llanfachreth**). Glasdir Forest Garden on left (see Coed-y-Brenin, page 50). Turn right at T-junction near car park for the **Precipice**

Walk (Don't miss this). **Nannau,** small 18th century mansion, on right. Keep to right at next two junctions, and then straight not right. Bear left at next junction (but turn right if you wish to visit **Cymmer Abbey**).

Turn left onto A470, and soon turn right with great care onto A493. Turn right in **Penmaenpool** near the interesting Nature Information Centre (The Penmaenpool-Morfa Mawddach Walk starts from here). Cross bridge over the head of the lovely Mawddach Estuary and turn left onto A496. Small parking space soon on right, near start of path heading northwards to Cwm-mynach and the Garth-gell Bird Reserve (see page 56). After 1 mile, Fiddler's Elbow car park on right. This is start of our **Walk 14**, page 156. Through village of **Bontddu** on A496. Fine views out over the Mawddach Estuary, and now return without further complications, to **Barmouth**, thus completing Tour 7.

Tour 8

Bala, Trawsfynydd and Celyn — Three Lakes in a Mountain Wilderness

40 miles. The runs along the lake shores and through the more sheltered valleys are fine for cyclists, but much of this journey is over wild open country, and along rather monotonous stretches of main road. For cyclists therefore, it is perhaps the least suitable of our ten tours.

Our route follows the south-eastern shore of Lake Bala before setting out from Llanuwchllyn over wild watershed country, up the valley of the Afon Lliw and down that of the Afon Gain. We then head for Llyn Trawsfynydd, for a short time closely following the course of the Roman Road known as Sarn Helen. We now pass the great Trawsfynydd Nuclear Power Station, and beyond, turn north-eastward to cross the little Afon Cynfal with its two attractive waterfalls. After climbing out of the Cynfal Valley, we move eastwards, skirting some of the lonely moorland of the Migneint, and heading between the twin peaks of the Arenig Range. We soon arrive at the fine Llyn Celyn Reservoir, and follow the western and northern shore before passing its massive grass-covered dam and heading down the valley to return to Bala.

Set out southwards on the B4391, from the bright little market town and tourist centre of Bala, and soon after lakeside car park on right, cross the outfall of Llyn Tegid into the River Dee (Afon Dyfrdwy), before turning right onto B4403. Terminus of the **Bala Lake Railway** on left. Now head down the south-eastern shore of **Llyn Tegid (Bala Lake)**. Pass three car parks, then through **Llangower** (car park on right, with jetty and picnic site). Pass two more car parks. At end of lake, bird sanctuary over to right, but naturally there is no access to this.

Bear right at entry to **Llanuwchllyn**, keeping on B4403. Straight, not left at end of village, and briefly onto A494. But soon fork left off A494, and go westwards parallel with Afon Lliw. In Dolhendre hamlet, turn sharp right, cross bridge over Afon Lliw, and turn left. Now move up the valley of the Afon Lliw, eventually crossing this stream and heading up over heavily afforested mountain country forming the watershed between the Afon Lliw and the **Afon Gain**.

Cross Afon Gain at end of woods, and follow down valley. Straight, not left, when climbing steep hill out of valley, and turn north-westwards. Fork right at diagonal X-rds. Course of Roman road (**Sarn Helen**) running parallel to right of our road. Turn right with care onto A470. (But turn left and then shortly right, if you wish to explore the road running along the southern side of **Llyn Trawfynydd**.) Head north on A470, and immediately after our joining it, go over X-rds (unless you wish to turn left to visit **Trawsfynydd** village). Keep straight, not right at major T-junction, keeping on A470, and keep heading north on A470, with views of Llyn Trawsfynydd over to left.

Car park on left immediately before **Trawsfynydd Nuclear Power Station** on left. Car park on left (in Utica) is start of our **Walk 11**, page 150. Straight, not right (but turn right if

SCALE 1:190 080 or 3 MILES to 1 INCH

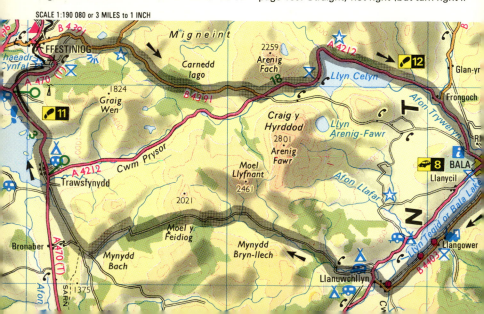

Bala Lake near the north-eastern end.

you wish to observe earthworks of **Tomen-y-mur**, etc. — however this is best seen from our **Walk 11**). Turn right at T-junction, keeping on A470. After 1¾m, straight, not left. But turn left for car park and picnic site beside Afon Cynfal. Walk from here, down-stream to waterfall of Rhaeadr Cynfal (see Ffestiniog, page 62), or up-stream to **Rhaeadr y Cwm**.

Almost immediately turn right at small offset X-rds just beyond Bont Newydd, off A470, and onto minor road (watch for this with great care). Fine view of dome-shaped Manod Mawr ahead, and then bear right onto B4391. After 1m, car park on right, with good views over Cynfal Valley and **Rhaeadr y Cwm** — path up to left leading to **Llyn Morwynion**, a lake with two sad stories involving maidens in distress.

Straight, not left, keeping on B4391 (Sign — Bala). Mountain country over to left is part of the wilderness known as the **Migneint**. Over bridge crossing the Nant y Groes stream, and then through thickly afforested country. The twin peaks of **the Arenigs** soon come into view — Arenig Fach ahead left, and Arenig Fawr ahead. Under electric power lines, and turn left onto A4212 (Sign — Bala).

Our road, the A4212, now runs between the two Arenig peaks, and soon starts its long winding course around the western and northern shore of one of Wales' most attractive reservoirs, **Llyn Celyn**. Almost immediately car park and picnic site on right. Then around the northern inlet to the car park by the satisfying little Capel Celyn (see Llyn Celyn, page 82). Past third car park. Past fourth car park, with Quaker Memorial Stone close by. Dam now on right, with car parks at both ends. This is start of our **Walk 12**, page 152.

Now continue on the A4212, down the valley of the Afon Tryweryn, a river which feeds into the Dee (Afon Dyfrdwy) at **Bala**. After crossing the Afon Tryweryn on a concrete bridge, our route runs into **Bala**, thus completing Tour 8.

Tour 9

Around the Aran Range — a high pass, and deep valleys — with tree-shaded torrents never far away

50 miles. The splendid pass, Bwlch y Groes, provides a worthy challenge for any cyclist, but beware of the descent from here — bicycle brakes must be in first-class order — and that goes for cars too! There are other hills to be tackled, but they pale into insignificance beside Bwlch y Groes. Cyclists are particularly advised to ask at Aberangell, if the forest road eastwards from there is open.

From Dolgellau our route heads north-eastwards over a modest pass to the west of the Arans, and drops down to Llanuwchllyn, a small village situated near the south-western end of Llyn Tegid (Bala Lake). Here we turn south-eastwards to climb up Cwm Cynllwyd to the high and lonely Bwlch y Groes, before dropping down again into the valley through which the infant Afon Dyfi (River Dovey) runs. We now continue down the lovely Dyfi Valley, through Dinas Mawddwy and Mallwyd, with a possible opportunity to turn westwards through the great Dyfi Forest. However this may not be possible, and our main route therefore continues to run down the Dyfi Valley almost to Machynlleth, but then turns northwards up the beautifully wooded Dulas Valley to the slate village of Corris. It is possible to divert here, further up the Dulas Valley into the very heart of the Dyfi Forest, but eventually we have no alternative but to join the A487, to return to Dolgellau over the Bwlch Llyn-Bach.

Set out eastwards on A470 from the busy market town of **Dolgellau**, and after about 2m, turn sharp left with care onto B4416. Small car park near river is best starting point for the **Torrent Walk**, which runs left from road on south bank of the rapid-flowing Afon Clywedog. Beyond interesting **Brithdir** church, straight, not left, leaving B4416. Immediately beyond this, earthworks of Roman fortlet to left of road (on private land). After 2m, fork right in Pont Llanrhaiadr hamlet, and then straight, not left where road becomes more open.

Over bridge crossing Afon Wnion and turn right with care onto A494. Over watershed and drop down into valley of the Afon Dyfrydwy (River Dee). Turn sharp right at entry to **Llanuwchllyn**, onto B4403. Over Afon Dyfrydwy and through village. Bear left near end of village and over second river bridge, and then turn very sharp right onto minor road (Sign — Dinas Mawddwy).

Now heading up spectacular valley of **Cwm Cynllwyd** (George Borrow came this way: see page 55). Fine views of Aran Fawddwy ahead right (see Aran Range, page 33). Fork left, keeping on wider road at Tŷ-nant. Pass beneath dramatic crags of **Craig yr Ogof**, and reach top of the finest pass in Wales, the **Bwlch y Groes**. Parking space on right provides splendid views back down Cwm Cynllwyd, and westwards to Aran Fawddwy.

Bear right — but turn left if you wish to divert to Llyn Efyrnwy (Lake Vyrnwy) (see Bwlch y Groes, page 43). Now, with great care, start very steep descent into the valley of the Afon Rhiwlech, with the sweeping crags of Craig y Pant over to left. After 1m, at bottom of steep descent, turn very sharp left. Path on right up to **Blaen-pennant Water-falls**. These are on the infant Afon Dyfi (River Dovey), which we shall now follow down the valley. Through minute village of **Llanymawddwy** — path up to right leads to Pistyll Gwyn (The White Waterfall). After 3m, straight, not right, in colourful hamlet of Aber Cywarch — but turn right if you wish to explore up **Cwm Cywarch** — limited parking space.

Enter **Dinas Mawddwy** by car park on left, turn left at small X-rds and bear left with care onto A470. Fork left, keeping on A470, and Meirion Mill soon appears on right — dont miss this. Keep on A470 through Mallwyd, passing Brigand's Inn and interesting little church on left. After 2m, turn right with care, off A470. Over Afon Dyfi into **Aberangell**, and turn sharp left. (But it is worth asking if the forest road to Aberllefenni is open to traffic. If so, this makes a delightful 'short-cut' across to Corris possible.)

Now heading south-westwards down the Dyfi Valley. Straight not left opposite Cem-

Dinas Mawddwy and the Dyfi Valley.

SCALE 1:190 080 or 3 MILES to 1 INCH

maes, and after 2m, bear right onto B4404. Keep on B4404 through Llanwrin hamlet, and after 2½m, turn right off B4404, onto minor road immediately **before** bridge over river. Now head northwards up eastern side of the wooded Dulas Valley. After 2m, **Centre for Alternative Technology** on right - don't miss this. Keep up east side of valley by using minor road northwards.

Through Esgairgeiliog hamlet, and up pleasantly wooded minor road and over small bridge at entry to **Corris.** Over small X- rds in Corris — but turn left if you wish to visit Railway Museum - or turn right if you wish to explore up valley to the **Foel Friog picnic site** and **Aberllefenni** — some grand forest

country up here. Head north from Corris, passing vast slate tips and bearing left in Corris Uchaf, before bearing right with great care onto A487.

After ¼m, pass Snowdonia National Park entry sign, and after a further 1¾m, pass a turning on left at Minffordd, which is the B4405 leading to **Tal-y-llyn** — a tempting diversion if you are still fresh. Now follow A487 through the Bwlch Llyn-Bach, with fine views up to left of the eastern crags of **Cadair Idris.** 2m beyond Minffordd, good viewpoint car park on left. Bear left onto A470 at Cross Foxes Hotel, and follow this road down into **Dolgellau,** thus completing Tour 9.

Tour 10

Two estuaries, two 'great little trains', and the splendid mountain country of Cadair Idris

55 miles. The words, 'Mountain Country', spell hard work for cyclists, but much of this tour follows comparatively easy roads around the outer bounds of the high country. The run from Arthog, along the northern flanks of Cadair Idris, does however contain some challenging sections, especially in its long climb out of the coastal country, onto the plateau above. There is also a long and steady climb beyond Cross Foxes Hotel, but the even longer homeward run down the delightful Dulas Valley will provide your final reward.

Our route starts from Machynlleth, and soon heads westwards beside the attractive Dyfi Estuary to the coast at Aberdyfi. From here we turn northwards, along the coast to Tywyn, before running up a valley to Abergynolwyn. We now break through a ridge between two valleys and turn southwards down the beautiful Dysynni Valley. On reaching the coast we run northwards past Fairbourne, and have a brief encounter with the lovely Mawddach Estuary, before climbing up to a plateau beneath the northern flanks of the great Cadair Idris Range. Having possibly called at Dolgellau, we turn southwards, beneath the eastern crags of Cadair Idris, and head down the beautifully wooded Dulas Valley, before finally returning to Machynlleth.

Leave the pleasant old market town of **Machynlleth** northwards on A487, and soon

SCALE 1:190 080 or 3 MILES to 1 INCH

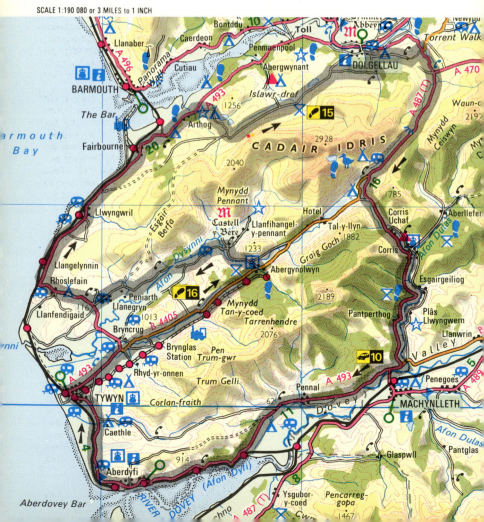

turn left onto A493, immediately beyond the Pen-y-bont, crossing the Afon Dyfi (River Dovey). Head westwards on A493 going through village of **Pennal**, and after 3m, the lovely Dyfi (Dovey) Estuary over to the left, with fine views to the mountains beyond. Through the attractive seaside village of **Aberdyfi (Aberdovey)** keeping on A493. After 2½m, straight not right, keeping on A493 (but turn right if you wish to visit the 'Happy Valley'). Keep on A493 through the small holiday town of **Tywyn**. Wharf Station on left is terminus of the fascinating **Talyllyn Railway**, and also has an interesting Narrow Gauge Museum. Do not miss a visit here, nor a trip on the railway. After visiting town, beach, etc., leave **Tywyn** on A493.

At entry to Bryncrug, turn right onto B4405, and follow this road out of village and up valley, running parallel with the **Talyllyn Railway**. After 3m, Dolgoch Station up to right, and path to beautiful **Dolgoch Falls** leads on from car park. After 1¾m, Abergynolwyn Station and public car park with picnic site, on right. This is start of our **Walk 16**, page 160, and also one of the starting points of the Nant Gwernol Walks (see Abergynolwyn, page 31).

Turn left off B4405 in **Abergynolwyn** (Sign — Llanegryn), but go straight ahead for access on right to Nant Gwernol Station, the terminus of the **Talyllyn Railway**, and starting point of the shorter Nant Gwernol Walks (see above). Over bridge crossing Afon Dysynni, and through narrow defile with river on left (see **Dysynni Valley**, page 61, for details of this rare example of 'an elbow of river capture'). Now turn left at offset X-rds (Sign — Bryncrug). (But turn right if you wish to visit **Castell y Bere**, and/or **Llanfihangel-y-pennant** and the ruined cottage where Mary Jones once lived.)

Now over bridge and head down **Dysynni Valley**. Fork right near **Craig yr Aderyn (the Birds' Rock)**, above to left. Recross Afon Dysynni and go through village of **Llanegryn** (but turn right up hill, go straight not left, and then turn left, if you wish to visit church — don't miss this). At end of village turn right with care onto A493.

Keep on A493 through **Rhoslefain**. After ¾m, pass Cae-du Farm on left (see **Owain Glyndwr's Cave**, page 92). Now run northwards along the coast. After ½m, **Llangelynnin Church** down to left. Through **Llwyngwril** on A493. Path to beach on left ½m beyond X-rds. After about 3m, keep on A493. (But turn left if you wish to visit cheerful seaside village of **Fairbourne**, with its attractive miniature railway running to the mouth of the Mawddach Estuary opposite Barmouth.)

After 1m, keep on A493. (But turn left if you wish to divert to Morfa Mawddach

Station, where there is a public car park, and from where it is possible to walk on a footpath alongside the railway, over the estuary bridge to Barmouth. Fine views up the estuary from here.) After 1¼m, **Arthog** church on left. After ¼m, watch for very sharp turn to right, where we leave A493, and climb steep hill and onto open mountain country, which forms a plateau beneath the high crags of Cadair Idris.

Llynnau Cregennen (The Cregennen Lakes) on left, good car park to right. Bear left at Y-junction beyond lakes. Great sweeping mountain-sides above to right. After 1¾m, straight, not left (junction not very apparent). Phone box on right after ¾m, and car park and picnic site beyond on left is start of our **Walk 15**, page 158. This uses part of the Pony Path (see **Cadair Idris**, page 44).

Gwernan Lake Hotel on left, and **Llyn Gwernan** on left, just beyond. Turn sharp right by Rhydwen Farm (but bear left and soon sharp left, if you wish to take the interesting **Tal y Waen Farm Trail**). Along quiet road and into woodlands, and after 1½m, fork left keeping on public road. Over stream and bear left just before reaching phone box. Down steep hill through woods, bear left by farm onto wider road, and down steep hill. Turn sharp right, and back up hill. (But turn down left if you wish to visit **Dolgellau**, only a short way ahead).

Up steep hill with woods, and straight not left at junction. Turn right with care onto A487 near Cross Foxes Hotel. After 2m, car park on right with fine views of the eastern flanks of **Cadair Idris**. After 2m, and heading through the Bwlch Llyn Bach, straight not right at Minffordd, keeping on A487. (But turn right onto B4405 for access on right to the Minffordd Path up **Cadair Idris**, and for road to **Tal-y-llyn Lake**, and Abergynolwyn, linking with an earlier part of our route.)

Now head southwards on A487, and after 2m, straight, not left, keeping on A487. (But turn left if you wish to take a quiet route down the eastern side of the valley, through **Corris**, and the hamlet of Esgairgeiliog, and passing the interesting **Centre for Alternative Technology**. This route is not described in detail here, as it is used (northwards) in our **Tour 9**.)

Heading southwards on A487, first passing the slate quarries of **Corris** over to left, and then into the wooded Dulas Valley. Tan-y-Coed car park and picnic site on right has access to **Cwm Cadian Forest Walks**. After about 1m watch for sharp turn to left for **Centre for Alternative Technology** at entry to **Pantperthog** hamlet — don't miss this. Now return to A487 and after 2m, turn left, over bridge crossing Afon Dyfi (River Dovey) to return to **Machynlleth**, thus completing Tour 10.

Walks

Walk 1
Yr Arwydd and two sandy bays on Anglesey's North-East Coast

Allow three hours

This walk takes us to the summit of Yr Arwydd, from which there are fine views out over Anglesey towards the distant mountains of Snowdonia. It then heads down towards the coast and passes along the dunes bordering Traeth Lligwy and Traeth yr Ora, two sandy bays much loved by those who prefer to be well away from the busy resorts. On returning to Brynrefail it passes a welcoming inn, the Pilot Boat, and a memorial to the Morris Brothers (see page 40), founders of the Cymrodorion Society.

The village of **Brynrefail** (114) (SH 48-86) is on our **Tour 1**, page 43, and is on A5025 five miles south-east of Amlwch.

(A) Start from Brynrefail car park just below the chapel on the south-western side of the road. Walk up a pedestrian ramp to the chapel and then after about 40 yards, take a stone stile on the right to a field path following the hedge. After three further stiles and a tumble of large sandstone boulders on the right, the path swings right for 150 yards to a ladder stile. Turn sharp left and keeping the wall and rock outcrop to the left, climb steeply on to the ridge and over an awkward ladder stile.

(B) The footpath continues between old wire fences over heather-clad rocks to a plank bridge and cultivated land. Turn half left over bridge through a fence gap and with the wire fence to the left as far as a small iron gate. Hedge now on right, climb a stone stile into yard of Caer Mynydd Farm, and then through gate to a stone track heading south-west. After 90 yards a junction with other tracks is reached. Turn left here and follow the surfaced track to the road. (Several 'permissive tracks' on the right lead to the summit of Yr Arwydd. Fine views of Anglesey and the mainland from here. It is also possible to walk on south-westwards to **Mynydd Bodafon**.)

(C) At the road turn left and follow it downhill 700 yards to the 14th century church of St Michael (see Brynrefail, page 43) which is well worth visiting. Now leave churchyard by the north gate and at Ty Bodafon, turn right for 25 yards, then right again down a lane some 650 yards to a farm track on the right. Cross the stile opposite, on the left, and follow footpath through gorse and heather via the stone tower of the Boston Sulphur Well. Path leads northwards into bushes, over a footbridge and, following a stream for 10 yards, swings left and heads for large barn on the skyline across heathland. A stile by the field gate leads to the A5025 road.

(D) Turn left on to A5025 for 200 yards to a T-junction. Turn left and follow road back to the car park at **Brynrefail (A)** thus completing a shorter walk, or at 300 yards from the

Traeth Dulas from our path near Traeth yr Ora.

junction turn right through a stile following path through four fields to the right of a house, and through a field gate by a stone wall; then continue to a wooden ladder stile. Follow the same line over the field until a similar stile is reached leading shortly to the shore of **Traeth Lligwy**.

At the northern end of the Traeth Lligwy car park a footpath sign points left, the path rising steeply through dunes to a headland before descending to Porth-y-Mor. Continue along the beach to a waymark where the path ascends the field edge to a grassy cliff-top walk and camp site.

(E) Swing half left and take the path descending through bracken to **Traeth yr Ora**. Then upwards again to the crest of the dunes. Here a track winds away from the beach upward to a farm, turns right and joins

a road. Keep on up the hill and, as the road turns sharp left, follow a footpath sign, through a cottage garden into a field. Ascend the field ahead, bearing left at the next waymark to a parallel hedge and upwards to a ladder stile and level ground.

(F) The ridge to the right at this point hides a view of the deep indentation of **Traeth Dulas**, but our path follows the wall to a stile and a descending farm track. Where it swings right a stile ahead leads into a field, then following the right hand edge, another stile, and with the hedge to the left continue to a wicket gate at the rear of the Pilot Boat Inn. Follow the A5025 road, up the hill to the left, passing a memorial stone and finely sited cross to the Morris Brothers (see page 40). After about 600 yards arrive at the **Brynrefail Car Park (A)**, thus completing Walk 1.

Walk 2
Porth Swtan, and Mynydd y Garn

Allow three hours

This walk explores a typically unspoilt part of north-western Anglesey, making use of quiet paths and also, where necessary, some stretches of lightly used roads. It follows both cliff-tops and gorse-covered hillsides affording panoramic views of the Irish Sea; but much of the walk passes through farming country, giving an impression of a way of life that persists, changing little over the course of many generations. Yet from the slopes of Mynydd y Garn walkers will see the intrusion of modern society in the uncompromising shape of nuclear reactors, a reminder that remoteness is an illusion.

The Porth Swtan Car Park (114) (SH 30-89) is on our **Tour 2**, page 112, and is situated approximately 12 miles north of Holyhead.

(A) From the **Porth Swtan** car park turn in the direction of the sea and after 80 yards branch right via a black wooden gate following the cliff-top track. As the track enters the second field strike diagonally uphill to the left of white cottages following a footpath through gorse to a stile on the right before the line of power cables. Turn right down the farm track to the steepled church of St Rhyddlad and then turn left up the lane to the road junction. Turn left again along the road, forking left at the junction.

(B) Where the road turns sharply left, opposite the track to Cae Mawr, branch right over a stile. The footpath crosses gorsy grazing land with fine views north to **The Skerries** by a fence on the right to a stile in a bog, then via an often wet track to a road. Turn right and 70 yards beyond Waen Lydan a stile on the left leads to a path climbing the north slopes of Mynydd y Garn parallel to a hedge and wall on the right. At the fourth stile head across the field in the direction of

0   200   400   600   800m   1   Kilometres

0   200   400   600   800   1000 yds   Miles   1

SCALE 1:25 000 or 2½ INCHES to 1 MILE

Porth Swtan, not far from the start of Walk 2.

Wylfa Power Station until the field wall corner is reached and continue with the wall to the left. Do not cross the next stile but turn right around the field edge, to a field gate and track leading left of Garn Farm to the road. Turn right along road for 200 yards to just before a school building in the small village of **Llanfairynghornwy**, where a track turns right at Point **(C)**.

(Only those capable of surmounting barbed wire barriers and a steep gorse and bracken covered hillside should use the next section of route. Others should continue along the road keeping right at next four intersections to reach Point (D), see below.)

(C) Having turned right on track, follow this for about 70 yards and climb the middle gate of three openings and keep hedge to the right through two fields, then turn left uphill towards the ruined Castell on the skyline. Level with Castell turn half left and head toward the corner of the field above the craggy outcrops where the wall topped with barbed wire can be climbed. If the steeply descending field on the far side has a growing crop, skirt it as near to the left as practicable and approach Plas-y-Nant. The path enters the garden by a gate and leaves on the south side where a well-defined but boggy track leads to Rhaid and the road at Point **(D)**.

(D) Turn right here and continue on the road to the village of Rhydwyn. At the T-junction follow footpath sign opposite indicating the farm track to Cae-dowtai, and on reaching this farm go to the right of the buildings where a stile leads to a field path following a stream. At its far end turn right on the track to Hafotty, go through the farmyard via a gate to a track leading towards a disused windmill.

(E) Turn left at a footpath sign before the mill and shortly enter a sloping field. Head for the stile to the right of a cottage and then join a track leading westwards to the road. Cross the road and take the track to Grugmor Farm, turning left at the farm to reach the bay and then climbing steeply right to a cliff-top path. Follow this path northwards until the road is reached at **Porth Swtan** and turn right for the car park **(A)**, thus completing Walk 2.

Walk 3
Conwy and the Sychnant Pass

Allow four and a half hours

This walk takes us from the historic town of Conwy, up into the unspoilt hill country to its immediate south and west, from whence there are fine views west to the Carneddau Range and north to the coast. Eventually we cross the small road running through the Sychnant Pass, and are treated to acoustic delights and further views, which on a clear day can reach as far as the Isle of Man and the mountains of Cumbria. We return along a ridge beside an Iron Age settlement, before dropping down to Conwy, passing quays, town and castle walls, and even Britain's smallest house.

Conwy (115) (SH 77-77) is on our **Tour 3**, page 114, and is situated at the mouth of the lovely Conwy estuary, near the north-east corner of the area covered by this guide.

(A) Start from Benarth car park, south of Conwy Castle and the railway line. Walk 50 yards east from the park along the road to kissing gate on right of road. Turn right (south) and walk up through field to stile in wood. Pause for good views of **Conwy** with its ancient castle and walls. Bear right over stile and continue southwards along edge of wood to stile and kissing gate. After 30 yards, turn right over stile and head south on marked path. After passing farm, turn left on to metalled road. Follow up road for 150 yards to footpath sign on right.

(B) Follow sign, through kissing gate and take path alongside hedge by the brow of the hill. Continue along ridge to caravan site where the path bears right down to ladder stile by large oak tree. Follow yellow way marks, and cross over stiles to service road. Continue on this road down to B5106.

SCALE 1:25 000 or 2½ INCHES TO 1 MILE

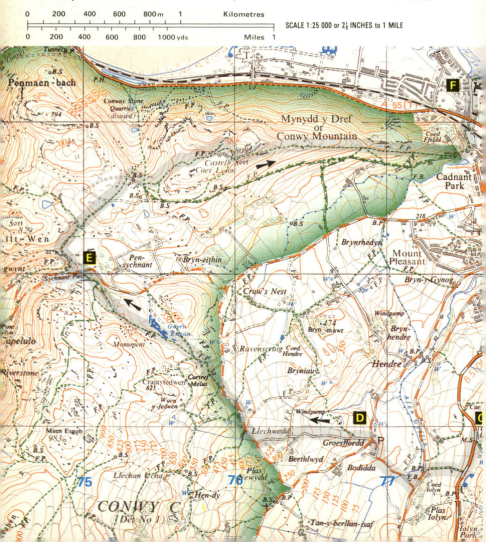

(C) Turn left on to B5106, follow for 200 yards and go through kissing gate on right. Before going down the field, pause awhile to take in the views of the **Carneddau Range**, with the 2000 foot Tal y Fan immediately ahead. Turn right down footpath, and after going downhill heading west, passing farm buildings on left, turn left on to metalled road. After 100 yards turn right at road junction, and follow road to Groesffordd village.

(D) Go straight over cross roads and proceed up the track past Berthlwyd Caravan Park. At the top, turn right on to metalled road going over cattle grid at Llechan Farm. Good views here of the North Wales coast. Continue for 200 yards, then fork left at footpath sign, up hill to Pen y Bwlch. At the top, take grassy path to the left of Gwern Engan Farm. Climb iron stile over wall and on past a water tank to footpath along by wood to gate at the top of the **Sychnant Pass**. Known in English as 'the dry valley', it also

The Sychnant Pass.

lives up to its other name, the 'Echo Valley', and has some splendid acoustic effects. There are fine views from here of Anglesey, and the Menai Strait.

(E) Cross the metalled road at the **Sychnant Pass** and take the wide track. Bear left for a few yards and turn right on to a wide track on to the Conwy Mountain. At the end of this track there are several paths. The path to the right, keeping alongside a wall, is the direct route back to Conwy, but we bear left following the ridge for a more interesting walk. There are fine views from this ridge of the Conwy estuary below, with **Deganwy**, **Llandudno** and the towering mass of the Great Orme beyond. On a clear day it is also possible to look far over the sea to the Isle of Man and the Cumbrian Mountains. Pass the Iron Age settlement of Castell Caer Seion, and continue down the path towards **Conwy**. Turn left on to road at the bottom of hill, by directional arrows. Go over railway bridge to A55 road. Cross A55 and along Morfa Drive, passing school on right.

(F) Turn right on to footpath alongside the Afon Quay, past boatyards. Go along quay-side, noting the quaint 'Smallest House in Great Britain' on right. Turn right at end of quay on to main road, cross this and continue down road between castle entrance and the Guildhall. Pass under arch and proceed to car park **(A)** on right, thus completing our Walk 3.

Walk 4
Aberconwy Lake Country
Allow four hours

This is a quiet walk, much of it through forest country, and much following the shore lines of two very beautiful lakes, Llyn Geirionydd and Llyn Crafnant. The car park and picnic site on the shore of Llyn Geirionydd where the walk starts, make an excellent base for exploring, and there is a Forestry Commission forest trail that starts from here. Canoe launching is allowed, and there is also a car park and forest trail to the north of the northern end of Llyn Crafnant.

Llyn Geirionydd (115) (SH 76-60) is on our **Tour 3**, page 114, and is situated about 12 miles south of Conwy on a minor road leading off the B5106 from Trefriw.

(A) Start from the car park near the southern end of **Llyn Geirionydd**, and head south-westwards on metalled road or along lakeside. Turn right onto track, cross stile and proceed along south side of lake. Bear left up forestry road for 300 yards and then turn right up path through forest. Cross three forestry roads and on reaching the top, at a level area,

make a slight diversion to a rock over to the left, from whence there is a splendid panoramic view including **Moel Siabod**, the Clwydian Hills and the Conwy Valley. Return to main path and turn left. Go down path and just before reaching the bottom, bear left and cross stile on to a metalled road. Telephone box now on right. Now go left along road, and bear right at Y-junction beyond Maes Mawr.

(B) Just before reaching Hendre, turn right off road, on to footpath. Follow this path to **Llyn Crafnant**, and then keep parallel with lake shore until reaching monument at north-eastern end. Follow metalled road north-eastwards until reaching forestry road branching off to right. **(C)** Proceed up forestry road and cross stile. Now follow path with old mine workings on right. Bear right to arrive close to a second monument, this one standing at the northern end of **Llyn Geirionydd**.

(D) Turn right by monument, passing house on right. Now follow down the western shore of **Llyn Geirionydd**. Leave shore near the southern end of lake, and eventually bear left on to forestry road. Then bear left on to metalled road and return on this to the starting car park **(A)**, thus completing our Walk 4.

| 0 | 200 | 400 | 600 | 800m | 1 | Kilometres |

SCALE 1:25 000 or 2½ INCHES to 1 MILE

| 0 | 200 | 400 | 600 | 800 | 1000 yds | Miles 1 |

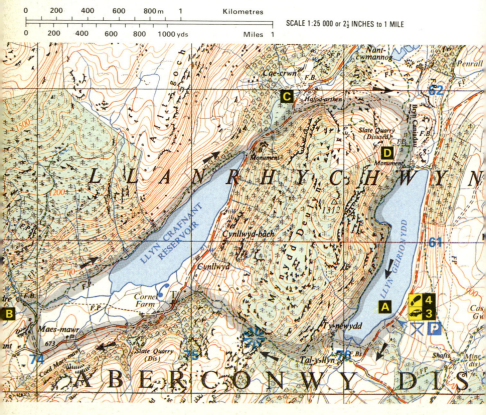

136

A view southwards over Llyn Crafnant.

Walk 5
Betws-y-Coed Forest Country

Allow three hours

This walk explores the forest country in the hills to the north-west of Betws-y-Coed, passing two lakes and the remains of several disused mines. Despite much afforestation there are splendid mountain views from several points along its varied route. Towards the end of the walk, the path drops steeply down to the Afon Llugwy at Miners' Bridge, and follows the course of this fast-flowing and very attractive river back to Betws-y-Coed.

The Afon Llugwy at Miners' Bridge.

Betws-y-Coed (115) (SH 79-56) is on **Tour 3**, page 114 and on **Tour 4**, page 116. It is situated on the A5, at the meeting point of several main roads.

(A) Start from the Pont-y-Pair car park, which is situated to the north of **Betws-y-Coed**, off the A5, just beyond the Pont-y-Pair. Proceed up small metalled road westwards for about 100 yards, and turn right on to path. Continue past yellow mark, down path and turn up past gateway. Walk up path to forest road and go along this noting the splendid views of the Conwy Valley over to right. Turn left up forest path, soon passing Aber Llyn, an old mine on right which once produced lead, zinc and a little copper. Proceed past mine buildings at the top, to the southern end of the lake, Llyn Parc.

(B) Turn left up forestry road for about 100 yards and then turn right up footpath through

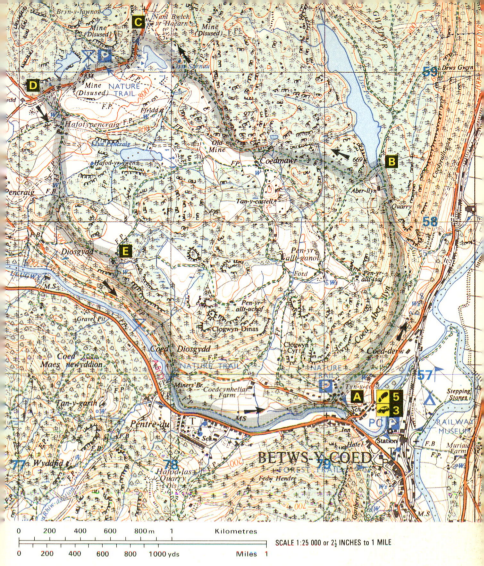

SCALE 1:25 000 or 2½ INCHES to 1 MILE

forest. Cross over two forestry roads and continue along footpath until reaching another forestry road. Turn left with Coed-mawr (the Great Wood) on left. Continue along road noting the fine view of **Moel Siabod** ahead. Take the first path to the right, and on reaching the top, which is about 1000 feet above sea level, take in the glorious mountain panorama from **Moel Siabod** in the south-west, round to the **Snowdon Range**, the **Glyders** and finally the **Carnedau** over to the north-west. Proceed down the path, passing a white cottage on right until reaching another path on the right. Ignore this path and go through trees on the left. Reach another forest road after only a few yards, and this leads to a metalled public road. Turn left on to this road.

(C) Cross car park on left (this is on our **Tour 3**, page 114), and beyond it is a lake called Llyn Sarnau. For no apparent reason,

this usually disappears in dry weather. Continue on metalled road for about half a mile, until another old lead mine is reached. On the left of the mine is a stile.

(D) Cross stile and follow markings down through fields. Cross second stile until, after a few yards, a forestry road is reached. Turn right and follow this road until another stile is reached. Cross field when there is a cottage on right and farm buildings on left. Immediately after the buildings, take footpath on right going down beyond a wall.

(E) Proceed first down steep path through mixed woodland, and then more gradually until a metalled road is reached. Cross over road and down through forest to the **Miners' Bridge**. But take the path on the left immediately before the bridge and follow the north bank of the Afon Llugwy back to the Pont y Pair car park **(A)** in **Betws-y-Coed**, thus completing our Walk 5.

Walk 6

Snowdon from Pen-y-Pass — an introduction to Yr Wyddfa itself

Allow seven hours

This walk makes use of two well-known paths leading to the very summit of Snowdon (Yr Wyddfa) ... the Pig Track and the Miners' Track, two of several routes that lead to the same unique objective (see page 103), and both of which are also described in leaflets issued by the National Park. These rugged paths have been trodden by countless thousands, and today they still provide one of the finest possible introductions to the joys of mountain walking in Snowdonia. However, do not be misled into thinking that no care is necessary. Always follow the advice given on the inside rear cover of this guide if leaving the road in this or in any other mountainous area.

Pen-y-Pass (115) (SH 64-55) is on our Tour 5, page 118, and is situated on the A4086, to the south-east of Llanberis and at the top of the Llanberis Pass. If you wish to avoid using this park, may we suggest that you use the Sherpa bus service from the free car park to the south of the A4086 near Nant Peris church (SH 60-58), 3 miles to the north-west.

(A) Start from the car park opposite the Youth Hostel and take the path on the right. This is the Pig Track, named after the high level pass, Bwlch y Moch, (Pass of the Pigs), and not named from the initials of the Pen-y-Gwryd Hotel (P.Y.G.), as was once popularly believed. The path is a little stony in parts, and although negotiable, strong boots or shoes are essential. Good views of the Llanberis Lakes and the Menai Strait ahead. The path eventually turns to the left and climbs to the ridge of Bwlch y Moch. Looking back it is possible to see the ridge of the Glyders, and ahead there are views to Y Lliwedd, with Snowdon to the right. Now at 1000 feet above the starting point and 2000 feet above sea-level. Pass track leading right, upwards to Crib Goch and the continuation of the Snowdon Horseshoe (see page 104), but do not take it.

(B) Follow the path which soon bears right, taking in the wide sweep of Llyn Llydaw below on the left. The path will soon start to climb, and after some time will eventually overlook the waters of Glaslyn, green-tinted by copper ore.

(C) A little further on, under the rocky slope of Snowdon itself, a path coming up the valley from the Miners' Track will meet our path (The Pig Track). If you wish to leave out the climb to Snowdon, turn sharp left here and refer to paragraph below, also starting with (C). However if you wish to

SCALE 1:25 000 or 2½ INCHES to 1 MILE

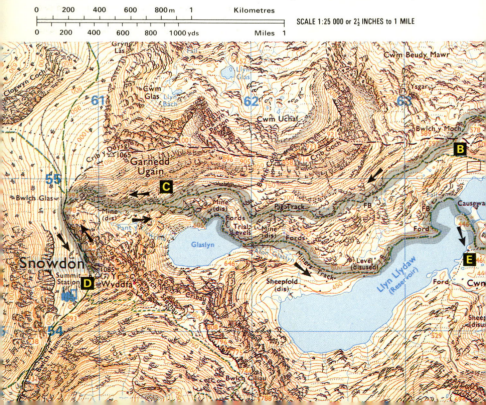

Walkers at the head of the Llanberis Pass, heading for Snowdon.

extend the walk to the top of Snowdon itself, continue up the Pig Track to the top of the steep zig-zag and then turn left to follow alongside the track of the **Snowdon Mountain Railway**. Extensive views can now be

had to the south and west of Snowdonia, and in a reasonably short distance the summit itself is reached.

(D) There are splendid views on every side from the summit of **Yr Wyddfa** (or **Snowdon**), and on a clear day it is possible to see the distant coast of Ireland, the Isle of Man and some of the Lakeland peaks, notably Scafell. Now retrace route alongside railway line, and turn right to descend the zig-zag path to return to Point **(C)**.

(C) Now fork right down the path into the valley, leading to the Miners' Track, so-called because miners once used to walk up here to the copper mines of **Cwm Dyli**, the ruins of which may still be seen above the shores of Glaslyn. Follow down the path and over a ridge and drop down to the northern shore of Llyn Llydaw. Follow this shoreline and when crossing the causeway across the lake, the dramatic cliffs of Lliwedd are in view straight ahead, with a track coming down to the left which is the end of the mountainous part of the Snowdon Horseshoe.

(E) From the end of the causeway climb away from Llyn Llydaw, and eventually pass to the north of little Llyn Teyrn (Lake of the Ruler), which also has ruined miners' buildings on its shores. Shortly after this there are views of **NantGwynant** (valley) down to the right, and ahead, **Moel Siabod** and the **Moelwyns**. Now follow comparatively easy path back to the car park at Pen-y-Pass **(A)**, thus completing our Walk 6.

141

Walk 7

Snowdon from the South, via the Watkin Path and Cwm y llan

Allow six hours

In its early stages this walk follows the well-trodden Watkin Path (see page 57), which is described in a leaflet issued by the National Park. After moving north-westwards parallel with the Afon Cwm llan, here enlivened with several waterfalls, it then heads westwards to Bwlch Cwm llan. From here a steady climb northwards along a steep-sided ridge, where care is required, takes us to a point from which the summit of Snowdon may be easily reached. We now descend south and south-eastwards, making use of the Watkin Path for our return journey to Pont Bethania, passing the interesting remains of old copper mines in Cwm llan on the way. The route of the Watkin Path passes through the great Snowdon National Nature Reserve and this is described in an interesting general leaflet on the Snowdon massif issued by the Nature Conservancy Council.

The Watkin Path is perhaps the hardest route up Snowdon, and the top, very steep section can be extremely dangerous in snow

Snowdon (Yr Wydffa) from Nantgwynant, near the start of Walk 7.

and ice, and during summer drought when it is very slippery. Always follow the advice given on the inside of the rear cover, if leaving the road in this or any other mountain area.

The starting car park is at **Pont Bethania** (115) (SH 62-50) on the A498, 3 miles north-east of **Beddgelert**. This is on our **Tour 5**, page 118.

(A) Cross the A498 road from the car park at Pont Bethania. Turn left and follow road for 100 yards . Now turn right through kissing gate on to metalled road. Follow metalled road for ¼ mile, and then keep left up a wide path. On right-hand side there is a fine view eastwards of **Llyn Gwynant**. As the path bears to the left a spectacular waterfall comes into view against the backdrop of Lliwedd up to the north. Continue on footpath which soon climbs alongside the waterfall. After passing some pools on right, the path levels out.

(B) Now leaving the Watkin Path, take the path which is immediately on the left, climbing steadily until it reaches a track, which was once the course of a railway line leading to the old mines at the head of **Cwm llan**. Turn right on to the track and after 300 yards take the path to the left going in a westerly direction. Pause awhile and look at the view. On the left is the spectacular peak of Yr Aran, whilst in front is the deep valley of **Cwm llan**, with **Snowdon (Yr Wydffa)** at its head. Continue up the path until reaching the ridge just beyond, which is called Bwlch Cwm llan. Here the path divides, one going westwards to **Rhyd-Ddu**, and the other one, going to the right up to Yr Wydffa.

(C) Turn right up this ridge-path, going northwards. As you climb more views are unfolded with the Nantlle Ridge, Mynydd Mawr and **Llyn Cwellyn** over to the left. In climbing up here take care to keep to the path as there are deep gullies on the right, above the crags of Clogwyn Ddu, which can be dangerous if mist happens to descend. After climbing to over 3000 feet there is a path leading to the left — this is the path to **Beddgelert** and **Rhyd-Ddu**. Continue straight on upwards through Bwlch Main, soon coming to a large pointed rock sticking up from the ground. This is Point **(D)**. If you wish to ascend the summit of **Snowdon (Yr Wydffa)**, take the short climb straight ahead, and then return to this point.

(D) Now starting our descent, using the Watkin Path, turn (eastwards) down scree path until reaching the ridge called Bwlch y Saethau (Path of the Arrows). Here again care must be taken in keeping to the path. Splendid views may be had from here, with Crib y Ddysgl and Crib Goch over to left, and Glaslyn and Llyn Llydaw below, with the

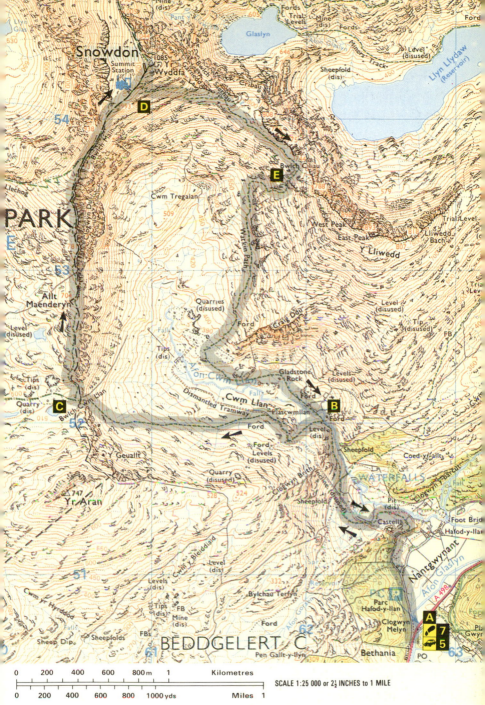

0 200 400 600 800m 1 Kilometres
0 200 400 600 800 1000 yds Miles 1

SCALE 1:25 000 or 2½ INCHES to 1 MILE

Glyders across the valley and Y Lliwedd ahead.

(**E**) Just beyond Bwlch Ciliau, turn right down the next footpath which takes a zig-zag course down to the old mines in **Cwm Llan**, then bearing left. Soon the Gladstone Rock will come into view on right. Here is a tablet recording the opening of the Watkin Path by W. E. Gladstone on September 13th 1892, when this great statesman was in his 84th year. Continue along path until it starts to descend, crossing the Afon Cwm Llan. Now arrive at Point (**B**), where the original upward path is met. After noting the fine views of **Cnicht** and the **Moelwyns** to the south-east, retrace the original path back to the car park at Pont Bethania (**A**), thus completing Walk 7.

143

Walk 8

Beddgelert Forest Country ... beneath Snowdon's Western Bastions

Allow two and a half hours

This walk starts from Rhyd-Ddu, below the western flanks of Snowdon, making early use of the lower part of the Rhyd-Ddu Path, one of the classic routes to Wales' highest mountain. There are fine views westwards out over Llyn y Gader, before our route turns abruptly southwards, and drops down into the Colwyn valley. Here it crosses the A4085, and heads up through the northern fringes of the great Beddgelert Forest, before returning north-eastwards along open hillsides to Rhyd-Ddu.

Rhyd-Ddu (115) (SH 57-52) is on our **Tour 5**, page 118, and is situated on the A4085, 4 miles north of Beddgelert and 9 miles south-east of Caernarfon.

(A) Start from the car park to the south of **Rhyd-Ddu**, and follow path northwards past the public toilets for about 50 yards. Now turn right through gate and go up hill in the direction of **Snowdon**. Go over stile and continue as track bends to the right. Pause awhile and look to the right for views westwards to the crags of Y Garn and the Nantlle Ridge with Mynydd Mawr further to the right (north west), and Llyn y Gader in the foreground below. Ahead is the Snowdon Ridge, Bwlch Cwm Llan and the peak of Yr Aran. Now along track and over two more stiles before reaching kissing gate on the Snowdon track.

(B) Turn sharp right at Pen ar Lôn, avoiding the track and stile immediately ahead. (Turn left here if you wish to follow the path to **Snowdon**.) Our footpath leads downhill over a stile and through gate to the farmyard at Ffridd Uchaf. Please keep strictly to right of way. Follow the track from the farm guest house to the A4085 road.

(C) Turn left on to A4085 and follow it for about 600 yards. Turn right into forest at the Pont Cae'r-gors Picnic Site notice. Keep straight going west for 600 yards, ignoring track to the right at 250 yards. After reaching junction of tracks take the right hand one going north-west for 650 yards, ignoring track on left at 350 yards. At the point where the track veers left, ignore the path going straight ahead and continue on the left hand track for ½ mile.

(D) Turn right at next junction of tracks and walk in a NNE direction until arriving at

View eastwards over Llyn y Gader to Yr Aran from beyond Point D.

small iron gate in wall. Now leave the forest and continue along path with grand views of the Snowdon Range with Mynydd Mawr to the left. Cross two streams and a stile. There are several white arrows on the rocks to indicate the line of this stretch of our path.

(E) When reaching the B4418, Nantlle road, turn sharp right over an iron stile and walk along the marked footpath which leads over another stile and footbridge, across a field, back to the A4085 and the **Rhyd-Ddu** car park (**A**), thus completing our Walk 8.

Walk 9

Beddgelert and the hills above Aberglaslyn

Allow five hours for main walk, or three hours for shortened walk

This walk sets out from Beddgelert up the valley of the Afon Glaslyn, and after making a brief aquaintance with lovely Llyn Dinas, heads south-south-west up over the Bwlch-y-Sygyn before dropping down into Cwm Bychan (the small valley), with splendid mountain views on every side. At Pont Aberglaslyn, the head of the now-drained Glaslyn Estuary, there is an opportunity to return direct to Beddgelert, on an old railway track. However, the main walk goes west up into the hills again, and then northwards along the eastern flanks of the massive Moel Hebog, before returning to Beddgelert.

Beddgelert (115) (SH 58-49) is on our **Tour 5**, page 118. and is situated at the junction of the A4085 and the A498 to the south-east of Caernarfon.

(A) Start from the car park in **Beddgelert** and turn left on A498 through the village. Turn right on to track just before reaching road bridge, and cross over footbridge which spans the Afon Glaslyn. Over road and stile,

across a field and over another stile onto metalled road (right of way). Turn right, and pass Cae Canol (Crusader Centre). Through gate where metalled road ends and round the back of Ty-hên. Turn left at footpath sign, and turn right past notice referring to the Sygyn Copper Mine. Pass Cae'r-môch cottage, with views over to left of Dinas Emrys (see Nantgwynant, page 90), and along by river until reaching shore of **Llyn Dinas**.

(B) Turn right on well-marked path up Afon Goch valley towards Bwlch-y-Sygyn, with views of **Moel Siabod** and the ridge from Moel Meirch to **Cnicht** to left. As you climb up Bwlch-y-Sygyn, keep to the higher path passing a derelict mine hut on right. At the top of the pass (bwlch) where footpaths cross, turn left (south) down Cwm Bychan, with fine views of Moel Ddu over to right, and the Glaslyn Estuary to the left (south).

(C) Pass derelict mine cableways and a sheepfold. From here there are views of **Cnicht** and the **Moelwyns** to the left and the **Rhinogs** to the far south. Continue down Cwm Bychan to car park at **Aberglaslyn (D)**. It is possible to shorten the walk by turning right from the Aberglaslyn car park, through the railway tunnel (right of way) and following the course of the old **Welsh Highland Railway** line to **Beddgelert**, thus returning to **(A)**.

(D) To continue on main walk, turn right

Dinas Emrys from beyond the Afon Glaslyn.

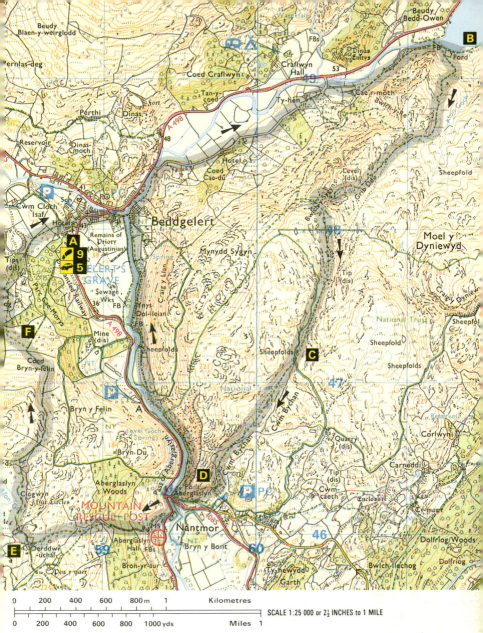

```
0    200   400   600   800m   1          Kilometres
|----+----+----+----+----+----|----------+----------|
0    200   400   600   800   1000 yds    Miles    1
                                   SCALE 1:25 000 or 2½ INCHES to 1 MILE
```

on to A4085 on leaving car park, cross bridge and turn left on A498. After about 150 yards turn right at footpath sign, and continue up on it through woods to gate and wooden bridge. At second gate turn right, and then left after 50 yards. Go up the stony path passing a large boulder on your left, and then through gap in wall. Keep stream on your right and cross stile at top of wood. Turn right up hill, through gap in wall and head for Oerddwr-uchaf farm.

(E) Stop here awhile and take in the superb views of the **Moelwyns** to the east and the **Rhinogs** to the south. On reaching the farm buildings turn right (north) and take the track

behind the farm. Cross the Afon Goch and pass the gap in the wall by the sheepfold. The path is indistinct here, but continue northwards with Moel Hebog over to the left. Go through gap in wall, and keep north along footpath to wall.

(F) Then bear left and make for gap between trees. Cross track through two gates (sign for Beddgelert) close to Bron Hebog. Follow footpath signs on posts. Bear right by old railway embankment, through iron gate, over stile and bridge by new housing estate at entry to **Beddgelert**, and follow road turning left into car park **(A)**, thus completing our Walk 9.

Walk 10

Around Yr Eifl, with fine viewpoints and an ancient British stronghold

Allow three hours

This walk encircles two peaks out of three of Yr Eifl, the triple peaks, which the English call 'The Rivals'. It also provides opportunities for walking up the main peak, Yr Eifl itself, and for visiting the Iron Age settlement of Tre'r Ceiri, from both of which there are outstanding views. But the circuit around the flanks of the Lleyn Peninsula's most prominent mountain group is a very pleasant walk in its own right, and should not be missed.

Our starting point car park (123) (SH 35-44) is on our **Tour 6**, page 120, and is located to the immediate west of a minor road, between trees and the road, a mile to the north of **Llithfaen**, which is itself 17 miles south-west of Caernarfon.

(A) Walk back from our starting point car park along road towards **Llithfaen** until the rough track leading north-east across the hillside is reached. Follow this track climbing gently for about 1900 yards until Bwlch yr Eifl is reached.

(B) *A possible diversion to the summit cairn on the left, keeping to the left of the transmitting station on the way up. This is without doubt the Lleyn Peninsula's finest viewpoint, and well worth visiting if the weather is reasonably clear.*

(B) From Bwlch yr Eifl continue downhill on a grassy track keeping just left of the power line until a ruined stone wall is reached **(C)**. The sure-footed can turn right here following the line of the wall and a faint track above crags dropping steeply down a gully, to arrive at **(D)**.

(C) Otherwise continue downhill between power lines and scree to left until next wall is reached, then turning right, away from wall following a track through bracken to iron gate in wall at stream. The footpath swings left over the shoulder of the hill and keeping to right of fence reaches Point **(D)**.

(D) A wicket gate leads the path between fences to a conifer plantation where a crawl beneath low branches is necessary for about 100 yards unless a diversion to the left of the trees is made to a gate and the lane. Turn

Yr Eifl from the starting-point of Walk 10.

right along lane to **Llanaelhaearn**.

(E) Then turn right near entry to **Llanaelhaearn** on to road signed to Nefyn. Climb out of **Llanaelhaearn** for about ½ mile, and then turn right off road following footpath sign. The stile leads to a grassy path climbing the hillside and after three more stiles the gradient begins to ease as the path reaches the plateau at Point **(F)**. *An optional diversion here leads to the right up the hillside to Tre'r Ceiri, an extensive Iron Age fort on the eastern summit (see **Llanaelhaearn**, page 67). Massive defence walls and dwelling foundations are visible and the fine views south to **Harlech** and the **Rhinogs** alone justify the ascent.*

(F) Returning to this point, continue south-westwards, the path gently descending, until it joins a track heading for **Llithfaen**. *Just before the first cottages the path swings north-west and then north indistinctly over rough heather-clad moorland to join the original track. Turn sharp left here and walk down track to return to car park **(A)**, thus completing Walk 10.

*There is a track leading directly from the cottages alongside a wall to return to the starting car park at **(A)**. Although this is not a designated right of way, it is possible that permission may be given for its use, if enquiries are made locally.*

Walk 11

Llyn Trawsfynydd Country ... Roman remains and a nuclear power station

Allow three and a half hours

This walk first goes eastward to pass close to two Roman sites which are themselves near the course of the Sarn Helen. After taking in some fine views, we head down towards the Trawsfynydd Nuclear Power Station, where there is an opportunity to divert to a small Nature Trail. *After passing a fish farm and the power station itself, we follow close to the northern shore of the great Llyn Trawsfynydd Reservoir, before returning through an extensive area of tranquil forest and farming country.*

Trawsfynydd (124) (SH 70-35) lies between Llyn Trawsfynydd and the A470, Ffestiniog to Dolgellau road, about 6 miles south of the former; but our starting point is the Utica Car Park (124) (SH 695-390) on the A470, 2 miles north of Trawsfynydd, and this is on our **Tours 7 and 8**.

(A) Start from the Utica Car Park and cross A470 to a chapel. 50 yards to the left (north), take a track to the right and go over railway bridge. Bear right through gate and across

The view south-westwards over Llyn Trawsfynydd from our lakeside path beyond Point C.

field to barn. Keep close to stream on right, and through gap in stone wall. Keep close to stream and head towards radio mast. But turn left up old farm track through gate on to road. Turn right along metalled road for about 600 yards until reaching the end where ruins of Roman amphitheatre are visible to right.

(B) Return back along road for about 80 yards and take path to left through felled forestry to stile (possible changes here by the time you come this way). Over bridge crossing small stream. Continue south-west along path noting large mound on left. This is the Roman fort, in the vicinity of the mound known as **Castell Tomen-y-mur**, but it lies on private land (permission to visit may possibly be obtained from the farmer). On reaching the top of the path pause awhile to admire the panoramic view which includes; to the north-east, the slate quarries of **Blaenau Ffestiniog**, and Manod Mawr; to the north-west, the **Moelwyns** and the **Stwlan Dam** nestling high up in the hills; to the west, the Lleyn Peninsula; and to the south-west, the **Rhinogs**, with the great reservoir, **Llyn Trawsfynydd** in the foreground to the immediate south. Keep to path which heads for power station. Go through gap in wall and bear left just before reaching wall in front. Cross stile and under tunnel beneath railway. Climb up steps, over stile and cross main A470 road.

(C) Beyond A470 go through small gate alongside cattle grid, leading to power station. Small nature trail on left. Return to road leading to power station and then bear left off road and up to dam wall. Walk beside dam wall, passing fish farm on left and the **Trawsfynydd Nuclear Power Station** on right. Our route now joins a metalled road. Eventually fork right off metalled road on to rough track just beyond power station, keeping alongside lake until reaching a gate almost at the end.

(D) Turn right at footpath sign near end of track and over stile. Bear right on broader grass path. This meets a forestry path. After a few yards along the path, bear left down another path by a yellow arrow. Pass over stile at end of path where it leaves the forestry. Pass under power lines and over three stiles. Now bear left, then right to Cae-Einion-Alun Farm and continue towards Bryntirion.

(E) But before reaching Bryntirion take signed path going sharp right. Follow path through two gates and along clearly marked route through bracken. Go through gap in stone wall and gate, to footpath sign. Turn left over stile and down to track over stream (Afon Tafarn-helyg) crossing wooden bridge. Continue past old barn and farmyard until reaching metalled road which leads back to A470 and our starting car park **(A)** at Utica, thus completing Walk 11.

Walk 12

Llyn Celyn and the Hesgyn Valley

Allow four and a half hours

This walk starts from the great dam of Llyn Celyn, with its memories of the village that once stood in the valley here before it was drowned. The walk immediately heads north-wards into the hills, and after crossing the lovely Hesgyn valley it encircles the slopes of Craig y Garn. There are fine views of Llyn Celyn, the Arans, the Arenigs and Bala from several points along the way. Although the walk passes several ruined farms, others have survived, and this quiet country provides a typical example of Welsh hill farming — a satisfying but an intensely hard way of life. Please follow the Country Code with your usual care, and respect the privacy of the farms that you pass through.

Llyn Celyn (124,125) (SH 88-40) is on our **Tour 8**, page 124, and is situated on the A4212, Trawsfynydd to Bala road, 4 miles north-west of Bala.

(A) Start from the car park near the north-eastern end of the **Llyn Celyn** dam, near the A4212 (SH 882-404). Walk east, down A4212 for about 400 yards. Turn left through gate and follow path upwards in a north-westerly direction. On reaching a ruined building turn right and follow path through bracken. Head northwards parallel with stream on right. Follow wall to the right for a little way when our path veers north-east through heather. Across a track and then veer round left on to a bridleway to the old farm of Cwm Hesgyn.

(B) From Cwm Hesgyn follow path to the right which crosses a bridge over the Afon Hesgyn. Beyond bridge turn slightly right and then left after a few yards. The path now climbs through the heather in a north-easterly direction. Before descending to Bwlch Graia-nog Farm, pause to admire the views of the **Arenigs** to the west and south-west, the **Arans** to the south, and **Bala** to the south-east. To the north and west lies a very lonely and unspoilt stretch of country, with the gradual contour leading up to Carnedd y Filiast (SH 87-44).

(C) After passing Bwlch Graianog Farm, continue along the bridleway passing the ruin of Ysgubor Bwlch-graianog (Ysgubor meaning 'barn'). Follow track east and then south-east to Nant Hir Farm.

SCALE 1:25 000 or 2½ INCHES to 1 MILE

View down the Tryweryn Valley from the grass-covered slopes of the Llyn Celyn Dam.

(D) A notice just beyond Nant Hir Farm directs us to the right, to the next farm up the hill, Maesygadfa. Go through farmyard, keeping to right of way, through gate and continue up road until reaching another gate. Do not go through this gate, but go through gate on right, and then immediately through gate on left. Continue south-westwards along track up hill and pass through gate at the top. Pass trees on right and continue through the ruins of Garn. Beyond this the path veers west to Traean-y- Garn Cottage,

and then north-west to a foot bridge.

(E) Here we recross the Afon Hesgyn, and then follow the path round to the right of the forestry before heading southwards down a rough track. About half way down watch carefully for a right turn leading along another path going westwards. This passes over two cart tracks and two small streams and then joins our starting path. Turn left on to this path and follow it down to the A4212. Turn right on to A4212 and return to starting car park **(A)**, thus completing our Walk 12.

Walk 13

Cwm Nantcol and the Gateway to the Rhinogs

Allow five hours

This walk starts from a car park and picnic place delightfully situated above the banks of the Afon Cwmnantcol and explores the hilly country on either side of the Cwm Nantcol, the foothills of the Rhinog Range. There are fine views from these hills, and a great sense of peace in the pastoral valley below them. There is a nature trail and a farm trail close to the car park, both of which are well worth following (see Cwm Nantcol, page 56).

The Cwm Nantcol Car Park (124) (SH 60-27) is on our **Tour 7**, page 122, and is situated 2 miles east of Llanbedr and 5 miles south-east of Harlech.

(A) Start from the Cwm Nantcol car park and picnic site (608-271) which is at the end of a small track leading from the road towards the river (The Afon Cwmnantcol).

Return from car park along track, crossing over cattle grid. Turn right up grassy slope to metalled road and turn right on to road. After 220 yards turn left up bridleway going north. Bear left keeping wall on left when meeting another footpath going north-east. Turn right along this path (path to left, and the next section of our own path is part of the Cefn-Isa Farm Trail — see Cwm Nantcol, page 56, for details). Cross over stile and head towards building named Fron-Dosdaidd. Pass this building on right and turn right.

(B) Beyond Fron-Dosdaidd take the track to the right uphill which then veers round to left. Turn left up path between walls going upwards and eastwards. Go through gate and turn right following grass bridleway. Take the right fork going eastwards. After going through four gates, bear left keeping wall on left. Pass through gate in wall straight ahead.

(C) After 150 yards turn right going south and passing large mound of bare rocks on the left. Go through gap in wall and then through gate. Take the left hand track still keeping south. Go through gate and follow track. Some fine views along this plateau, with **Bardsey Island** to the west, **Yr Eifl (The Rivals)** to the north-west and part of the

| 0 | 200 | 400 | 600 | 800m | 1 | Kilometres |

| 0 | 200 | 400 | 600 | 800 | 1000 yds | Miles 1 |

SCALE 1:25 000 or 2½ INCHES to 1 MILE

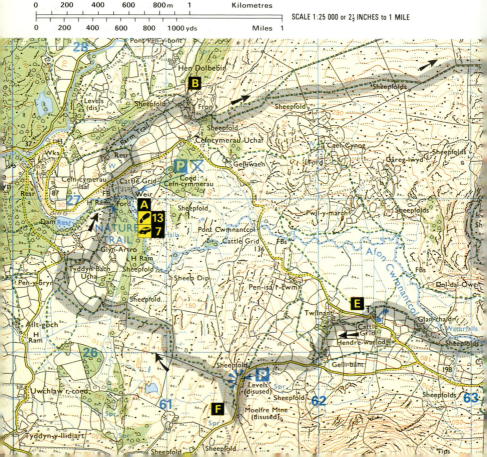

Nantlle Ridge to the NNW, whilst immediately below the Afon Cwmnantcol meanders down the valley towards Llanbedr and the sea. Across the valley, directly ahead is the mountain Moelfre.

Take the path below the ruin which is on the left, passing old mine on left, and then go through gap in wall. Go over stile. Y Llethr which is the highest point in the **Rhinog Range**, can now be seen to the south-east, with Rhinog Fach to the east. Continue south and south-south-east passing through gap in wall. Turn left through gate and through two wall openings. Turn right onto metalled road and over Pont Cerrig crossing Afon Cwmnantcol. Road up to left (north-eastwards) leads to Maes-y-garnedd, a farm where Oliver Cromwell's brother-in-law was born (see Cwm Nantcol, page 56). A path beyond this goes over the **Bwlch Drws Ardudwy**.

(D) Immediately after bridge, turn right over stile. Head in a direction slightly south of west. Cross bridge over small stream and go over stile. Go through gap in low wall and then through gap in higher wall. Turn left over stream and head for gate in wall. Pass through gate and then fork right down to building. Pass through gate on right. Turn

left and continue north-westwards. Do not go through gate ahead, but veer right keeping wall on left. Go through gate. Turn left through gate below school and go through another gate, which leads to a metalled road.

(E) Cross road and go through gate on to a footpath. After reaching Twll-y-Nant Farm turn left through small gate. Continue south-westwards up field and go through gate in wall. Cross stream and continue up footpath to metalled road. Turn right and now walk along road, soon going through gate across road. When reaching top of road, look back to the **Rhinog Range** with the deep cleft between the two Rhinogs, known as **Bwlch Drws Ardudwy**, once crossed by an old drovers' road. Looking north, the Hebog and Snowdon ranges can also be seen. About 400 yards **before** next gate across road, go through gate in wall on right.

(F) Follow path in a north-westerly direction. Go though gate in wall on the right. Continue north-westwards, then veer left through gap in wall, and on to bridleway. Cross over stream. Bear left, go through gap in wall, bear right and through wall on right. Go through gate and gap in wall. Go through another gate and bear right going through gate to left of Tyddyn-bach Farm. Turn right on to track and just before cattle grid, turn left down track between walls, passing through two gates. Go north down field over stile and then cross over bridge crossing Afon Cwmnantcol. Continue through woods until reaching track. Turn right on to track and return to car park **(A)**, thus completing our Walk 13.

The Rhinogs above Cwm Nantcol, from our road near Point F.

Walk 14
The Mawddach Estuary, Bontddu and the Gold Mine Country

Allow four hours

This walk follows the shore of the lovely Mawddach estuary for some distance before heading northwards beyond the small village of Bontddu. It then runs parallel with the fast-flowing Afon Hirgwm, passing the entrance to the small but famous Clogau St David's Gold Mine, traditional source of Royal wedding rings for several generations. Beyond here the walk heads north-eastwards into mountain country where there are the remains of earlier mines, once linked to the estuary by an old tramway. At various points on this section there are splendid views to the north before the walk eventually turns south and south-westwards to return to the starting point through partially wooded country. This last section also provides fine views — this time southwards, out over the Mawddach estuary to Cadair Idris.

Bontddu (124) (SH 66-18) is on our **Tour 7**, page 122, and is situated on the A496, 4 miles west of Dolgellau. The walk starts from a car park on the right of the road just before the entrance to **Bontddu**.

(A) Start from Fiddler's Elbow car park (SH 67-18), just to the east of **Bontddu**. Fine views from here out over the Mawddach estuary to the **Penmaenpool Nature Reserve** on its southern shore, and beyond to the crags of **Cadair Idris**. Turn left on to A496, and walk eastwards along it for about 250 yards. Then turn right down footpath past house called Rhuddallt, and follow yellow signs.

(B) Turn right at next footpath which is well marked, and follow parallel to the shore of the Mawddach, keeping to the path as there are fast-flowing and dangerous tides in this estuary. Bear left over footbridge and then right, keeping fence on right. Now bear right through woodland keeping small river, the Afon Hirgwm, on left. Continue up track to A496 road in **Bontddu**.

The Mawddach Estuary near Bontddu.

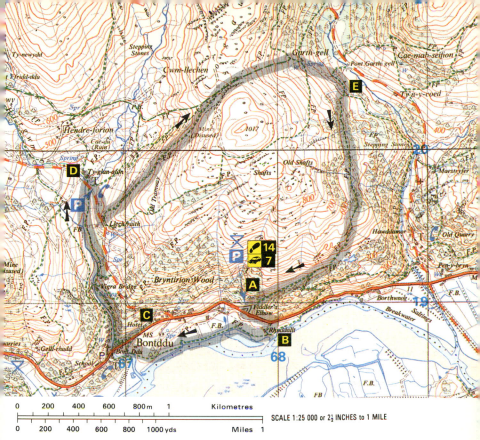

(C) Cross A496, and follow left (westward) along it for a few yards, before turning right into side road which runs parallel with A496. Pass a well on right and then turn right following footpath sign immediately beyond well. Climb up steps with buildings to right and go through gate. Continue up hill through woodland. Bear left at forked paths and go through kissing gate, following signs. At the next forked footpath (where left footpath goes over bridge), take the right fork. Keep bearing left on to rough road with Afon Hirgwm on left. Where rough road forks, bear right (the left fork enters the Clogau St David's Gold Mine — not open to the public at time of writing — see Bontddu, page 42). Continue up path through kissing gate, cross field and through another gate, which leads to a metalled road.

(D) Turn right along road. Continue for 300 yards and then turn left up a footpath just beyond house. After a few yards with another house in front, turn sharp left up grassy path. After a few yards the path veers right (north-east). Pass through gate, and continue along path with wall on left. Go through gate, and as path veers round to right there are splendid views of Cwm Llechen to the north, with Diffwys beyond to the north-west. Follow path which goes between two walls and a gate. Then follow a wider path and through gate. Just before reaching mine spoil-heap go through small gate on left. Turn right and follow path which runs parallel with wall on right. After wall ends, continue straight ahead and follow yellow arrows. Continue downwards passing through gate. Cross over rough track and follow marked path. Go through gap in wall on right and follow rough track downwards on the left, keeping Garth Gell on right.

(E) Just before reaching kissing gate, turn right on grassy path, pass through gap in wall and pass old building on left. Follow yellow arrows heading south. Pass through small gate and then through gap in wall. After passing through another gate, climb the small knoll on left and admire the fine views ahead, encompassing the Mawddach estuary with Dolgellau to its east, Penmaenpool to the south-east, and the whole of the Cadair Range to the south and south-west. Return to path, continue south, and pass through gate. Our path now descends south-westwards. Note attractive small reservoir below to left. Pass through gate. Ignore the next gate on left with yellow arrows and continue alongside wall on left. Now go through gate on left with yellow arrows. Continue down track to return to starting car park at Fiddler's Elbow **(A)**, thus completing Walk 14.

Walk 15
Cadair Idris from the North

Allow five hours

This walk makes use of one of the well known paths that lead to Penygadair, the highest summit of the rugged **Cadair Idris** *Range — the Pony Path. We have deliberately avoided using the Fox's Path for the descent, as this is extremely hazardous. But whichever route you choose, always follow the advice given on the inside rear cover of this guide.*

The starting point for this walk is a small car park (124) (SH 69-15) on the north side of a minor road running from **Arthog**, past the **Llynnau Cregennen**, north-east back towards **Dolgellau**. This is on our **Tour 10**, page 128.

(A) Start from the car park, turning right (south-westwards) over a bridge and along the road for about 50 yards. Turn left through gate at footpath sign. Follow stream on the right, passing Ty Nant on left. Follow well-marked footpath to gate in stone wall. Continue to well-marked path and climb up the zig-zag to the 'bwlch' (pass).

(B) At this point we are at 1842 feet above sea-level and have actually climbed 1200 feet from the starting car park. Here is a chance to rest awhile and view the impressive panorama, with the Pony Path descending south-westwards into the **Dysynni valley**, where **Castell y Bere** and **Craig yr Aderyn (The Birds' Rock)** lie; and over to the north, the distant outline of the **Rhinogs**. Now follow the left footpath going eastwards, and continue climbing past the cairns, keeping fence

SCALE 1:25 000 or 2½ INCHES to 1 MILE

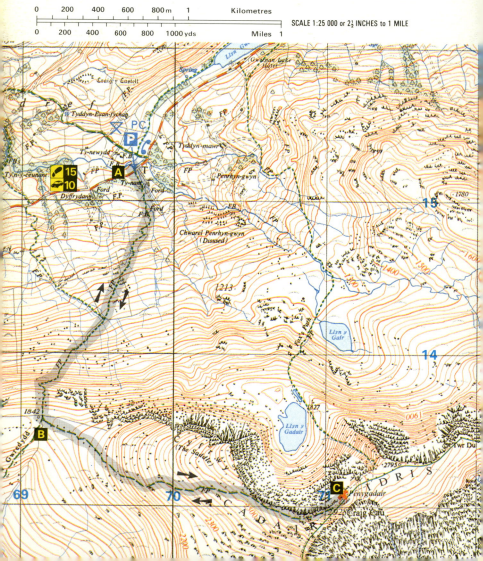

The crags of Cadair Idris from the starting-point of Walk 15.

to the left. The Minffordd Path soon comes into view coming over a crag on the right, and this meets up with our path at the very summit, Penygadair **(C)**.

On a clear day there are splendid panoramic views to be had from this mountain top, with Plynlimmon over to the south, and to the north-west, the Mawddach estuary leading to Barmouth and the sea, with **Yr Eifl (The Rivals)** and the Lleyn Peninsula beyond. The rugged outlines of the **Snowdon** and **Glyder** ranges can be seen to the north, while to the north-east lie the **Arenigs** and the **Arans**. Victorian visitors came here in their thousands, and on the summit will be found the remains of a stone refreshment hut, erected here by some enterprising caterer.

(C) Having avoided the temptation of using the dangerous Fox's Path for your descent, make a return by the same paths that were used for the ascent, to arrive back at the starting car park **(A)**, thus completing our Walk 15.

Walk 16

Dysynni Valley Country...home of Prince Llywelyn and Mary Jones

Allow three hours for the short walk or five hours for the long walk

This walk explores the lovely Dysynni valley, with its views of the dramatic Birds' Rock, and the romantic Castell y Bere, once the home of Prince Llywelyn. It also passes not far from the home of a humbler citizen of Wales, Mary Jones, who once walked all the way to Bala in her search for a bible in Welsh, no mean feat for a young girl, in the days when roads were almost non-existent.

Abergynolwyn (124) SH 67-06) is on our **Tour 10**, page 128, and is situated on the B4405, 6 miles north-east of Tywyn and 11 miles south-west of Dolgellau. The walk starts from Abergynolwyn Station and this can also be reached from Tywyn on the attractive **Talyllyn Railway** (see page 106).

(A) Start from the car park at Abergynolwyn Station, which is on B4405, ½ mile south-west of **Abergynolwyn**. Turn left (south-west) on to road and walk along grass verge for about ⅓ mile. Cross road where woodland ends on right and follow footpath sign on right. Follow track up through woods on a zig-zag course to the top, where there are old farm buildings on left and a house called Rhiwerfa on right. The track now meets a metalled road which leads downwards. Follow this road until reaching gate. Beyond gate, bear left along road for ¼ mile, and after second gate, bear right. Pause here awhile to admire the beautiful **Dysynni valley** and the **Cadair Idris** massif beyond to the north-east.

(B) Follow path leading to a derelict barn. Pass through gate on left and through field

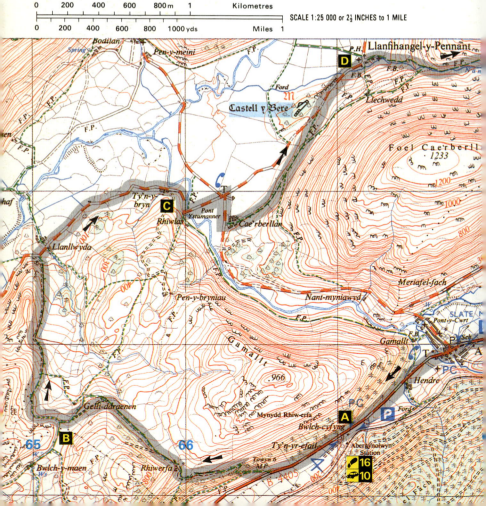

SCALE 1:25 000 or 2½ INCHES to 1 MILE

Abergynolwyn ... a slate-quarrying village cradled in the hills.

keeping wall on right. Follow path down to metalled road. Turn right and walk along metalled public road for ¾ mile. After about half way, turn round and look down valley. This view includes on left, the rock **Craig yr Aderyn** (the Birds' Rock), so-called because it is the only known territory where cormorants come inland to breed. Continue along road passing farm on right until a bridge **(C)** is reached, the Pont Ystumanner.

If you wish to take the shorter walk, leave road just before bridge, following sign on right of bridge, passing the front of the house, Rhiwlas. Through gate and follow path parallel with the Afon Dysynni back to **Abergynolwyn** and take B4405 back to station car park. (See Dysynni Valley, page 61 for details of a rare physical occurrence that has taken place between the two valleys which are linked here.)

(C) To take the longer walk, cross the Pont Ystumanner, follow road for about 300 yards, and turn right on to road signed to Abergynolwyn. After another 200 yards, turn left through Cae'rberllan farmyard, through gate and follow footpath to a Y-junction of paths. Take the left path to the road below **Castell y Bere**, a ruined fortress on a dramatic rocky outcrop, and once the home of Prince Llywelyn. Now go further down the road to **Llanfihangel-y-pennant (D)**, with its delightful little church.

(D) From here it is possible to go beyond to Tyn-y-ddôl (off map to north, about ½ mile from Llanfihangel) to visit Mary Jones' Cottage (see Llanfihangel, page 76). But otherwise turn right in **Llanfihangel** going eastwards along a track beside river. Follow track past derelict farm, Nant-yr-eira. Continue over stile and through gate. Turn right off track by yellow post. Down through woods on zig-zag path marked by yellow posts. Over stile, cross field, and over another stile on to metalled road.

(E) Turn right on to B4405 at Y-junction near the Pont Cedris. Return by B4405, through **Abergynolwyn**, to Abergynolwyn Station car park **(A)**, thus completing our Walk 16.

CONVENTIONAL SIGNS

1:190 080 or 1 INCH to 3 MILES

ROADS
Not necessarily rights of way

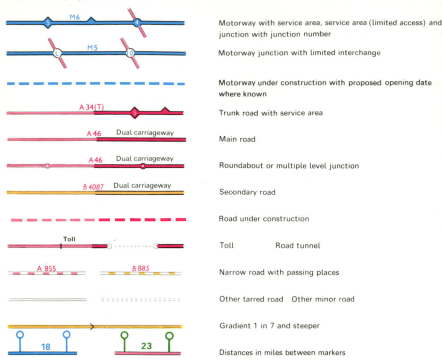

M6	Motorway with service area, service area (limited access) and junction with junction number
M5	Motorway junction with limited interchange
	Motorway under construction with proposed opening date where known
A 34(T)	Trunk road with service area
A 46 Dual carriageway	Main road
A 46 Dual carriageway	Roundabout or multiple level junction
B 4087 Dual carriageway	Secondary road
	Road under construction
Toll	Toll Road tunnel
A 855 B 885	Narrow road with passing places
	Other tarred road Other minor road
	Gradient 1 in 7 and steeper
18 23	Distances in miles between markers

The representation of a road is no evidence of the existence of a right of way

PRIMARY ROUTES

These form a national network of recommended through routes which complement the motorway system.
Selected places of major traffic importance are known as Primary Route Destinations and are shown thus **BANGOR**
Distances and directions to such destinations are repeated on traffic signs which, on primary routes, have a green background or, on motorways, have a blue background.
To continue on a primary route through or past a place which has appeared as a destination on previous signs, follow the directions to the next primary destination shown on the green-backed signs.

RAILWAYS

Standard gauge track	Road crossing under or over
Narrow gauge track	Level crossing
Tunnel	Station

WATER FEATURES

(boat) (hovercraft)	Ferry routes for vehicles (subject to change)
Canal	
Marsh	

Short ferry routes for vehicles

Lake   Bridge   Ferry

Slopes   Cliff

Flat rock

Transport for vehicles

Light-vessel

Low water mark

Foreshore

High water mark

Dunes

ANTIQUITIES

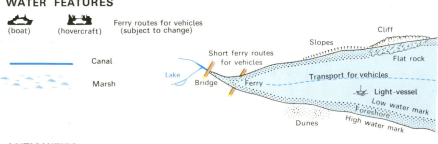

✳ Native fortress	Site of battle (with date)	Roman road (course of)
Castle · Other antiquities	CANOVIUM · Roman antiquity	

𝔪   Ancient Monuments and Historic Buildings in the care of the Secretaries of State for the Environment, for Scotland and for Wales and that are open to the public.

BOUNDARIES

 + — + — + — + — National

— — — — — — — { County, Region or Islands Area

GENERAL FEATURES

Buildings

Wood

Lighthouse (in use)

Lighthouse (disused)

Windmill

Radio or TV mast

▲ Youth hostel

⊕ + Civil aerodrome { with Customs facilities / without Customs facilities

Ⓗ Heliport

✆ Public telephone

✆ Motoring organisation telephone

+ Intersection, latitude & longitude at 30' intervals (not shown where it confuses important detail)

TOURIST INFORMATION

✝ Abbey, Cathedral, Priory

🐟 Aquarium

⛺ Camp site

Caravan site

🏰 Castle

Cave

Country park

Craft centre

❀ Garden

⚑ Golf course or links

🏛 Historic house

ℹ Information centre

Motor racing

🖼 Museum

Nature or forest trail

🦆 Nature reserve

☆ Other tourist feature

✕ Picnic site

Preserved railway

Racecourse

Skiing

Viewpoint

Wildlife park

🐘 Zoo

AREA COVERED BY THIS GUIDE

WALKS AND TOURS

Applicable to all scales

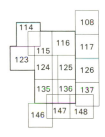

🔦1 Start point of walk

➡ Route of walk

Featured walk

🚗1 Start point of tour

➤ Route of tour

Featured tour

1:50 000 ADJOINING SHEETS

114		108
115	116	117
123	124	125	126
	135	136	137
	146	147	148

CONVENTIONAL SIGNS   1:25 000 or 2½ INCHES to 1 MILE

ROADS AND PATHS

Not necessarily rights of way

M I or A 6(M)	M I or A 6(M)	Motorway
A 31 (T)	A 31 (T)	Trunk road
A 35	A 35	Main road
B 3074	B 3074	Secondary road
A 35	A 35	Dual carriageway

Narrow roads with passing places are annotated

Road generally more than 4m wide

Road generally less than 4m wide

Other road, drive or track

Unfenced roads and tracks are shown by pecked lines

.... Path

PUBLIC RIGHTS OF WAY

Public rights of way may not be evident on the ground

} Public paths { Footpath / Bridleway

+ + + + + Byway open to all traffic

+ + + + Road used as a public path

DANGER AREA
MOD ranges in the area
Danger!
Observe warning notices

The indication of a towpath in this book does not necessarily imply a public right of way
The representation of any other road, track or path is no evidence of the existence of a right of way

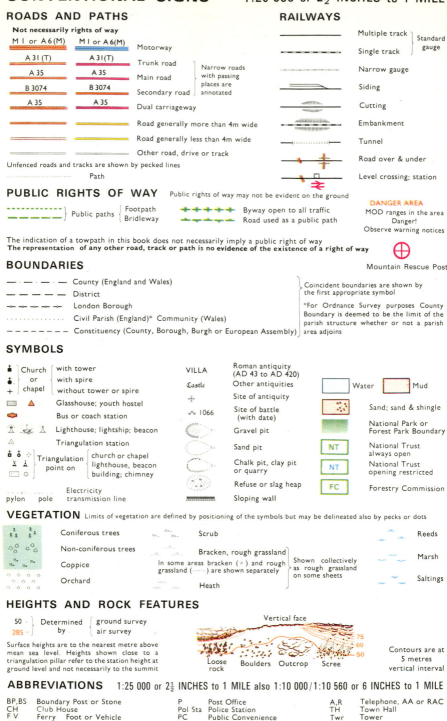

Mountain Rescue Post

RAILWAYS

———————	Multiple track } Standard gauge
— — — — —	Single track
⋯⋯⋯⋯	Narrow gauge
	Siding
	Cutting
	Embankment
·····──·····	Tunnel
	Road over & under
	Level crossing; station

BOUNDARIES

— · — · — · — County (England and Wales)

— — — — — District

⊸⊸⊸⊸⊸ London Borough

·············· Civil Parish (England)* Community (Wales)

— — — — — — Constituency (County, Borough, Burgh or European Assembly)

Coincident boundaries are shown by the first appropriate symbol

*For Ordnance Survey purposes County Boundary is deemed to be the limit of the parish structure whether or not a parish area adjoins

SYMBOLS

Church or chapel { with tower / with spire / without tower or spire

Glasshouse; youth hostel ▲

Bus or coach station

Lighthouse; lightship; beacon

Triangulation station △

Triangulation point on { church or chapel / lighthouse, beacon / building; chimney

Electricity transmission line
pylon   pole

VILLA — Roman antiquity (AD 43 to AD 420)

Castle — Other antiquities

✤ Site of antiquity

✕ 1066 Site of battle (with date)

Gravel pit

Sand pit

Chalk pit, clay pit or quarry

Refuse or slag heap

Sloping wall

Water   Mud

Sand; sand & shingle

National Park or Forest Park Boundary

NT — National Trust always open

NT — National Trust opening restricted

FC — Forestry Commission

VEGETATION

Limits of vegetation are defined by positioning of the symbols but may be delineated also by pecks or dots

Coniferous trees

Non-coniferous trees

Coppice

Orchard

Scrub

Bracken, rough grassland

In some areas bracken ( ) and rough grassland ( ) are shown separately

Heath

Shown collectively as rough grassland on some sheets

Reeds

Marsh

Saltings

HEIGHTS AND ROCK FEATURES

50 · — Determined by { ground survey
285 ─ —   { air survey

Surface heights are to the nearest metre above mean sea level. Heights shown close to a triangulation pillar refer to the station height at ground level and not necessarily the summit

Vertical face

Loose rock   Boulders   Outcrop   Scree

Contours are at 5 metres vertical interval

ABBREVIATIONS   1:25 000 or 2½ INCHES to 1 MILE also 1:10 000/1:10 560 or 6 INCHES to 1 MILE

BP,BS	Boundary Post or Stone	P	Post Office	A,R	Telephone, AA or RAC
CH	Club House	Pol Sta	Police Station	TH	Town Hall
F V	Ferry Foot or Vehicle	PC	Public Convenience	Twr	Tower
FB	Foot Bridge	PH	Public House	W	Well
HO	House	Sch	School	Wd Pp	Wind Pump
MP,MS	Mile Post or Stone	Spr	Spring		
Mon	Monument	T	Telephone, public		

Abbreviations applicable only to 1:10 000/1:10 560 or 6 INCHES to 1 MILE

Ch	Church	GP	Guide Post	TCB	Telephone Call Box
F Sta	Fire Station	P	Pole or Post	TCP	Telephone Call Post
Fn	Fountain	S	Stone	Y	Youth Hostel

Maps and Mapping

Most early maps of the area covered by this guide were published on a county basis, and if you wish to follow their development in detail R. V. Tooley's *Maps and Map Makers* will be found most useful. The first significant county maps were produced by Christopher Saxton in the 1570s, the whole of England and Wales being covered in only six years. Although he did not cover the whole country, John Norden, working at the end of the 16th century, was the first map-maker to show roads. In 1611-12, John Speed, making use of Saxton and Norden's pioneer work, produced his *'Theatre of the Empire of Great Britaine'*, adding excellent town plans, battle scenes, and magnificent coats of arms. The next great English map-maker was John Ogilby, and in 1675 he published *Britannia, Volume I*, in which all the roads of England and Wales were engraved on a scale of one inch to the mile, in a massive series of strip maps. From this time onwards, no map was published without roads, and throughout the 18th century, steady progress was made in accuracy, if not always in the beauty of presentation.

The first Ordnance Survey maps came about as a result of Bonnie Prince Charlie's Jacobite rebellion of 1745. It was, however, in 1791, following the successful completion of the military survey of Scotland by General Roy that the Ordnance Survey was formally established. The threat of invasion by Napoleon in the early 19th century spurred on the demand for accurate and detailed mapping for military purposes, and to meet this need the first Ordnance Survey one-inch map, covering part of Essex, was published in 1805 in a single colour. This was the first numbered sheet in the First Series of one inch-maps.

Over the next seventy years the one-inch map was extended to cover the whole of Great Britain. Reprints of some of these First Series maps incorporating various later 19th century amendments, have been published by David & Charles. The reprinted sheets covering most of our area are Numbers 24, 31, and 39.

The Ordnance Survey's First Series one-inch maps evolved through a number of 'Series' and editions, to the Seventh Series which was replaced in 1972 by the metric 1:50 000 scale Landranger Series. Between the First Series one-inch and the current Landranger maps many changes in style, format, content and purpose have taken place. Colour, for example, first appeared with the timid use of light brown for hill shading on the 1889 one-inch sheets. By 1892 as many as five colours were being used for this scale and at one stage the Seventh

Series was being printed in no less than ten colours. Recent developments in 'process printing' — a technique in which four basic colours produce almost any required tint — are now used to produce Ordnance Survey Landranger and other map series. Through the years the one-inch Series has gradually turned away from its military origins and has developed to meet a wider user demand. The modern detailed full colour Landranger maps at 1:50 000 scale incorporate Rights of Way and Tourist Information and are much used for both leisure and business purposes. To compare the old and new approach to changing demand, see the two map extracts of Caernarfon on the following pages.

Modern Ordnance Survey Maps of the Area.

To look at the area surrounding our Landranger Sheets 114, 115, 116, 123, 124, 125, and 135, the Ordnance Survey 1 inch to 4 miles **Routemaster** Sheet 7 (Wales and the Midlands) will prove most useful. An alternative will be found in the form of the **O.S. Motoring Atlas**, at the larger scale of 1 inch to 3 miles.

The Ordnance Survey publishes a **Tourist Map of Snowdonia and Anglesey** at ½ inch to 1 mile scale. To examine the Snowdonia area in more detail and especially if you are planning walks, the Ordnance Survey special **Outdoor Leisure Maps of the Snowdonia National Park** at 1:25 000 scale (2½ inches to 1 mile), are all ideal, as they show public rights of way information. They are as follows:

    16 — *Conwy Valley Area*
    17 — *Snowdon Area*
    18 — *Harlech & Bala Area*
    23 — *Cadair Idris Area*

Standard series maps at 1:25 000 (2½ inches to 1 mile) are also available for the rest of our area. Most of these maps are in the modern Ordnance Survey **Pathfinder** series, which carry rights of way information. The Pathfinder series is replacing the old 1:25 000 **First Series** mapping, which does not show rights of way.

To place the area in an historical context the following O.S. **Archaeological and Historical Maps** will also be found useful: **Roman Britain, Britain in the Dark Ages, Britain before the Norman Conquest, Monastic Britain, and Ancient Britain.** Ordnance Survey maps are available from officially appointed agents (local agents are shown on page 26, under 'Useful Addresses'), and from most booksellers, stationers and newsagents.

See following pages for extracts relating to Caernarfon, taken from the First Series one-inch map, and the latest Landranger map.

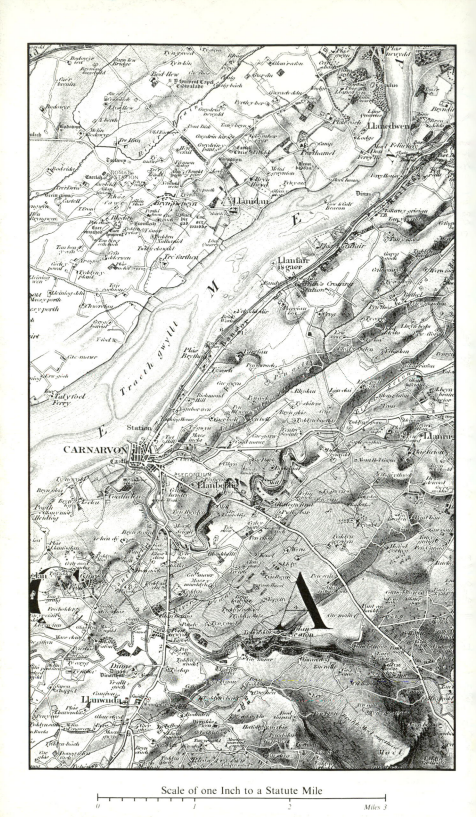

Scale of one Inch to a Statute Mile

0   1   2   Miles 3

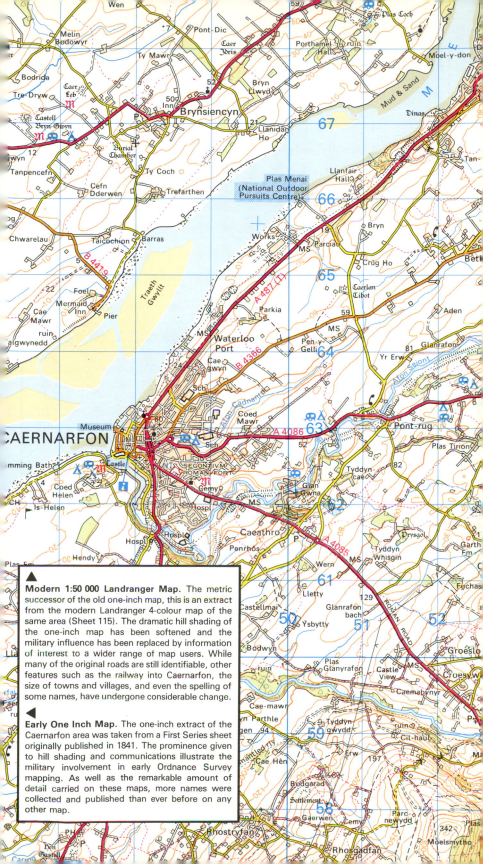

Modern 1:50 000 Landranger Map. The metric successor of the old one-inch map, this is an extract from the modern Landranger 4-colour map of the same area (Sheet 115). The dramatic hill shading of the one-inch map has been softened and the military influence has been replaced by information of interest to a wider range of map users. While many of the original roads are still identifiable, other features such as the railway into Caernarfon, the size of towns and villages, and even the spelling of some names, have undergone considerable change.

◄

Early One Inch Map. The one-inch extract of the Caernarfon area was taken from a First Series sheet originally published in 1841. The prominence given to hill shading and communications illustrate the military involvement in early Ordnance Survey mapping. As well as the remarkable amount of detail carried on these maps, more names were collected and published than ever before on any other map.

Index

Further Reading . . .
A List of Books.

General

Beazley, E. & Brett, L. *Shell Guide to North Wales*. Faber & Faber

Beazley, E. & Howell, P. *Companion Guide to North Wales*. Collins

Condry, W.M. *Exploring Wales*. Faber & Faber

Fletcher, H.L.V. *North Wales* (The Queen's Wales)

Rees, V. *Shell Guide to Mid-Western Wales*. Faber & Faber

Rhys Edwards, G. *Snowdonia National Park Guide*. H.M.S.O.

Art, Architecture & History

Barber, C. *Mysterious Wales*. Paladin

Bowen, E.G. *Saints, Seaways and Settlements in the Celtic Lands*. University of Wales Press

Dyer, J. *Prehistoric England & Wales*. Penguin

Grimes, W.F. *The Prehistory of Wales*. National Museum of Wales

Hawkes, J. *Guide to Prehistoric & Roman Monuments in England and Wales*. Cardinal

Margary, I.D. *Roman Roads in Britain*. Phoenix House

Soulsby, I. *The Towns of Medieval Wales*. Phillimore

Sylvester, D. *A History of Gwynedd*. Phillimore

Tooley, R.V. *Maps and Map-Makers*. Batsford

Wilson, R.J.A. *A Guide to Roman Remains in Britain*. Constable

Wood, E.S. *Field Guide to Archaeology in Britain*. Collins

Fiction, Literary Interest and Early Travellers

Borrow, G. *Wild Wales* Collins Classics

Defoe, D. *A Tour Through England and Wales*. Penguin

Firbank, T. *I Bought a Mountain*. New English Library

Giraldus Cambrensis. *Itinerary of Wales 1188*. Everyman's Library

Jones, G.& T. (Ed.) *The Mabinogion*. Everyman's Library

Pennant, T. *A Tour in Wales*.

Natural History

Breeze-Jones & Thomas. *Bird Watching in Snowdonia*. John Jones

Condry, W.M. *The Snowdonia National Park*. Fontana

Saunders, D. *Guide to the Birds of Wales*. Constable

Shaw, D.S. *Gwydyr Forest in Snowdonia*. H.M.S.O.

Railways, Roads, Industries, etc.

Beazley, E. *Madocks and the Wonder of Wales*. Faber & Faber

Christiansen & Miller, *The Cambrian Railways (2 vols)*. David & Charles

Dodd, A.H. *The Industrial Revolution in North Wales*. The University of Wales Press

Jenkins, J.G. *The Welsh Woollen Industry*. National Museum of Wales

Lee, C.E. *The Welsh Highland Railway*. David & Charles

Lindsay, J.A. *A History of the North Wales Slate Industry*. David & Charles

Rees, D.M. *Mines, Mills & Furnaces*. National Museum of Wales

Rolt, L.T.C. *George & Robert Stephenson*. Penguin

Rolt, L.T.C. *Thomas Telford*. Penguin

Walking and Climbing

Marsh, T. *The Mountains of Wales*. Hodder & Stoughton

Poucher, W.A. *The Welsh Peaks* Constable

Mountain Rescue Handbook Mountain Rescue Committee

Safety on Mountains Central Council for Physical Education